STAMFORD ADVOCATE

FOUNDED 1829

Supplement   STAMFORD ADVOCATE, WEDNESDAY, SEPTEMBER 16, 1942.   Civilian Defense Supplement

AN AMERICAN TOWN
GOES TO WAR

by
Tony Pavia

TURNER PUBLISHING COMPANY
Paducah, Kentucky

Prepared with the Cooperation
of the
Stamford Defense Council

TURNER PUBLISHING COMPANY
Publishers of Military History
412 Broadway • P.O. Box 3101
Paducah, KY 42002-3101

Editor: Amy Cloud

Library of Congress Catalog Card No.
95-080568

ISBN: 978-1-59652-777-5

Printed in the USA
Additional books available from
Turner Publishing Company
Paducah, Kentucky

TABLE OF CONTENTS

DEDICATION

This book is dedicated to a special generation of men and women who served their country without question or condition. They left the comfort of their homes and the company of their loved ones to fight in distant lands. They endured pain, hardship, and loss without complaint. They placed the interests of others before their own, knowing that the fate of millions rested with their efforts. Finally, this book is dedicated to the memory of those who made the supreme sacrifice by giving their lives for their country.

Charles Acker, Army, 1943
Edgar J. Albert, AAF, 1944, France
Nicholas Armalfitano, Army, 1944, Italy
Frank Argenio, Army, 1943
Raffaele Arruzza, Army, 1944, Europe
Albert W. Austin, 1943, Italy
Arthur Austin, Navy, 1945, Pacific
Raymond Avery, Army, 1944, France
Benny Babula, Army, 1944, Italy
Savros Batsos, Army, 1945, Germany
Gustave Belasco, Navy, 1942, Pacific
Howard Bernes, Army
Basil Bernychny, Army
Peter Bennitt, Army, 1944, France
Percy Blackwell, Marines
Henry John Blomquist, Army, 1944, E.T.A.
Alfred Bocuzzi, Army, 1943, Pacific
Frank Bonjiorno, Army
Alphonse Brach, Navy
Richard Branch, AAF, 1945
Charles Brooker, Army
Arthur Craig Brown, Navy
Walter Brzoska, AAF, 1945, E.T.A.
Robert Buchanan, Navy, 1945
John Henry Byrne, Navy, 1944
Patrick Byrnes, AAF, 1943, Pacific
Raymond Cahill, Army, 1944, France
Frank Calderone, Army, 1945, France
Daniel Callahan, Navy, 1942, Pacific
Anthony Candilmo, AAF
Louis Cappossela, Army
Roger Carlino, AAF, 1944, Greece
Rocco Carlo, Navy, 1944
Anthony Castelli, Army, 1945, Germany
Robert Joseph Cavanaugh, AAF, 1945, Philippines
Leonard Chrostoski, Army
Raymond Clark, AAF
Richard Cody, Army, 1945, New Guinea
Thomas Conforti, AAC
Francis Connolly, Army, 1944, Belgium
John Conroy, AAF
John Constable, Army, 1945, Germany
Robert Cornell, Army
Thomas Coughlin, Army
William Coyle, Army, 1945, Germany
Carl Creiger, Army
Salvatore Crocco, 1945, Germany
Darill Crosby, Army
Richard Cullen, Army, 1945, Italy
Louis Czako, Navy, 1945, Pacific
Michael D'Agostino, Army, 1944, Germany
Marino D'Aquilla, Navy
Arthur Daly, AAC

Lockwood Darling, Army, 1944, E.T.A.
Warren DeCamp, Jr., Army, Italy
Rocco Dedonato, Army, 1944, France
David DeFelice, Marines, 1945, Okinawa
Joseph Delvecchio, Jr., Navy, 1944
Julio Demares, AAF, 1944
Angelo DeMasi, Army
James DePreta, Marines, 1943, Tarawa
Emmit DeVincent, Navy, 1944, Africa
K.L. Diffenderffer, Navy
Donald Donahue, Army, 1944, Germany
James Donohue, Army, 1945, Germany
Charles Downing, Marines, 1944, Palau
Milton Dubvrosky, Army, 1944, Germany
O'Henry Durandi, 1944, France
John Dzioba, Army, 1945, Belgium
Warren Ericson, Navy
John Francis Egan, Jr., Army, 1945, Germany
Oswald Fabrizio, Marines, 1945, Okinawa
Joseph M. Farrell, Army, 1944, Italy
George Feilding III, Army, 1945, Philippines
Charles Fell, Navy
Gabriel Fillak, Army, 1944
William Fowler, Navy, 1945
Myles Fox, Marines, 1943, Tulagi
Stephen Fuda AAF, 1944, Philippines
James Gaffney, Army, 1945, Belgium
Arthur Gallyse, Army
Lewis Gautrau, Army, 1944, Germany
Patrick Gentile, Army, 1943
Jeremiah Gerardi, Army, 1945, Luxembourg
Daniel Gervasio, AAF, 1945, Germany
Joseph Giordano, Army, 1945, Belgium
John Goral, Coast Guard
Harvey Gordon, Navy, 1945, Pacific
John Grabowski, Army, 1944, Italy
Joseph Grabowski, Navy, 1944, Pacific
Lionel Gregoire, Army, 1945, Germany
Homer Griffiths, Navy
Matthew Guzda, Marines, 1942, Guadalcanal
William Harper, Army
Prentice Hatch Jr., Marines, 1943
William Hayes, Army, 1945, E.T.A.
Henry Henrickson, Marines, 1944, Saipan
Adrian Henry, Army, Pacific
Vincent Horan, AAF, 1941, Pearl Harbor
Charles Howes, RCAF, 1944, E.T.A.
Leonard Hrostoski, Army, 1944, Italy
George Hyland, Marines, 1945, Iwo Jima
Edward Ianazzi, Army, 1944, Austria
Emilio Intrieri, Army
Patsy Iovino, Army, 1943
Herbert Johnson, Army, 1943

Everett Jordan, Army, 1944, E.T.A.
Victor Kalander, Army, 1945, Germany
Elmer Kalman, AAC
Basil Kernychny, Navy, 1943
Charles Kewer, Navy, 1945, Pacific
Benjamin Kijek, Navy, 1943, Pacific
Frank Kijek, Navy, 1944, Atlantic
Benjamin J. Kisczkiel, AAF
John Koceniak, Army, 1945, France
George Kovacs, Jr., Army, 1944, Germany
Peter Kowalski, AAF, 1945
Chester Kopodlowski, Navy, 1945
Edmund Kulka, Navy
Yale Kweskin, AAF, 1943
Harry LaChance, Army, 1944, France
Donald Lannan, Army, 1945, Germany
Irving Lanyon, Marines, 1944
John Lapinski, Army, 1943, Africa
Everett Larson, Marines, 1942, Solomans
Archer B. Lord, Army, 1943
Joseph Lorenti, Army, 1945, Belgium
Edred Loveland, Army, 1945, Luzon
Frederick Loveland, Jr. Marines, 1942, Solomans
Roswell MacMaster, Army, 1944, Burma
William Malizewski, Marines, 1945, Iwo Jima
Myron Mantell, AAF, 1943, Caribbean
Joseph Matlack, Navy, 1942, Pacific
Joseph Mattera, Army, 1945, Burma
David MacDonald, Army, 1944, France
Michael Meno, AAC
Nicholas Mercede, Navy, 1943
Ellis Middleton, AAC
Jere Ambler Miller, Army, 1944, France
Vough Miller, Army
Max Micha, Navy, 1944, Pacific
Michael Mishley, AAF, 1942, Philippines
David Mixsell, Army
Edward Molino, Army, 1944, Italy
Raymond Morris, Army, 1944, Holland
John Mownn, Army, 1945, Philippines
John Mrus, Army, 1945, Philippines
Joseph Mugan, Army, 1945, Europe
Pierce Joseph Mullen, Army, 1944, France
Frederick Murphy, Jr., Navy, 1943
Thomas Murray, Army, 1944
Sidney Neuger, Army, 1945, Leyte
Arthur Nielsen, AAF, 1944, Germany
Douglas Northrop, AAC
Alexander Novash, Army
Michael O'Connor, Army, 1944, France
Clifford Olson, Army, 1944, France
William O'Neill, Navy
Carlo Pangia, Army, 1945, Germany
Benjamin Parente, Army
Thomas Pastuscak, Navy
Elmer Francis Peaston, Navy, 1943, Pacific
Ernest Peck, Army, 1943
Dr. Charles Pecoraro, Army, 1942, Pacific
Kalman Perlman, Army, 1944, Burma
Anthony Pezzimenti, Army, 1943, Africa
Vito Phillipse, Army
John Pierson, Navy
John Polinsky, Army, 1944, France
Francis Poltrack, Marines, 1944, Pelileu

Benjamin Praeger, Army, 1944, Europe
Joseph Price, Marines, 1944, Saipan
Charles Quick, Army
Louis Radocy, Army, 1944, Italy
Charles Raymond, Jr., AAF, 1943
Aaron Resnick, Army, 1945, Belgium
Winthrop Roche, Army, 1944, France
Julio Rodriguez, Army, 1944, France
George Roth, Army, 1945, Iwo Jima
Robert Rotunno, Marines, 1945, Iwo Jima
Peter Russo, Army, 1944, Italy
Joseph Ryan, Navy, Pacific
Hugh Francis Rush, Marines, 1944,Bougainville
Peter Sabino, Army, 1944, Italy
John Scalzi, Navy, 1945
Herbert Schacht, Navy
John Joseph Scipioni, Army, 1944
Harry Schopf, Army, 1945, Pacific
Silvio Joseph Sessa, Army, 1944, France
Edward Shaw, AAF
Hugh Sheldon, Army, 1945 Germany
Jack Singer, AAF, 1943, Pacific
Charles Skarberg, Army 1944, Anzio
William Skura, Marines, 1945, Okinawa
Stuart Smith, Army, 1945, Pacific
William Smith, Army, 1945, Germany
Pasquale Spina, Army, 1944, Germany
George Spon Jr., Navy, 1945
Winston Statewhite, Army, 1944, Burma
Daniel Stolfi, Army, 1945, Luxembourg
Deron Sundar, Marines
Elmer Svenningsen, Army, 1945, Europe
George Stobridge
Dominick Tamburri, Army, 1944, Italy
Joseph Tamburri, Army, 1945
Lawrence Tracy, Army, 1944, Europe
Robert Tracy, Army,1942
Vincent Tripodi, Navy, 1945, Okinawa
Edward Tuminski, Army, 1943, Europe
Alfred Turner, Army, 1945, France
Frank Touri, Army
Amerigo Ucciferri, AAC
Aggie Joseph Umile, Army
Frank Valenzano, Army, 1942, Philippines
Leonard Volpe, Army, 1945
Charles Vonderlieth, AAF, 1943, Europe
Richard VonEgidy, Marines, 1945, Iwo Jima
Harry Waldron, Navy
Thomas Walsh, AAF, 1944, India
Virgil Wardwell, Jr., Marines, 1944
Walter Waring, Army, 1944, Italy
William Wasco, Army, 1944, France
Robert Wasserman, Army, 1945, Luzon
Carl Weiant, Jr., Navy, 1942, Atlantic
Leonard Weiss, AAF, 1944, Germany
Roy West, Jr., Army, New Guinea
William White, Jr., Marines, 1945, Iwo Jima
Charles Wichert, Marines
Stanley Williams, Army
Robert Winkler, AAF, 1944, Germany
James Winslow, Navy, 1944, Pacific
Stanley Wisnewski, AAC
Walter Yeruc, Army, 1944, France

ACKNOWLEDGMENTS

No project of this magnitude can be completed without the patience, goodwill and friendship of others. Several people assisted me at all levels of this book and justly deserve recognition. I would like to thank the following people fortheir valuable contributions to this work.

- My students: Jennifer Chiapetta, Josh Fedeli, Anna Norgren, Matt Rende, Jennifer Ritchie, and Rebecca Sobo for encouraging me and assisting me in the initial phases of the book.
- Justin Calvillo, Michele Ruscoe, and Rosemarie Ruscoe for the magic of their computer talents.
- Judy Betty, Cathy DeBartolo, Danielle Manegio, Rita Miller, Gay Nilson, not only for helping me to organize these stories, but also for their keen eyes, observations, and suggestions.
- Joe Pavia for his wild goose chases at the library and veterans memorials in search of obscure information and other minutae.
- Ernie DiMattea of the Ferguson Library Staff for their cooperation, patience and assistance.
- To the "Stamford Advocate" for its extremely important role in chronicling our city's history during the Second World War and also for their generosity in allowing me to use photographs that appeared in the paper (1941 - 45).
- To the VFW's, the Springdale, Fred Robbins, and the Homer Lee Wise Posts for assisting me in identifying and locating area veterans.
- To all of the Veterans and their families for their kindness and support and also for allowing me to share their experiences with others.
- To John Obuchowski, Jerry Lambo, Hawley Oefinger, Sarge Pia, Charlie Guinta, Al Benevelli, and Flavio Foglio for being there at the beginning.
- To Evans Kerrigan, for his knowledge, expertise, encouragement, and confidence in me.
- To Jim Ryan, for some of his photographs and Mark Martini for his cover design.
- To Jeff Bouvier, for his help in editing the material.
- To Ralph Chianelli, who designed and formatted the book and stoically endured countless changes and updates, while never losing his sense of humor.
- To my family: Mom, for her unwavering support, Matt, Bobby, and Jason, for tolerating their Dad's obsessive behavior, and most of all to my wife, Robin, who patiently supported this endeavor long after it should have been completed and who also, without fail, provided good, sensible advice and guidance.
- Special thanks to Dad, Bo and Uncle Ray.

Mike Pavia

Bob Lowler

Ray Collins

On December 6, 1991, over eighty students sat motionless in the small auditorium at Stamford High School as they listened to the accounts of five local World War II veterans. Hawley Oefinger spoke about Pearl Harbor, Jerry Lambo about the Bataan Death March, Charlie Guinta about Iwo Jima, and Al Benevelli about the invasion of Sicily. At one point the fifth veteran, Tony Pia, pointed to a young man seated in the audience and said, "That's exactly where I was seated when we listened to FDR's speech declaring war on Japan." You could feel the reaction from the students. They were listening to five living history books. I will remember that day for the rest of my life. It affected both me and these young people profoundly.

Later, when I discussed aloud my longtime desire to compile a book of oral histories from local World War II veterans, a student looked at me and with a puzzled expression asked, "What are you waiting for?" At that exact moment I made a commitment. Little did I know that this commitment would take me almost three years to fulfill.

- PREFACE -

These are the stories of men who went off to war. All of the men are from the same town, – Stamford, Connecticut – but their stories are universal. They could come from any city, state or township in America. Like any other town of its size, Stamford contributed on every level and in every theatre of World War II. Its citizens fought in every corner of the globe and participated in one of the most important chapters in our history.

Sixteen million Americans served their country during World War II. Over 10,000 of these came from Stamford. Since the population of the town at that time was about 60,000, this means that roughly one out of six citizens answered his country's call to duty. This figure does not include factory workers, civil defense volunteers or the countless others who contributed to the war effort.

There were local boys present at Pearl Harbor on the morning of the attack. Scores of others participated in every amphibious assault in the Pacific. On D-Day there were local boys in the air, at sea and on the beaches of Normandy, one whose plane is exhibited in the museum at Ste Mere Eglise. Some were witnesses to the tragic mass suicide at Saipan and the awesome destruction of the Atom Bomb. The town has multiple winners of every honor from the Silver Star to the Medal of Honor.

Unlike any other war, every single person in Stamford was touched by World War II. Everyone had a spouse, sibling, friend or family member in harm's way. Many families had multiple siblings in action. One family, the DePreta's sent seven sons off to war. Only six returned. Three other families lost more than one son.

Many other lives were touched by tragedy. Almost two hundred local men lost their lives in the great conflict, each of them affecting not just a family, but also a neighborhood and a community. When James DePreta was killed in 1943 the entire Cove section mourned along with his family. The same can be said of the West Side when Mike D'Agostino died; the South End when it lost the Kijek brothers and Glenbrook when it lost Douglas Northrup. It was not uncommon for a neighborhood, even a single street to lose several of its boys in any one year of the war.

This was a war of massive proportions which was fought in several corners of the world and yet reached the cities, towns and neighborhoods of America. It was a war that was blind to race, creed or ethnic origin. In Stamford, people from all backgrounds made sacrifices and people of all classes and social standing suffered the loss of loved ones.

In the end Stamford recovered from its losses. Many of those who returned from the war, went back to work, settled down, raised families and went on to live long and productive lives. Some who were raised here moved away and never again returned. Others moved here from other places and became integral parts of the community over the next fifty years. In each case, they were significant participants in the events that changed history and shaped the modern world.

- INTRODUCTION -

As a typical "Baby Boomer" growing up in the late 1950's and early 1960's, I was surrounded by living reminders of World War II. Our fathers, mothers, friends, and neighbors were all involved in some way with the war effort, whether it was as a soldier, nurse, factory worker, or civil defense volunteer. And many of us, if not touched personally by it, were at least aware of someone who had lost a friend or family member to the war.

References to World War II were present in every part of our culture. Our common language contained such phrases as D-Day, Iwo or Bataan. President Eisenhower led the war effort and President Kennedy fought in it. Every Sunday we were treated to an afternoon TV schedule that included such movies as <u>Guadalcanal Diary</u>, <u>Twelve O'Clock High</u> and <u>The Purple Heart</u>. Each of these movies seemed to remind us that we were living in the greatest country on earth and among a special breed of people who pulled together and emerged victorious over totalitarian forces.

As I grew into my teens the collective memory of World War II began to fade and Vietnam took center stage. As it began to consume the nation's attentions it appeared, at least in the public's mind, that the difference between right and wrong, good and evil, had been clouded. The heroes of the past were replaced by cultural icons from the "New Generation".

As the seventies grew into the eighties, the wounds of our most recent war had begun to heal and new generations were raised with other references to history. To this younger generation, the historical benchmarks became Watergate, the Hostage Crisis, the Challenger explosion and, most recently, The Persian Gulf War.

As we enter the 50th anniversary of our involvement in World War II, it becomes more and more important to preserve the memories of this time period. It is important to remind some, particularly our young people, that their grandparents once led this nation in a great struggle to defeat the forces of aggression. They should know that the "old man" across the street, the retiree around the corner, the man in the Senior Citizens home, and even the "guy that drives too slow", was, at one time, risking his life so that future generations might live in freedom. It is vital that our young people have some link to this era. That link lies in the stories of the survivors.

In this book I have attempted to gather the stories of some of the people of Stamford whose lives were touched by World War II. I would have loved nothing more than to have compiled the definitive comprehensive work on our city's role in World War II. This would have included a directory of all Stamfordites who served their country, a compendium of award winners and biographies of the nearly two hundred men who gave their lives during this struggle. However, with the time and resources available, this job became impossible.

Unknown to many, few if any records of our local citizens in World War II still exist. In fact, to this date, I can locate no central list or directory of Stamford World War II veterans. Improbable as it seems, no one, not the Armed Services, Veterans Administration or National Archives has this information. The State of Connecticut Military Library's records are incomplete as are those of Military Personnel Records in St. Louis whose files were partially destroyed by a fire in 1973. When I talked to the historian at the Adjutant Generals' Office in Hartford, he informed me that I would have more luck compiling a list on Civil War veterans.

Sadly, the only general list of local World War II veterans that existed was the one that adorned the walls of the old Honor Roll on the Town Green. When it was removed during the 1970's to make way for more elegant designs, a portion of our history was lost.

The local newspaper, "The Stamford Advocate," has proved to be the only consistent source of information about this era. However, even the "Advocate" had its limitations. Many times information about our soldiers such as their location or theaters of action was inaccurate, incomplete or withheld for security purposes.

Thus it appears that much of the history of this era lies in the memories of its people. The interviews I have done do not represent a comprehensive work on a town's involvement in World War II. They merely represent different views of the war as seen by those who witnessed this dramatic chapter of our history.

This project, since the start, has itself been a battle against time and limited resources. In the fifty years since we were drawn into "The Great War" countless survivors have died or moved away. Not a single week has gone by when the obituary hasn't contained the name of a veteran of World War II. The greatest frustration has been the knowledge that in a short time the richest sources of historical information about this era will all be gone.

If nothing else, I hope that this book will inspire others to pursue this study before it is too late. All over Stamford and all over the nation there are parents and grandparents, uncles and aunts with important stories to tell. Their experiences and accounts are the richest and most important historical resources available.

Since so much of our local and national heritage can only be obtained through oral history, we must not allow these stories to go untold.

- ABOUT THE INTERVIEWS -

I have done my best to gather personal interviews from a variety of battles, theaters and branches of service. These accounts were not taken verbatim from a transcript. In many cases they were edited, condensed and patched together from recorded interviews and subsequent conversations. Many times after a two or three hour visit and long after the recorder was turned off, the subject would remember an important detail or anecdote. Other times I would receive a phone call later to clarify or amplify a story. Some of these people had not talked about these events for close to fifty years, and the interview often opened a torrent of memories.

In all cases I have tried to maintain the exact wording of these men and women. In cases when this was impossible or impractical, I have done my best to preserve the flavor of the stories as they were related to me. A transcript was given to each of the subjects for approval. In very few cases did they request a change.

Another relevant point must be made about the subjects themselves. Early on in the project I was warned that everyone would inflate his or her own importance in the war effort, that stories would be exaggerated. I found exactly the opposite to be true. Many were reluctant to tell their story and even more reluctant to take credit for anything heroic. They were much more willing to praise "others." Very few volunteered information about decorations they received in combat. In most cases I had to pry it out of them. Other times a wife or relative would pull me aside and tell me. In one case after a three hour interview with one of the men, I found a photograph of him being awarded the Bronze Star. When I asked about it the subject said, "You're not going to make a big deal out of that are you?" This was the typical reaction I got to such an inquiry. I interviewed one man for hours and was long finished with his account when I stumbled upon an article in the newspaper in 1945 which announced that he had been awarded the Silver Star. He simply never mentioned it to me. He still hasn't. Many of the men who were wounded did not want me to mention it. Their typical attitude was that others had suffered more and that in comparison their troubles were minor.

These men slept out in the cold for months on end, lived through blizzards and typhoons, suffered chillblaine and jungle rot, ate cold food and drank warm beer. They were forced to leave behind their parents, siblings, wives and in some cases their children. They endured hardships that are inconceivable to most people today. Some still suffer nightmares about their ordeals. Yet when asked about their contribution to history they dismiss it by saying that they simply did their "job." They cannot conceive of what they have done as being in any way extraordinary. All of them consider themselves "lucky". "The real heroes" they say, are "all dead." Why, they wondered, would anyone be interested in what they did fifty years ago?

In reading their stories you will not hear about valiant or heroic deeds, nor will you hear graphic tales of blood and death, but rather of common, humble men and women describing a job that they knew was important to their country. Through these humble and underrated accounts you will conclude, as have I, that these truly were extraordinary people and that the rest of us owe them a debt that we can never truly repay.

1

The USS Arizona at Pearl Harbor, December 7, 1941.

CHAPTER ONE

PEARL HARBOR:

THE DAY THE WAR CAME HOME

Like people in most towns across the nation, the citizens of Stamford followed the war in Europe and Asia with a mix of caution, apprehension and indifference. Although new breakthroughs in the art of warfare could render the town's numerous wartime industries vulnerable, there seemed, at least in 1939, to be no immediate danger. The war was a world away.

As we entered 1940 the public's focus seemed to turn more and more toward the war. As democracies began to fall, hometown factories tightened security, serious thought was given to spies and saboteurs, a Draft Board was formed and an Air-Defense Command was established.

As U.S. relations with the Axis deteriorated in 1941, an Air Raid Warden was named, volunteers were enlisted and a program for the defense of the town was outlined. And yet, the war seemed so far away.

On December 7, 1941, the Japanese attacked Pearl Harbor and, after years of debate, the United States, finally entered World War II. On that fateful morning there were several young men from Stamford who were stationed in Hawaii.

The first local man reported to die in World War II was Sergeant Vincent Horan of the 78th Pursuit Squadron of the Army Air Corps. Horan, a 1938 graduate of Stamford High School, was killed in action at Wheeler Field during the Japanese attack. He was only 20 years old.

The second area man reported dead was Ensign William Thomas O'Neill, Jr. A 1933 graduate of Stamford High School, O'Neill was stationed on the Arizona and perished when the Japanese destroyed the ship.

Everett J. Hyland, who was aboard the U.S.S. Pennsylvania, was the first local man to be wounded in the war. During the attack he was assigned to anti-aircraft guns. When a bomb exploded on the ship, Hyland was hit by shrapnel which tore out bones in his elbow and left thigh and wounded him in the chest, back, and face. Hyland remained hospitalized in both Pearl Harbor and San Francisco for months.

With tragic swiftness, the war had finally come home.

- JOHN OBUCHOWSKI-

It was by accident that John Obuchowski ended up in Hawaii. When he enlisted in 1940, his first choice was the Philippines but there were no more openings. Instead he chose Pearl Harbor believing it would be the opportunity to see an exotic land.

On the morning of December 7, 1941, Obuchowski decided to sleep late and skip breakfast. The night before, as an accordion player for the popular Army Forces Band, John had played before an audience made up of top army brass including General Walter Short, one of the commanders later blamed for the success of the Japanese attack.

The next morning he was awakened by the sound of planes strafing Schofield Barracks.

The first explosion woke me up and I instinctively glanced at the wall clock. It read 7:55 AM. It was shortly followed by another explosion. Someone hollered, "Japs are bombing and strafing us". Carl R. Boone and me in our undershorts ran out on the third floor landing, and saw a (VAL) Japanese dive bomber flying about fifty feet overhead with his canopy opened, staring down at us. I still recall seeing the pilot's face and mustache.

We were issued M-1 rifles, automatic weapons, and assigned to guard Wheeler Field and Schofield Barracks water filtering plant, fearing sabotage.

I don't remember exactly what was running through my mind. There is no explanation for it. You reacted instinctively. Danger didn't enter your mind. Most of the fellows I've talked to felt the same way. Total shock. Even when the bombs were dropping you felt, "It must be some mistake".

A few days later, I was relieved from guard duties, to entertain the wounded servicemen at the Army and Navy hospitals, Mrs. Ann Etzler vocalizing and me on the accordion. I also entertained troops in the northern mountain regions of Koli Koli pass, the flight path that Japanese aircraft flew to bomb Pearl Harbor, and other military installations on the island of Oahu December 7, 1941.

It never dawned on me what an important event this was. Recently I ran into an old buddy who said, "John, you never told me you were at Pearl Harbor". It never occurred to me to tell him.

Maybe two or three weeks after the attack things settled down. We were allowed to go into town. We always had to carry our gas masks. When I finally did see the full damage at battleship row I couldn't believe it. You had to see it. Oil all over the water, debris on top, battleships turned over. It was all too much. I thought the Japanese had us by the throat.

In November of 1942 John was transported
out of Pearl Harbor. He thought that the war would be
over for him. At the time John could never have known that
he was about to witness one of the pivotal battles in the
Pacific. He was on his way to Guadalcanal.

We were happy; we thought we were going back to the States. We said "OK, we did our job now we're going home." The next thing I know we're on Guadalcanal. I had never heard of the place. All of a sudden we're getting strafed by Japanese Zeroes. We jumped right into the latrine holes we were digging.

For the next three years Guadalcanal was our home base but the next few months were unforgettable. Because I was with the band, we were assigned to the medics as "litter bearers" (*stretcher carriers*). Sometimes we had to go right out during a fight to carry the wounded away. I was assigned to Hill 43 and an emergency hospital. A lot of the time we were under fire and had to go into the shooting zone. Later our commander put us in for a citation.

When we first got to Hill 43 we were short of supplies. We didn't even have stretchers the first week we were there. We had to make stretchers out of tree branches, shelter halves (tents) and even used Japanese communication wire to hold them together.

One time we went out to carry off a soldier who was hit. He must have been at least 6'3" and weighed over 200 pounds. We put him on the stretcher and all of a sudden Japanese snipers opened up on us. We took cover behind a tree. All of a sudden, the soldier who was unconscious jumped up, ran about 50 feet or so and collapsed. We finally got him to a hospital and when they examined him they told us that he had been shot 7 times. They evacuated him and I never found out what happened to him.

We had an older guy we all looked up to. He was a seasoned combat veteran, a line soldier. He used to take care of all of us kids, keep an eye out for us. One night he was hit and we had to evacuate him. We were all shaken up. He was wounded badly and they had to amputate his leg. We stayed with him the entire time. Then we had to sit him down in a foxhole and we covered him with blankets. The doctors said that he came through the operation well and that he would be O.K. But the next morning when we woke up he had died.

During the lull in the fighting on Hill 43, the doctors sent my friend Dube and I to get water for the wounded. We had to walk to the bottom of the hill, which was maybe two or three miles with five gallon cans for the water. We didn't expect too many problems but on the way down Japanese snipers opened fire on us and we had to take cover. We weren't even armed. Even though a squad accompanied us down to the watering hole this was one of the scariest times for me because the fire got even worse as we approached the watering hole. On the way back we were fired on again and again by the Japanese and forced to take cover. This little trip for water ended up taking us over 4 hours.

Very often, up on that hill, B-17's had to drop food and supplies to us. The natives wouldn't carry supplies to Hill 43 because of the sniper fire. During combat our daily ration up there was a small can of meat and a piece of chocolate.

Some of the airfights we saw were incredible. I wish I had a camera. You could see the Zeroes, the P38's, F4U's, everything. Then when the anti-aircraft went off you had to be careful not to get hit by falling shrapnel. You had to worry about that too. We also had personnel bombs to worry about. These were bombs with long rods on them. When the rods would hit something the bomb would ignite along the ground and fragments would fly everywhere. That's when I started thinking — "Hey, this is a war."

There were a lot of other things to worry about. You had to deal with malaria, huge bugs and lizards, even a tidal wave. Every night one of us was assigned to put the mosquito nets around everyone. It's amazing how you live through all of these experiences. You sleep in the mud. Rain every day. It was so humid that your clothes would have mildew on them. Then when we slept on the beach the crabs would come out at night and bother us.

One time our supply ship was sunk. So for three weeks in a row all we had was pancake mix. After a while some guys tried to sneak into the New Zealanders' chow line because they had meat.

But what I won't forget is the smell and the first time I actually saw death. Eventually you had to get used to that. But even with all that death around you what really shook me up was seeing a young guy I knew, dead. He was 18 years old, a beautiful kid from Wisconsin dead. I didn't sleep well for weeks.

After Guadalcanal was secured our chaplain organized a group from our division that would trade with the Melanesian natives for souvenirs. One time a bunch of us traveled to the Savo Island, which was about 20 miles northeast of Guadalcanal. We arrived there about 10:00 a.m. and were scheduled to leave at 2:00 p.m. One of the guys, a regimental photographer, talked a few of us into going to another village which was about 4 miles away. We went to the village and got back too late. The boat had left without us. For three days we were marooned on Savo. While on the island, we lived under primitive conditions in native thatched huts, sleeping on straw mats, and eating strange foods from Japanese mess-kits. During evening hours, the islanders would entertain us. The chief would carry a lighted torch, and, followed by young Polynesian boys, would enter our shack to sing tribal war chants, and a few bars of "You Are My Sunshine". We were all pleasantly surprised and enjoyed the show.

After spending three days and three nights on the island, we became very

Obuchowski (back row, third from left) on Guadalcanal with a captured Japanese flag.

apprehensive about our chances of ever being rescued. It was all so bizarre. On the fourth day, a Navy ship cruised close to the island. Ken Hoser, with the aid of semaphore code, attracted their attention. The ship approached us and catapulted a line to shore, with a small skiff attached. The islanders loaded the skiff with bananas, native wood carvings, mats, and other things. As we all climbed into the skiff, the entire village waved us farewell.

Once aboard the ship, the Captain informed us that their original mission was to rescue a downed pilot, not us.

When we arrived at Lunga Point in Guadalcanal, about a twenty mile trip, we were placed under arrest, and immediately driven to our home base. Our Commanding Officer read us the Articles of War. He charged us with desertion, and called for a General Court Martial. None of our fellow bandsmen were in sight, which seemed strange. Then, as we executed an about-face, the entire band greeted us with the song, "Hail, Hail, the Gang's All Here". No words can describe our relief to find out that the joke was on us.

In 1943 I was back in the band and travelled all over the Pacific, New Zealand, New Caledonia and Vella La Vella.

When we got to Vella La Vella, the Japanese must have found out we were being transported, because we got to the beach and they really let us have it. We were stuck on the beach for about 4 hours. That night they started dropping flares — that was eerie. Here it is at 2:00 a.m. and everything was lit up. I found a pit with some sand bags around it. There was an anti-aircraft gunner in the pit. I dove in with him. He kept right on working.

Now, of course, I say, hey, this was an important battle, but at the time, especially after Pearl Harbor, I thought we were losing.

In 1945, I was on my way home on furlough. When that was over we were supposed to go back to the Pacific. Then we heard the news that the war was over. I had enough points to get out of the Army so I never had to go back to the Pacific.

After his discharge John worked for Pitney Bowes for a few years until joining the Stamford Fire Department where he worked until his retirement. John finally did get that citation. In 1981, he received his Bronze Star for "meritorious service in ground combat."

In December of 1994, almost exactly 53 years after the day that would forever change his life, John passed away at the age of 73.

- ELWOOD LICHACK-

On December 7, 1941, Lichack was a 1st Class Gunners' Mate aboard the U.S.S. Pennsylvania, the flagship of the navy fleet and the headquarters of Admiral Husband Kimmel. The Pennsylvania was usually moored in Battleship Row, right next to its sister ship, the Arizona. But on that eventful morning, it was in dry dock for repairs.

That morning I was awake at 0315 hours (3:15 am). I had the armory watch 0400 to 0800 (4:00 am to 8:00 am). The armory is located on the third deck - port side aft. My duties were to issue small arms (guns) with ammunition to our crew in the event of hostile boarders. With the world situation being what it was and with 40,000 Japanese Nationals on the Island, boarders were a great possibility as we regarded most of them as spies.

At approximately 0755, General Quarters was sounded over the intercom with the words, "Man your battle stations, this is no drill." I could hear the noise from the torpedoes exploding which were concentrated on the U.S.S. Arizona BB39, our sister ship, and other battlewagons. Within minutes I was in the 5" .25 caliber gun shop alongside the port side of our smoke stack. I got the firing locks to our guns and assigned a gunner's mate to install the firing locks to the four guns on the port side. I installed the firing locks to the four guns on the starboard side, made the electrical connections to the firing locks and had the gun captain remove the safety latches from the guns. Our ammunition hoists were open, ammunition was coming up, and firing commenced at all available targets. Because we were in dry dock, we could not fire at low flying targets since it meant firing in the direction of our own fleet. While we concentrated on the higher altitude planes, our .50 caliber machine guns were engaging the lower flying planes. It was a day of "hell", but I don't think any of us had time to be scared.

We took two bombs, and lost over 20 men. But we were lucky compared to the Arizona. If we weren't in dry dock, it could have been us. At the time we didn't know how long the attack would last. For all we knew the entire island was being invaded. I didn't leave my gun for days. We ate and slept right at our stations.

The battle lasted approximately two hours with hundreds of planes involved. Each of us were furious that these Japanese were allowed to surprise us. We had radar, the Japanese did not. Washington was breaking the Japanese code, they had to know something. Had we been able to meet the Japanese fleet at sea, at night, history would be different.

I saw battleships burning, ships listing and sinking. The Arizona burned for weeks. I heard the explosion of a bomb and saw the bow of the U.S.S. Shaw disappear. Ford Island was in ruins with many fires raging. I witnessed two destroyers in dry dock with us being hit by bombs just as we were. Flames engulfed them, their torpedoes were exploding on their decks, and their torpedo tubes were flying a hundred feet in the air.

The funny thing is that a few days before the attack, a couple of gunners mates from the Arizona were teasing me about taking the gun covers off the anti-aircraft. You see, because we were the flag ship, everyone had to follow our lead. Every day we took our covers off at a different time. So these guys were teasing me, saying "Who's running that ship anyway." That morning, our gun covers were off before the attack.

After the attack, we were taken out of dry dock and sent to California. Over the next few years, I was stationed aboard the U.S.S. Mount Vernon, the U.S.S. Manila Bay and travelled all over the Pacific.

In April of 1945, I was on the LST (*Landing Ship Tank*) during the invasion of Okinawa. We transported the marines there and took the wounded out. I stayed there until the war ended.

Ironically, my two worst days came the day the war started and the day after the war ended. Of course, the Pearl Harbor attack was the day before we entered the war. The day after the Japanese surrendered, we were actually attacked by a group of kamikazes. We were in Bruckner Bay (*Okinawa*) when one of our support ships was hit by an airplane. It actually took the whole bridge out. It came very close to us.

In late 1945, I went ashore and a few of us took a jeep to Hiroshima. As we got closer and closer to the city, we could see more and more damage. By the time we got right into the city, there were only a few things standing. We walked into a news building. The building was standing and still had a staircase. We walked up the stairs and looked out and saw that the city was deserted and everything was leveled.

When I came home in 1945, my daughter Ellen was two years old. This was the first time I ever saw her.

Mr. Lichack and his wife raised two more children in Stamford, and upon his retirement from the U.S. Navy in 1956, he had reached the rank of Lieutenant Commander.

- ENSIGN WILLIAM THOMAS O'NEILL -

When he entered the service William O'Neill was a resident of Darien. However, he was raised in Stamford, and like Vincent Horan, had attended Saint John's School on Atlantic Street. Voted "BEST LOOKING" by the Stamford High School Class of 1933, he went on to attend Fordham University and graduated four years later.

After college, O'Neill joined the U.S. Navy and left for Pearl Harbor on Christmas Day 1940 and was stationed aboard the "Arizona". His parents never saw him again.

Today the name William T. O'Neill is etched in the wall of the Arizona Memorial which honors the men who died aboard the ship during the attack on Pearl Harbor.

- HAWLEY OEFINGER-

Hawley Oefinger graduated from Stamford High School in 1938. After working for Shick, Electrolux and the Stamford Fire Department, he enlisted in the U.S. Navy in 1940. After serving in the North Atlantic for 10 months as a radio operator, Hawley was transferred to Pearl Harbor in November, 1941.

In November of 1941 the Navy was looking for a radioman for a detail detached duty. They wouldn't tell us exactly what it was for. I said, to hell with it. I'll get off this ship. So I end up in Pearl Harbor. I got there only about one week before the attack.

On December 7, 1941, I was in the Naval Radio Station. We were on four hour shifts. I was just about to come on watch from 8:00-12:00. Things were quiet. Normally every message was sent in code. Nothing was sent in plain language so most of the time I didn't even know what message I was receiving. You'd hand the message over to a young sailor who would run down and give it to the skipper who would put it in a machine that would translate it into plain language.

Well, I came on duty at the wrong time. All of a sudden every message was coming in plain language. That's when I knew something was wrong. Then we got the code—I can't remember it. Maybe it was WPL-49. That told all personnel in the U.S. Navy to dump their practice ammunition overboard and load up their guns. By the time we did that there was so much trouble we didn't know where to start. It was like trying to put out a fire with no water.

I had to stay at my post until well past 12:00, but I could hear the banging and the crashing outside. You could see smoke rising from the ships. I knew there was serious trouble but there was nothing I could do but hope that I was in a place that didn't get hit.

It was utter chaos. Confusion. Fires everywhere. For the rest of the day the messages were in plain language. I don't know exactly what I was thinking while I was on duty but it took at least a day or two to realize how much trouble we were in.

I was only at Pearl Harbor for about another few weeks then I went back east to rejoin my ship. To this day I still don't know why they sent me out to Hawaii for only five weeks.

Before Pearl Harbor I had originally signed up for one year in the Navy but I was gone for six. In February of 1941, after attending underwater sound school, I was assigned to a "tin can" (destroyer), the U.S.S. Dallas, a World War I ship, leaks and all. I called FDR every name I could think of. Then we became part of what was called the Neutrality Patrol. (*The Neutrality Patrol convoyed both American and British merchant ships. In some cases, these ships reported the positions of German subs to the British.*)

Our job was to escort merchant ships from Newfoundland to Europe. In all, before the war, we made nine trips. I spent most of my time topside because I figured if the ship went down I'd have at least a 50-50 chance. Down below I'd have no chance. We'd be zig zagging along when all of a sudden you'd heard - BARROOMM and you'd see one of the ships shiver and then down it would go. The German subs would patrol in wolf packs. They'd wait for the right time and then they'd hit the convoy.

I was in convoys with the Reuben James and the Kearny. (*The highly publicized sinking of these two ships in October of 1941 helped to lead the U.S. into an undeclared war on Germany prior to Pearl Harbor.*) The Kearny was the first to get it but it was a newer ship and didn't sink. The Reuben James was about 200 miles south of us when it got hit but we heard that it went down fast.

We usually had a convoy of about 55 ships but I'd say an average of about 30 made it. The subs would come up in the middle of our formation and we couldn't detect them with our underwater equipment. We'd only pick up the sounds of the other merchant ships.

One time the skipper came down to me and asked me to tune into a news station. FDR came on and said "I say A-gain and A-gain not a single U.S. ship is convoying British ships". We all had to laugh at that one. But I do have to say that FDR was 100% behind the Navy.

After the war started I spent the next few years patrolling the Atlantic with the U.S.S. Dallas.

Then, in November of 1942 we actually went to North Africa. We transported a group of rangers up the Sebon River near Casablanca. We ran the ship aground, the rangers got off and captured an airport (Port Lyautey).

We returned to the North Atlantic and I was there until 1944 when I became a radio instructor back in the states. When the war was over I was back on the Fire Department and a month later it was like I was never gone.

Hawley worked for the Stamford Fire Department where he became the Superintendent in charge of communications for the Police and Fire Department. He retired in 1987 after 47 years with the city.

- EMILIO ATTANASIO -

Emilio Attanasio enlisted in the U.S. Navy in 1939 and was stationed at Pearl Harbor from December of 1940 to the Spring of 1942. Just prior to the attack, however, his squadron was sent to Midway Island.

I was with a Patrol Bomber Squadron (VP21). We flew in a twin engine sea plane that was equipped to carry bombs and torpedoes. We flew from 6:00 a.m. to 6:00 p.m. and our primary job was to sight and report any surface craft or aircraft in the vicinity. We had roughly a 500 mile quadrant to patrol. We did this every day.

Three weeks before the attack, just as we were getting into our bunks, we had an alert. We were told to get down to the hangars immediately and arm the planes as fast as we could. Then we were told it was only a drill. The skipper told us he needed to know exactly how long it would take to get the planes armed and ready. That's the first time we suspected that something was in the wind. We thought something was brewing, but we expected at least a declaration of war.

Shortly after this, we left Pearl Harbor and got to Midway around November 30th and then a week later, of course, there was the attack. We got hit at Midway that same night. A little after lights out, we were told to get down to the hangars to muster. Just as we got there, someone yelled, "scatter." We were being shelled. There was a plane that was supposed to go on patrol in the morning, but it was in for a repair. When the plane blew, the hangar went up too. It was one of the biggest fires I ever saw. Later we were told that we were shelled by a destroyer and a cruiser. The funny thing is that our planes had gone out on patrol that morning and never even saw them.

On Midway, the Japanese used to broadcast messages to us over the radio. They used to tell us that as soon as they finished taking Wake Island, they were coming to get us next. Well, they were held up at Wake so that was fortunate for us.

It wasn't until February that we got back to Pearl Harbor. When we got there, the ships were in the same position as when they got hit. They were still pumping water out of some of them. One was capsized; one was on its side. The Arizona was almost completely submerged. There was oil all over the water. It was like that until the end of 1942.

I'll never forget the trip back there. About ten or twelve of us flew back to Kaneohe Bay, and the next morning they took us by truck back to Pearl Harbor. We were all in a great mood, glad to be getting back from Midway, which was out in the middle of nowhere. We were laughing and joking. But when the truck arrived at the landing, everything just stopped. Nobody said a word. We just kept looking around and couldn't believe what we saw. All of those beautiful battlewagons, such powerful machines just reduced to nothing.

One of my friends was on the Arizona. Later he told me that he got up that morning and decided to go up on deck instead of going to breakfast. Just as he was getting there, bombs began to fall and the next thing he knew, he was in the water with his shoes off.

When we got back to Ford Island, our hangar was completely destroyed. If we were there on December 7th, we would have been mustering at around 8:00 a.m. My hammock and mattress were there and when I got back, there was very little left of them.

After his discharge from the Navy in 1945, Mr. Attanasio worked for Chance-Vought, an aircraft manufacturer. After the company moved to Texas, he worked with American Cyanamid until his retirement in 1980.

- DOUGLAS PERRY -

Douglas Perry enlisted in the Army Air Corps and was sent to Pearl Harbor in 1939 as a Control Tower Operator. On the evening of December 6, 1941, Sergeant Perry was invited by a friend to spend the night on the Arizona but because he was on duty the next morning, he declined and returned to base.

When the attack began the next morning Perry was in the control tower at Hickam Field. The Japanese flew close to the control tower and riddled it with machine gun fire. However, neither Perry nor the other officer in the tower was hit. Instinctively, he took out his sidearm and began firing at the planes. Later, out of frustration, he began throwing anything within reach at the low flying planes, including his staplers and paper weights. Like many others that day at Pearl Harbor, Perry later said that he would never forget the faces of the Japanese pilots that strafed him and attacked the base that morning.

Later, from the control tower, he was one of many to sight periscopes in the harbor. They turned out to be two Japanese mini-subs which were subsequently captured.

After the war, Perry worked with the Stamford Rubber Company and Metropolitan Life Insurance Company. He was a pilot in the Civil Air Patrol in Stamford and flew reconnaissance flights until the agency was disbanded.

- WALTER GRABARZ -

Walter Grabarz had originally intended to join the Navy, but when there were no openings in early 1941, he enlisted in the U.S. Army. He was sent to Virginia for artillery training and arrived in Pearl Harbor just four months before the attack.

When I arrived in Hawaii, it was so beautiful that I remember thinking I could spend the rest of my life there. Our outfit specialized in anti-aircraft and our job was to protect the airport at Hickham Field. A week before we knew something was up because we were sent to Hickham, and actually started making our gun emplacements all over the field. We set everything up, sand bags and all, and our guns were loaded with live ammunition. We were supposed to stay there for three weeks, but for some reason, they sent us back to Fort Shafter after only one week. We were suspicious because we never had live ammunition, only for target practice at the other end of the island. We had a premonition. A lot of guys were saying, "Something's cooking. Why do we have live ammo?" Then all of a sudden we're pulling back. I've read a lot about Pearl Harbor since then and I've never seen this explained.

On Sunday morning, December 7th, I was up early and went downtown to catch a bus. I figured I'd go to the beach and relax for the day. At about 7:30 I was waiting for the bus and all of a sudden I saw a big cloud of smoke. I knew it was coming from the direction of Pearl Harbor. Then a major came running up to me and said, "Soldier, where are you going? The Japs are bombing Pearl Harbor. Get back to your outfit."

When I got back, we hooked up a 37mm anti-aircraft gun to our truck and mounted a .50 caliber machine gun on the back. Then we started driving out to Hickham Field on the King Kumahamah Highway. There were about 14 of us in the truck and out of nowhere a ZERO came after us. As we were moving in we saw the bullets hitting the road and heading right for us. The kid on the .50 caliber machine gun froze; he couldn't do anything. Then a lieutenant grabbed the gun and started firing. The plane veered away from us and the lieutenant swung the gun around and kept firing. He hit the plane but the funny thing is that he actually shot it down by the tail. The plane exploded into flames and crashed.

As we drove by the harbor during the attack, you could see that parts of the water were on fire and these poor guys were trying to get out. You could hear them screaming for help and there was nothing we could do. It was like trying to save a drowning man if you couldn't swim. There was just nothing we could do.

We finally got to Hickham Field and that's when we really got sick. Guys were screaming, some were crying, planes were destroyed, things were in flames. There was a staff car on fire and there was the driver still behind the wheel, dead. Then we got into our gun emplacements, but by the time we got there, the worst of it had ended. As soon as the day was over we had to go out and help. There was so much work to be done.

The crazy thing is that the Japanese hit just about every other hangar. The empty hangars weren't touched but those with planes and other valuable equipment in them were destroyed. They must have known just where everything was.

Then the rumors began to fly. We were told that the Japanese had already landed on the north side of the island and they were coming for us. We were on alert for about a week. We worked in four hour shifts and got very little sleep for a few weeks.

We stayed at Pearl Harbor for more than two years after the attack and most of our work was rebuilding and cleanup. (*Grabarz was stationed at Pearl Harbor until June of 1944 when he shipped out. In June of 1944 Walter Grabarz left Pearl Harbor and was headed for Saipan.*)

We didn't know where we were going. Maybe this was the most fearful time for me, knowing that I was going into battle but not knowing exactly where. Finally, when we were half way across the ocean, we found out.

We were attached to the Second and Fourth Marine Divisions because they needed more antiaircraft support. The landing on the beach was terrible. We lost a lot of men. We went in on LSTs and had a heck of a time. We were stuck on the beach for a couple of days, but after a while our fear disappeared and was replaced by anger. You realized that it was either you or them.

What I remember the most are the dogfights that were taking place over our heads as we went in. Then I saw an American pilot bail out, and the Japanese didn't even give him a chance. They all moved in and shot him while he was coming down in his chute. I called them every name I could think of. If there were any curse words in the book, I used them all up that day. Later the Americans did the same thing to the Japanese.

After we drove the Japanese off the beaches, they retreated into caves. Then the Marines tried to flush them out with explosives. But they couldn't go near the mouth of the caves because it was too dangerous. So they had us line the antiaircraft guns and fire right into the caves. This kept the Japs away from the entrances and gave the Marines a chance to blow the cave. Then when the Marines drove them to the northern end of the island, they began to commit suicide. Women and children were even thrown off the cliffs.

Even when we secured the island, it wasn't safe. We were assigned to protect the airfield and every night a Japanese plane would fly over. We called him "sewing machine Charlie." It was a reconnaissance plane. It didn't attack, but it would aggravate the hell out of us because we'd have to stay on alert and sit up all night. I was in charge of the antiaircraft section so I told the guys that I would pull duty all day, and they could rest. Then they'd be on alert all night.

So, one day, I heard this plane. It was very high, but I knew by the sound that it wasn't one of ours. It circled the airport. Then all of a sudden, it swooped down and began firing. The bullets were hitting all over. I think six men got hit. I was sitting in a chair and as the bullets were hitting the coral, my first thought was to hit the ground. When I looked up at the chair I'd been sitting in, it had a hole right in the middle of it.

I ran over to the turret machine gun. It had four .50-caliber guns mounted on it, along with a 40 mm antiaircraft gun and was our only protection. As the plane was coming in again, the Second Lieutenant told me to fire one round every three seconds. I said to the other guys, "I don't care what he says, I'm putting it on automatic." We pushed the gun and hit the plane clean and knocked it out of the sky. *(Grabarz was decorated for "extraordinary courage and leadership displayed during the aerial attack on Saipian airstrip." He received the Bronze star.)*

We stayed on alert permanently after that. At night, snipers would shoot at us and try to sabotage the air strip. One night we put up flares and lit up the entire area. While we were in our trenches, I could swear I saw what looked like a tree trunk, move. I was so tired I didn't know if I was seeing things, so I said to the kid next to me, "Keep an eye on that thing." It moved again. Then I yelled out for the password which was "June." We heard a voice answer, "Joonya." The kid next to me was yelling, "Shoot! Shoot!" When he got a little closer, we all opened fire. Then the kid wanted to go out and check to see if he was alive. I told him he could go out if he wanted to, but the rest of us would wait until morning.

Finally, in February, 1945, they were rotating troops, and I was lucky enough to be sent home on leave. I was discharged a few days before VJ Day.

> *While he was on leave, Grabarz married Helen Ostaszewski of Stamford, whom he had been engaged to for four and one half years. After the war, he worked at Connecticut Light and Power Company and Pitney Bowes where he and his wife worked until their retirement in 1982. Grabarz and his wife now live in Marietta, Georgia.*

- THE BLACKOUTS -

> *As with most towns and cities, Stamford had a number of blackouts as part of its civil defense program. The "Advocate" reported all of the blackouts to be a success – with minor safety hazards. During one of the blackouts, the newspaper reported that Mrs. Nellie Gross, an 84 year old citizen, fell down a flight of stairs. She was brought to the hospital and reported in "fair" condition. During another blackout an overzealous citizen was arrested and fined $25 for throwing stones at a house which had a hallway light burning. One of the stones crashed through a window and struck a woman on the head.[1]*

- AUDREY HORAN VIVIAN -

Vincent Horan was killed at Wheeler Field on the morning of December 7, 1941. He was the son of Timothy and Elizabeth Horan of Hubbard Avenue. The oldest of six children, he attended St. John's School and enlisted in the Army Air Force immediately after his graduation from Stamford High School in 1939.

This interview was with Audrey Horan Vivian, Vincent's younger sister, who was sixteen years old at the time of his death.

Vincent was a wonderful older brother. We all looked up to him. I don't think I've met a young man of that age who's been as mature, responsible and ambitious as he.

I can still see him sitting in a chair looking at the Sunday comics, laughing to himself. He had such a sense of humor, and being the oldest, he was always up to something. One night my father's boss came to supper. My father used to tell us that when his boss got mad he would take his hat, throw it up in the air, and then step on it. So that night my father walked his boss in, took his hat and coat and put them in the closet. As soon as the two men walked into the dining room, Vincent ran over to the closet, grabbed the man's hat, threw it up in the air, and stepped on it. We were in hysterics.

In high school he worked all the time, at the Roger Smith Hotel and Western Union, so he never had time to be involved with sports. But he was Sports Editor of the "Siren," the school newspaper. At Western Union he met Dougie Northrop. Dougie was about four years older than my brother, but they became good friends and Vinnie idolized him.

Vincent Horan

After high school, Vincent wanted to be an FBI man so he actually sent a letter to J. Edgar Hoover asking him what it would take to join the FBI. He got a letter back saying that he needed at least four years of college. Next he wrote to Notre Dame, and I remember him getting a big thick catalogue from them. But my parents couldn't afford college at that time.

Someone suggested that he go into the Army Air Force because he loved air planes so much. His hero was Charles Lindbergh, and he'd read anything he could about flying. In fact, when our parents went out and he took care of us, I remember him telling us to listen every time a mail plane flew over. He had visions of being a pilot some day. Then, when Dougie (Northrop) became a flyer, that became Vincent's goal.

My mother and father didn't want him to

go in. Dad fought in World War I. He was shot in the leg and gassed in the Argonne Forest. So from the day Vincent left, my father was always concerned about him. In fact, he was always anxious to hear from Vincent, always waiting for a letter to arrive. When he left Vincent at Fort Slocum, my mother was so upset, we just couldn't console her. Then when he was shipped to Hawaii, we just knew we weren't going to see him for a long time.

On the way out to Hawaii, Vinnie competed in some boxing matches. We got a letter saying that he fought a 25 year old sailor and won by TKO. He won ten dollars and sent it home. When my father found out about this, he wrote Vincent immediately saying he didn't want him boxing any more.

Once he got out to Hawaii, he loved it. He loved the outdoors and the beach so much, he wrote us a letter saying that it was "the next best thing to heaven."

He wasn't even supposed to be in Hawaii in 1941 because he was originally told that his third year of service would be back in the states. But when his first two years were up, they wouldn't let him come back because they said he was needed there. He was so upset that he couldn't get back home to see us. Back then, you couldn't just pick up a phone and call.

When Pearl Harbor was bombed, there was a lot of confusion. We heard about it that Sunday and didn't know whether or not Vincent was all right. The next day was a holy day so that morning my mother and I walked to Sacred Heart Church, and then I went right to school. That day there was Hawaiian music on the radio, and it went right through me so badly. I couldn't listen to that music for years after that.

That night, my younger brother answered the telephone. It was the Postal Telegraph, and they said they had a message from the War Department. Frank called my mother to the phone and without so much as a word, they just read the telegram over the phone...We regret to inform you that your son, Vincent Horan, has been killed in battle. My mother fainted. There was no preparation for this. It was the first we heard of it.

Ed McCullough was an editor at "The Advocate" and a close family friend. He had gone to Western Union after the attack and told them that if any message came for the Horans to call him first. But this message was not sent Western Union; it was sent Postal Telegraph. They didn't have any messengers so they just read it over the phone. Mr. McCullough came right over to the house, and then the police arrived. They went right down to the telegraph office to make sure the message was really there. *(One day later, "The Stamford Advocate" reported that he was killed at Hickam*

Horan on Waikiki Beach in 1941 with actress Dorothy Lamour

Field. He may have been confused with a John Horan from Tarrytown who was also killed at Pearl Harbor.)

He was the only one in his squadron who was killed. The War Department later told us that, during the attack, he was running down the hangar line, and he was hit in the chest by shrapnel from one of the bombs that the Japanese dropped. He lay there for hours before anyone could reach him. He died from loss of blood.

Before the attack, we hadn't heard from Vincent in over a month. My parents were very concerned because he was normally so good about writing. After his death, we received a letter from him saying that the reason we hadn't heard from him was that they were on alert and had relocated to another airfield. During this time, he had been sleeping under the wings of the planes. I don't know if they were expecting something to happen. In early December, they brought everything back to Wheeler and called the alert off. He also said, "I don't know where I'll be next because they've already sent quite a few men to Corregidor." We were thankful that he didn't end up there because we may never have known what happened to him.

They sent us all his belongings in a box, including his watch, his ring and his favorite suit. The watch was in pieces, and it didn't even have a strap on it. Apparently, when the Japanese strafed the base, the bullets went right through his locker. His shoes were still covered with red clay.

When he was out there, he and another boy bought a car. After the war, the friend came to visit us. He told us that a few days after the attack, he was driving the car and it kept making a funny noise. Finally he looked around, and in the rear hubcap he found a bullet hole and inside it was a bullet. That was what was making the noise.

After Vinnie's death, Dougie Northrop became the leader of a B-29 squadron in the Pacific. On one of his bombing raids, he wrote my brother's name on a bomb and released it. He sent us the pin from the bomb. It reads, "Vinnie. Dropped on Tokyo. April 2, 1945." April 2nd was Vinnie's birthday. We wrote Dougie back to ask him if he knew this, but before he ever got the letter he was killed. *(Northrop was reported missing on April 27, 1945. His plane went down in the Pacific.)*

My mother and father were crushed by Vincent's death. My father became ill and died a few years after the war. My mother lived a long life and died at the age of 89. She rode in some of the Veterans' parades for years and was involved with the VFW and American Legion. She even had the honor of christening a ship, the "U.S.S. Stamford Victory," in honor of my brother (March, 1945). Because of Vincent's death, she received $12 a month until the day she died.

I'll always remember how Vincent used to dance me around the room while I stood on top of his feet. I was a little girl and would think how wonderful it was to have a big brother like this. When he was out in Hawaii, he wrote and told me that he would be back in the states in time to take me to my Senior Prom. Kids would laugh at that today, but I was thrilled. I absolutely adored him.

Audrey Horan married Donald Vivian and raised five children. A street on the east side of High Ridge Road was later named Horan Avenue, but was taken during the construction of a new high school in the early 1960's. For a while there was talk of naming it Horan High School, but ultimately it was given the name of Rippowam. In June of 1973, a small park, on Washington Blvd., just north of Bridge Street, was dedicated to the memory of Vincent Horan. There, a bronze plaque which sits atop a rock stands as a lasting reminder of the first Stamford man to lose his life in World War II.

- *JUNZO NOJIMA* -

Junzo Nojima was born on the island of Kikaikajima in Japan and came to live in Stamford in 1926. Six years later he opened one of the first Japanese owned restaurants in the state, the "K & J Three Decker Restaurant" on Atlantic Street. However, in the days immediately following Pearl Harbor the restaurant was vandalized, and later closed and even after it reopened business was slow. In an interview with the "Advocate" in 1981, Nojima said "I cannot blame the public. They thought I was the enemy. And after awhile my customers came back." The business survived the anti-Japanese sentiment and in fact thrived in its downtown location for forty years.

Over the years, Junior, as he was known to friends, was active in the community and received the Honorary Police Chief Award for his service to Stamford. His most significant and lasting contribution was his work to beautify the Mill River Park. In the late 1950's, in order to show his love

for Stamford and its people, Nojima planted over 150 Japanese cherry trees that now line the river. For years he also watered each tree by hand, using a single bucket and carrying the water from the Mill River.

Nojima prospered in Stamford and later moved back to Japan to live in a mansion that he had built for himself there. But after living there a short time, he missed his adopted town and returned to Stamford.

In 1983, Junzo Nojima died at the age of 83. The trees stand as a constant reminder of his devotion to Stamford. To many in the Japanese-American community he will always be remembered as "Hana Saka-jiji", a character in the Japanese tale, "The Man Who Made the Cherry Blossoms Bloom".

---

1 "Hurler of Stone During Blackout Fined". Stamford Advocate, April 2, 1942, p.1.

CHAPTER TWO

THE FALL OF THE PHILIPPINES

Early in 1942, as the Japanese were rapidly advancing in the Pacific, the nation's attention turned toward the Philippines. Over 70,000 Filipino and American troops were surrounded by the Japanese and in desperate need of food and supplies. After a valiant defensive stand, the Allied troops were forced to retreat to the Bataan Peninsula. On April 9, 1942, ravaged by dysentery, malnutrition, and the realization that the reinforcements promised to them would not arrive, the brave defenders of the Philippines finally surrendered.

What followed was one of the worst atrocities of the entire war known as the "Bataan Death March". The Japanese forced the surviving defenders, many of them sick and wounded, to march in the hot sun almost 90 miles to Camp O'Donnell. On the way thousands died, some beaten, shot and, clubbed to death by their conquerors.

The remaining prisoners were herded into prison camps where the abominable treatment and conditions continued. Over the next three years, hundreds died each week. Toward the end of war the Japanese decided to move the prisoners to the mainland. The journey to Japan was a nightmare. Prisoners were packed so tightly that some became depraved. Others were killed when these unmarked prisoner ships were mistakenly bombed from the air or torpedoed by the Americans.

When the war finally ended in August of 1945, only about 4,000 survivors of Bataan remained. These men had endured almost three and a half years of an agonizing captivity, longer than any other American prisoners in the war.[1]

- JERRY LAMBO -

Jerry Lambo enlisted in the Army Air Corps in 1940 at the age of 18. He was trained as an aerial gunner and sent to the Philippines as a member of the 27th Bomb Group. He had been there for only eighteen days when the war broke out. Because the planes had been diverted to Australia, Lambo was transferred into the infantry and took part in the infamous "Death March" and was a prisoner of the Japanese until the end of the war.

When we were sent out to the Philippines in November of 1941, we felt like we were going to the safest part of the world, like all of the danger was in Europe. After the Japanese attacked we were forced into what MacArthur called a "strategic withdrawal". We called it retreat and we kept on retreating until we reached Bataan. For what little we had, we did a good job against the Japanese. We had no planes. All we had was artillery. I had a 1903 Springfield rifle with World War I ammunition. The safest place to go was the Bataan peninsula because we had the shores pretty well defended. If they wanted us they would have to come inland over the mountains.

We had our backs to the beach and a few 155 mm guns behind us, and we held them right there. The only thing they could do was shell us every day and they shelled the hell out of us. By the second month the cavalry was gone. We had eaten all the horses and were on starvation rations of one meal a day. A lot of us survived on sugar cane and some peanuts we found. But morale was still high. Some guys said that this would be another "Dunkirk"; but how could it be? We had nowhere to go.

The bombs got bigger until they started dropping blockbusters on us. One of the shells came in and I was hit with shrapnel in both of my legs. The medics took the shrapnel out, wrapped me up and sent me right back out. I was fortunate, though, I was able to stay healthy enough to maneuver around. We had all lost a lot of weight. I started out at about 185 pounds but I must've still weighed about 160 pounds at this point. By the end of the war I was down to 127 pounds. There wasn't a lot of medication with all the diseases going around like malaria and beri-beri. But basically before the Death March we still hadn't lost that many men, maybe 1200 in combat, and we were still in pretty good shape. Along with us was the Filipino Constabulary or "Home Guard". There were probably about 200,000 of them on the island but a lot less than that were with us.

By April our commander, General King, had no choice. He had to surrender. We were all told to report to Marvielis and by the time we got there the Japanese were already there and we had already come to the terms of surrender. Then they gathered us all together and later they started us on the march.

When we surrendered, we had no idea what was in store for us, and looking back on it now, we were fortunate that we didn't know. If we knew we were going to be there for three and a half years under those conditions, none of us would have made it. In fact, during the last year of the war we were all at the point of giving up. A lot of us were saying, "This thing is not going to end. We're all going to die here." You just reached a saturation point and our health was deteriorating.

For the next eight days they marched us 85 miles. They marched us during the day in the hot sun. Never at night. They were marching their own troops at the same time under our cover because they probably figured that the American guns on Corregidor would not fire on them if they were near us.

They marched us from sunrise to about five o'clock. They gave us one bowl of rice per day and it was heavily salted so it would make you even more thirsty. And we had very little water. They'd stop once a day and some would be able to get water from a very little spigot. But not everybody got water every day. Some of the guys would go crazy and try to dive for these little puddles on the sides of the road. The Japanese would kill them. They were punishing us for being inferior. According to their code, we shouldn't have surrendered. So we were dirt. Any one who fell out of formation was killed. Mostly bayonetted. They didn't want to waste ammunition on us. These were "The Tiger of Singapore," General Homma's troops and they were mean. *(Homma was executed as a war criminal after the war.)*

The Filipinos were good people. They'd try to give us some food along the way like bananas, or other fruit but the Japanese would beat them. Others lined the road and would holler, "Hey Joe," and give us the "Victory" sign with two fingers.

I think that the guys who survived were either young and healthy or had a will to live. I felt I was too young to die and I always told myself, "I'll live just to spite these bastards." The most important thing, though, was that you had to have a sense of humor. You had to find little things each day that were funny. A man without a sense of humor was lost. It was survival of the fittest. You did everything to help a buddy. If he couldn't get up you'd help him up. But you could never feel sorry for him. Never! You could help to a certain degree but if a guy felt sorry for himself there wasn't much you could do for him. There were also some guys, and you couldn't blame them, that just gave up. Some were older and were ready to return home when the war broke out.

After eight days we got to Camp O'Donnell. The camp was being built for the Filipino Constabulary but was never finished because the war broke out. It was supposed to be a temporary layover for us but we were there for about a month and men were dropping like flies. While I was there I got malaria and was sick for days. At one point they put me in a building that was for men who were dying but I was determined to live and soon I was back with the other guys.

One of the guys who was with me in the Philippines was a friend from New Canaan named Sammy Russo. He was going to enlist in the Navy but then changed his mind and joined the Army Air Corps. He was in the same squadron as me. He never made it out of Camp O'Donnell.

We had burial detail there every day. The prisoners would have to carry the dead out to open graves. We used to bet on how many would be taken out each day. Some days it was 30. Some days it was 40. Some of the guys that survived the death march died here. The vast majority of the men died in the first year and a half. They'd give us rice with weevils in it. Some guys would complain about it but we'd say, "Hey, don't complain. We got meat today."

Later we were sent to the main camp, Cabanatuan. By the time we got there we started to get a little medication and a little more food. We were farmers out there and we ate pretty good because we had vegetables and things. But I didn't want to stay there. The camp itself wasn't so bad but I didn't want to be a farmer. You had your ass in the air and your head down all day. I didn't want to stay there so when the Japanese started to ask for volunteers to go out on work details , I went. They wouldn't tell you where you were going because nobody wanted to go to Nichol's Field. This was the worst detail in the world. The Japanese marines were there and they were tough. They'd kill you if you swallowed wrong.

I was lucky to be sent to Clark's Field. We had barracks there, bunks, running water, showers, and we ate good. It was the best detail. Most of the guys there were happy. They divided us into 30 man details. I was in charge of mine and was what they called a "honcho". I was lucky because we had a guard that was good to us. We called him "Nick the Greek" because the guys all said that he looked like a Greek. Every hour we got a short break and we used to sit down to talk. I wanted to learn Japanese and he wanted to learn English. We'd talk a little each day and through trial and error we were able to communicate. By the end of the year I spoke pretty good Japanese.

But some guys didn't want to learn and some of them couldn't even count in Japanese. And that was important because every day at roll call we'd have to count off. Every morning and every night we had to do this. If you didn't know your number the guards would whack you on the head. We had this young kid from New Mexico, Garcia, who wouldn't learn to count. And he'd be right in the front line, in front of the guards, every day. And every day they'd count off and when he didn't know his number, whack, he got hit in the head. We'd say, "Garcia, at least get in the back of the line or something." But every day he'd be in front and, whack, he'd get it again. Every morning and every night he'd get it. The Japanese guards used to burn, especially Lieutenant Osaka, he was a son of a bitch. He'd come down, with his boots all shined up, his saber hanging and he'd yell and scream and Garcia would get it. And on top of it he'd never fall down. The best thing to do was let them knock you down. Then they'd leave you alone. But Garcia would never go down. We'd say, "Garcia, for Christ sakes, fall down." But he wouldn't. He drove them nuts. I can see it like it was yesterday.

After a while when the guards hit you you'd learn to roll with the punch and fall down and pretend they hurt you. But you might not be in the mood to fall down and you'd say, "Go ahead you bastard, hit me again." There was one guard there who we called Mickey Mouse. He'd yell and scream at you all day. One day I was on his detail and it was right before quitting time and he started yelling at me. I smiled and then swore at him. I figured that since I was smiling at him he wouldn't know what I said. But he knew, and he beat the living hell out of me. But most of the time we had good guards at Clark's Field.

On weekends we'd play them in baseball. We beat them all the time and one week they announced that there would be no more baseball. One of the guards told us that we shouldn't have won all the time. So we begged them to play again and this time we let them win every game.

Judo was a big thing too. When they'd teach us we'd pretend we didn't understand and, bang, we'd sneak a shot at them. We'd give them a rabbit punch to the head or neck. Then when they came at us we'd fall right down.

We had a real scavenger with us named MacCormick. He could take anything and do something with it. One day we saw him carrying a log from a papaya tree. We asked him what he was doing with the log and he said, "You'll see." He sliced it up thin and fried it in oil and it tasted like french fries. After that we used to steal diesel oil and put it in our canteens. Then we'd put potato skins and charcoal in the oil to clean it. Then we'd ask the Japanese if we could take some branches from the papaya trees and they'd think we were nuts. We'd slice up the log, soak it for a few days and then fry it. It was one of our treats.

We also had our own tea. Somebody discovered that if you boiled guava leaves it was like tea. It was bitter but at night it was our tea. It's amazing what you do to survive. Before the war I wouldn't even eat rice.

I was finally kicked out of Clark's Field for "riding the sick book." If you didn't want to work you'd say you were sick. Then they'd send you to the doctor. He was an American, Doctor Kerns. Well, a friend of mine, a guy from Westport named Cosmo, taught me a little trick. He'd close his mouth and rub his tongue against his gums. The friction would cause your mouth to get hot. When the doctor put the thermometer in, you'd have a temperature. Cosmo used to get off five and six days at a time.

I'd do anything to fool the Japanese so one time I told the doctor I had an ear infection. The doctor was puzzled, he couldn't find anything wrong. At the same the Japanese were getting on his ass about the number of sick men there were. Doc Kerns did everything. He cleaned my ear, gave me pain killers but I was in there for fourteen days. Finally he kicked me out and told me never to come back. The Japanese checked the sick book and shipped me back to Cabanatuan. Then a month later they asked for volunteers and guess where I ended up? Clark's Field. As I walked through the gate Old Doc Kerns looked at me and said, "Oh Jesus not you again".

As the war moved to the Philippines they started moving us to Japan by freighter. I think we were the next to last boat to leave. Our ship was the "Noto Maru" but we called it the "Binjo Maru" or "Shit Ship". The trip took a few weeks. This was probably the worst part for me. Worse than the "Death March". They stuffed us down the hatch. There were probably about 1200 of us below deck and we were packed so tightly you could hardly move. We had to sit with our knees up against our chest and pushed right against one another. And it was so hot down there because they'd only open the hatch a few times a day. There was no room to walk. You had to crawl over people to get water or defecate. Guys were starved and half crazed because they had no water.

These ships were not marked so we had to worry about American fire from bombers or submarines. The ship right after us was hit by the Americans and 2400 died. *(In total over 5,000 American prisoners were killed on these ships by American fire.)* We were told that when the ship was hit many of them rushed to get on deck and were machine gunned by the Japanese. I think two guys from Stamford were killed on that ship.

Finally we got to Hanuwa, Japan. It was in the mountains and it was cold. We were issued work clothes and shoes and a paper raincoat coated with wax, and sent to work in the Mitsubishi Copper Mines. We worked in the mines with civilians. They worked like hell and so did we. Sometimes we actually felt sorry for them. They got nothing. At least we got three cigarettes a day. We used to cut each one of them into 4 parts. Then we'd hollow out a piece of bamboo and use it as a cigarette holder so we didn't burn our fingers. Sometimes a guy would say, "If that's too hot for you now I'll take it." I was rebellious in the mines and took my share of beatings.

In Japan they were short on rice so for the first ten days they gave us millet, but it was like eating buckshot. We couldn't digest it and our average weight loss the first week was 7 lbs. Finally they switched us to barley. Once they had us picking locusts. We didn't know why. The next day they were in our barley.

We had an interpreter there. He was a Japanese college professor and could speak English. He would talk to us every day and tell us what was going on in the war. All of a sudden he was gone. We didn't see him for ten days. When he finally returned he told us that he was placed in solitary confinement for aiding and abetting the enemy. But he told us not to worry. He was a Christian and he was praying for us.

At the end of the war I got hurt in the mines. One of the cars ran over my foot. The Japanese doctor there, we called him Dr. Cyclops, never let you off work. His cure for everything was work. But my foot was hurting so badly that I had to go see him. Cyclops wrapped my foot and kept me out of work for ten days. A lot of guys teased me that I did it on purpose but it hurt too much to do that on purpose.

We knew something was up when one day the commander told us that we didn't have to work. Then he told us that the war was over and he didn't see any reason why we couldn't be friends.

Then one day, American B29's flew over and air-dropped food on us. We ate too much and got sick. Later, the Navy rescue team liberated us and they wouldn't let us eat too much at a time.

I don't know how many of us are still left. We have a New England chapter of the Defenders of Bataan and Corregidor. At the reunion a few years ago there were about thirty of us. A year later there were only eighteen.

A lot of people ask me about the experience and how it affected me and I always give them the same answer. I wouldn't do it again for a million dollars but I wouldn't take a million dollars for the experience.

Lambo returned home in 1945 and raised his family in Stamford. For over twenty five years he was the Golf Professional at Rockrimmon Country Club and is presently retired. He was activated again for service during the Korean War and served for one year until they realized that he was a disabled veteran. He was awarded the Purple Heart, the Bronze Star, four Battle Stars, Presidential Unit Citation, the Philipine Presidential Unit Citation with two Oak Leaf Clusters and in 1979 was honored as the Grand Marshal of Stamford's Veterans Day Parade. Today he is on a 100% disability as a result of his combat wounds and the beatings inflicted by the guards. He is one of a rapidly dwindling number of "Death March" survivors alive today.

- THE PHILIPPINE LOSSES-

When the Japanese overran the Philippines, several families waited anxiously for word about their loved ones who were stationed there. By the end of 1942, seven Stamford men, Mike Mishley, Frank Valenzano, Harvey Gordon, Horton Kimble, Lt. Walter Winslow, Albert Ives, and Alfred S. Bocuzzi were reported

missing in action. As news of the atrocities in Bataan trickled back to the United States, hope for the safe return of these men grew dim.

At the end of the war, Albert Ives, Horton Kimble, and Walter Winslow were liberated from Japanese prisons. The others, however, were not so fortunate. Mike Mishley and Frank Valenzano died in Japanese internment camps in 1942. Harvey Gordon survived the death march and the internment camps, only to be killed in 1945 when the Japanese freighter, which was transporting 1800 American POW's back to mainland Japan, was sunk by the Allies. Finally, in December of 1945, news of the last of the men was announced. Alfred Bocuzzi, missing in action since 1942, had died on December 4, 1943, when he was being transported to a prison camp on Cuyo Island.[2]

- THE ODYSSEY OF JOHN BALOG -

One of the most daring exploits of the war took place when a squadron of PT Boats, known as the Mosquito Boat Unit, evacuated General MacArthur from the Philippines and transported him safely to Australia. One of the brave men who risked his life to rescue the legendary General was John X. Balog of Stamford. Balog was the Chief Pharmacist's Mate aboard PT 41, which also evacuated President Quezon from the Negros Island.

Balog joined the U.S. Navy in 1931, at the age of 17. When America entered the war, he was stationed in Manila. On March 11, 1942, as the American defenses on the Philippines were collapsing, the squadron evacuated MacArthur from Corregidor and took him to Mindanao. From there, MacArthur was taken to Australia. En route, three of the other PT Boats were sunk by the Japanese and PT 41 was encountered by a Japanese cruiser, which it sunk. Balog's PT 41 anchored in Mindanao and the crew hid there in the hills for weeks. They then joined up with about 50 other aviators and soldiers who managed to escape from Corregidor. While on the island, they lived on caribou meat and coarse brown rice.

Some of the men managed to repair a damaged Catalina plane that had crash landed there, and Balog was among the seven passengers who were designated to make the attempted flight off the island.

On May 2, 1942, with the Japanese bearing down on Mindanao, the plane lifted off and flew over 1600 miles to Australia where Balog's odyssey finally ended.

Balog and 23 others were awarded the Navy Silver Star with Oak Leaf Cluster for their courageous journey. He was promoted to Ensign and was later assigned to the Naval Hospital in Norman, Oklahoma until his return to Stamford after the war.[3]

---

[1] Donald Knox. Death March. (New York: Harcourt Brace Jovanovich, 1981), p.5.

[2] "Stamford Men Held in Jap Camps." Stamford Advocate, January 28, 1944, p.1.

[3] "Stamford P.T. Boat Hero of Pacific Returns Home." Stamford Advocate, June 27, 1944, p.6.

CHAPTER THREE

WAR ON THE PACIFIC

After the crippling attack on U.S. air and naval forces at Pearl Harbor it appeared as though the formidable Japanese navy would remain unchallenged in the Pacific. But within a year the US rebounded and the stage was set for some of the epic naval battles of history.

Never before had naval battles been fought on such a scale with huge fleets of modern sea craft and aircraft waging war from miles apart. In fact, when the US squared off against the Japanese on May of 1942 at the Battle of Coral Sea, neither fleet ever laid eyes on the other. Similarly, a few weeks later when the U.S. and Japanese forces met again at Midway, most of the work was done by airplanes that had been transported by carriers. At these two great battles the US navy inflicted damage from which the Japanese navy would never recover.

Massive naval battles continued throughout the Pacific and ultimately American naval superiority was a decisive factor in dislodging the Japanese from their island holdings and crushing the Japanese war machine.

- RALPH "CAPPY" COPPOLA -

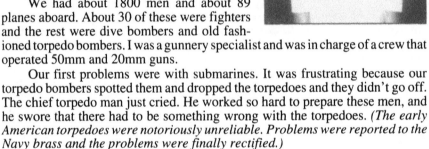

Ralph Coppola graduated from Arnold College with a degree in Physical Education. He enlisted in the U.S. Navy in 1941 and was sent to the Naval Training Station in San Diego as a recruit trainer. In 1943, he was assigned to the Aircraft Carrier U.S.S. Independence.

I stayed at the Naval Training Station for about seven or eight months, but I was anxious to get out on a ship. Finally, I was assigned to the Independence, which was newly built and not even seaworthy yet. We left from New Jersey and had to go through the Panama Canal and from there out to the Pacific.

We had about 1800 men and about 89 planes aboard. About 30 of these were fighters and the rest were dive bombers and old fashioned torpedo bombers. I was a gunnery specialist and was in charge of a crew that operated 50mm and 20mm guns.

Our first problems were with submarines. It was frustrating because our torpedo bombers spotted them and dropped the torpedoes and they didn't go off. The chief torpedo man just cried. He worked so hard to prepare these men, and he swore that there had to be something wrong with the torpedoes. *(The early American torpedoes were notoriously unreliable. Problems were reported to the Navy brass and the problems were finally rectified.)*

The first real action we saw was when we were attacked by Japanese dive bombers. Although we had two destroyers covering us, we had to try to outmaneuver the planes. The Japs didn't dive low enough. The bombs were hitting all around us, but they couldn't get a direct hit. They managed to blow two of our radio antennas off, but other than that, we were lucky that there was no more damage. During this attack, one of the officers became ill, and I was given the job of running the starboard quarter guns. After the attack, we really came together as a crew. We realized that everyone had to do their job for the ship to survive.

We had three or four more confrontations with the enemy. Each time it was against airplanes. It was such an unusual situation, that you really didn't have time to think. You just reacted. Planes would be diving on the ship, bombs would be dropping and you really didn't comprehend everything that was going on.

Once we had a Kate dive at us with a torpedo. He was coming in nice and slow and our gunners knocked him out of the air. Then the Zeroes came in and started machine gunning us. We could see the red flashes of fire blinking at us as the plane came in. We shot the plane down and assumed we weren't hit.

But the next day we had a fire drill on the ship, and when we rolled out the hose, there were bullet holes in it. In another attack, we thought we got off easy, but later down below, we found all of the band's musical instruments were destroyed.

Our biggest and most spectacular battle, though, was against Truk, a huge Japanese base. We attacked on one side, and the Enterprise attacked on the other. It turned out to be a real hornet's nest, and we had to stay at our battle stations from

4:00 a.m. to dark. The Japanese kept coming and coming and coming, and all the while, we had to keep our planes refueled and in the air. That night, the sky was filled with planes, and it looked like a fantastic fireworks show. We lost maybe 15 or 20 pilots, which was a lot, but it turned out to be an even bigger disaster for the Japanese. It wasn't as big a rout as the Turkey Shoot, but it was a big, big day for the U.S.

During the battle, we had a destroyer on our quarter called the "Farragut." They had been out in the Pacific for a long time and were a highly disciplined crew. They stayed right in the quarter position and picked off four planes that were attacking us. It was a tremendous shooting exhibition. A plane would come in, the Farragut would turn to face it and BOOM, down it would go. Later, when the Farragut had to get fuel for us, our band played for them, and we sent over ice cream and movies for the crew. For a while we were all up on deck cheering for them. I still can't get over that marksmanship.

The strangest thing happened at Truk. We hit a Japanese Betty, and it went down on our starboard quarter. The plane was floating in the water, and the pilot got out. He had a white scarf wrapped around his neck. I can see it today. Then he stood on the wing of his plane, took out his revolver and began shooting at us. He was killed immediately, but that always made an impression with me. It showed the tenacity and religious fervor of the Japanese. This guy had no chance against us, yet he took out his gun and tried to fight his way out.

In 1943, we supported the invasion of Tarawa, and it was the saddest event I remember. After days of bombardment from all the planes and battle wagons, the Marines went in and still got cut to shreds. The whole ship was crying. The fire from the Japanese bunkers was so tremendous that most of our guys never even got to shore. We stood at our battle stations, but there was nothing we could do to help.

It was during this stretch when we finally got hit. It was around nightfall when we picked up a few Japanese Bettys coming over the horizon and right at us. By the time we got to general quarters and started shooting, it was too late. We got hit by a torpedo right there in my quarter. We were hit badly and lost quite a few men, but we were lucky to get out of there alive. Thank God they only hit us with one torpedo. It made a hole the size of a room.

When we got hit, I was up in the catwalk with a lot of the men from my battery. I saw the torpedo coming. I saw this big wake, and it was headed right for us. The men on one of the 40mm guns were just blown right off the side. It bounced on the top deck and went right over the side. I was blown inward from the catwalk and knocked unconscious. I don't remember anything after that.

When I woke up, all I saw was the red lights with shadows moving around in front of them. Finally I picked up my head and saw that I had blood all over me. Then the Chaplain said to me, "How are you?" and I said, "Am I in hell?"

I had shrapnel in my head and up and down my leg. My pants had been torn right off. Then, when they tried to stand me up, I realized that I had broken my leg, too. But, overall, I was very lucky. Some men were burned badly in the blast, and that was a horrible sight that we weren't prepared for. And, sadly, I had to write eleven letters to families whose sons in my crew were killed in the attack.

The ship was damaged and trying to limp back at about three knots. We had two destroyers escorting us in, and after a stop on an island right on the equator, we finally made it back to Pearl Harbor.

At the end of 1943, I was commissioned as an officer and moved off the

Independence. I was sent to Panama where I remained until the end of the war.

Thinking back on it now, the thing that amazes me the most is that the U.S. was able to take seventeen and eighteen year old kids, untrained and undisciplined, and mold them together. In three or four weeks, they were expected to match up against the Japanese, who had battle hardened and highly disciplined troops that had over ten years experience. In time, we welded together as a fighting unit and learned that we all had to cooperate with each other to survive. And we proved that we were up to the task!

> *Upon returning to Stamford, Ralph went to work at the liquor store that his father had opened with the money he had sent home from the Navy. He soon took over the store, renamed it "Cappy's," and operated it for over forty years.*

- THE PRINCETON -

During the great naval battle in Leyte Gulf, the carrier "Princeton" was hit by a 550 pound bomb dropped from a Japanese "Judy." The bomb went right through the flight deck and detonated on the hangar deck and the resulting blast and fires forced the crew to abandon ship. Several naval vessels converged on the ship and began to rescue the crew members. Others turned their fire hoses on the burning carrier in an attempt to fight the flames. A few hours later, just when the fire seemed to be under control, a huge explosion rocked the ship, killing almost all who remained on board and an additional 229 who were on the light cruiser "Birmingham," which had drawn close to the ship in an attempt to tow it.

When the Princeton was sunk that day, three Stamford men were on board. Seaman First Class Kenneth Hall, Ensign John J. O'Connor, and Aviation Machinist's Mate John A. Miller were all reported missing. Before long, however, all were reported to be safe. Miller, a veteran of 11 battles, was injured when the force of a Japanese bomb knocked him some 30 feet away from where he was working and burned him on his hands and arms. After receiving first aid, he made his way off the sinking ship and floated in the water without a life preserver for four hours before being rescued.[1]

| Kenneth Hall | John Miller | John O'Connor |

- JOE D'ADEMO -

Joe D'Ademo was seventeen years old when he enlisted in the U.S. Navy. He left the states in 1944 and was stationed aboard the USS Lexington, one of the most proficient aircraft carriers in the war. The "Blue Ghost" was so named because Tokyo Rose proclaimed the ship to be sunk some 49 times. It was involved in several Pacific battles and was awarded 11 Battle stars, the Presidential Unit Citation, and the Philippine Liberation Medal. At the end of the war, the Lexington was credited with destroying over 1,000 Japanese planes and sinking over one million tons of Japanese vessels.

In his two years aboard the "Blue Ghost," D'Ademo saw action in such places as Saipan, Tinian, Iwo Jima, and the Philippines and at one point was at sea for seventeen consecutive months.

I went into the Navy in April, and by June of 1944, I was picked up by the Lexington in the Marshall Islands. It was like a city. We had a cobbler shop, a gym, a coffee and ice cream shop, a movie theater, and a tailor. That's how big it was.

We had over 3,000 men and 126 planes. I was an aviation mechanic 3rd class. I gassed up the planes before they took off. Once the planes were off, I would stay on the hangar deck and my general quarters station was as a firefighter.

In 1943, before I was assigned to the Lexington, it was torpedoed. The first week I was on board, it got hit by a kamikaze, and 30 men were killed, almost all of them were pilots. They were in the ready room waiting to make a raid on the Marshall Islands when it hit.

I was on deck when it happened. It's one of those things I don't like to think about. The plane dove out of the clouds and hit the iron structure. I dove into an opening and hurt my shoulder. But a guy I was talking to just a moment before was killed instantly.

I saw the son of a bitch. You wanted to strangle him, but there was nothing you could do. You didn't have much warning because they'd usually hide in the clouds. You might hear them, but you never saw them. *(During this time, Joe also witnessed the famous Marianas "Turkey Shoot." In June of 1944, the Japanese took a desperate gamble and sent hundreds of planes after American aircraft carriers. The gamble failed and in two days, the Japanese lost almost 400 carrier planes and 3 carriers.)*

It lasted two days and two nights. We worked in shifts, but it was impossible to sleep. At night the sky was all lit up like Christmas. Planes were moving in and out, and at the end of it, the Admiral ordered all of the landing lights to be turned on so that the pilots would see where we were.

Around this time, a ship right along side of us, a jeep carrier, was sunk by a plane. The guys were jumping overboard, and there was nothing we could do. We could only save about twenty of them.

I remember watching as our planes were chasing a Japanese Zero. I was on the starboard side of the ship cheering like I was on the 50 yard line of a football game. "Go get 'em. Go get 'em." I got so excited that I jumped and put my foot through the wing of an airplane. I got out of there in a hurry.

After this, we went to the Philippines in Leyte Gulf. We really destroyed the Japanese fleet there. For a few days, twenty four hours a day, we were shooting down planes. We were part of the 5th fleet, and we had the Admiral aboard (Marc Mitscher). We used to watch him to get an idea of what was going to happen. If we had a general quarters (alarm) and he disappeared, we knew we were in for trouble.

When we were in Leyte, the native women walked around bare breasted. So one day, the Admiral sent in a bunch of tee shirts for them to wear. The next day, the women came out in the tee shirts, but they had cut holes in the front so their breasts were still out.

One day an officer was walking around smoking a cigarette. I was standing watch, and the smoking lamp was off because they were bringing in gasoline. I went up and said, "sir, you have to put your cigarette out." He said, "Oh, okay, Son, keep up the good work." It turned out to be Admiral Halsey.

Sometimes we would carry P.O.W.s to the troop ships. One time we had about two hundred of them and were taking them to the stockade. One of our guys just came up and grabbed ahold of one of the prisoners and killed him right there. He was court–martialed. It turned out that he had a sister that was on the Bataan Death March. Most of the time, though, there were no problems with P.O.W.s. But it did get us mad that when we went to get chow, they always ate first.

The battles at Saipan and Iwo were probably the roughest, but the worst thing that happened was when we were hit by a typhoon. The ship was listing so bad that we had to tie the planes down. We didn't lose any, but I was more scared then than in any battle. *(This typhoon in December of 1944 took more than 800 men, damaged 21 ships and destroyed about 150 planes.)*

In 1945, after Iwo Jima, we went to the Navy yard for an overhaul. We were there when the war ended and were sent to Hokkaido and later Tokyo. The guys on board donated clothing and shoes for the American P.O.W.s. When we went ashore the city was pretty well chipped up. The bombers really did a job. We also went by truck to Hiroshima and later Nagasaki. The cities were leveled, and the people were walking around like they were in a stupor. They acted polite to us, but you could tell they couldn't stand us. I couldn't blame them.

We've had about seven or eight reunions since the war. But in 1975, we went back to Pensacola and actually got to go aboard. When I first saw the ship, I just cried. I hadn't seen it in almost 40 years. Then they took us all out to sea. What an incredible feeling.

Today I wouldn't give up my experiences for all of the money in the world. At the time, you were scared, of course; but to see that many Americans, and how they held together, is something I'll never forget.

Joe D'Ademo came home in 1946 and worked with his father as a mason for several years. He later opened a gas station in the Cove which he operated for more than 25 years.

The "Blue Ghost" remained active until November, 1991, when it was finally decommissioned. Today it is located in Corpus Christi, Texas, where it holds the distinction of being active longer than any other aircraft carrier in the history of the U.S. Navy.

- JOHN FEULNER -

John Feulner entered the US Navy in February of 1941, someten months before the attack on Pearl Harbor. When the US entered the war he was a Fireman Third Class on the USS Hornet, the aircraft carrier which transported the planes for the Doolittle Raid and one of the premier aircraft carriers of the American fleet. Aboard the Hornet and later the USS Coos Bay he saw action at Midway, Guadalcanal, the Phillipines, Saipan, and Bougainville.

My job was down in the fire room (boiler room). I was five decks below the flight deck and below water. In fact, all day you could hear the water rushing by you. It took 9 boilers to power the ship and they had to heat the water to nearly 900 degrees superheated steam to provide steam for the engine. In each of these fire rooms you had a crew of 4 just to run the boiler. It was hot down there and we worked in shifts of 4 hours on and eight hours off. But when you had General Quarters you were on duty with no relief at all and it seemed like you were down in that room forever. At one point in the war, around Guadalcanal, we were on General Quarters for 48 hours without a break!

I reported for service on the Hornet in Norfolk, Virginia, in October of 1941. We trained there for the next few months until the war broke out. Before we left, we had to try and fly two B-25's off our deck. At the time we didn't know why and we were wondering what the heck we were doing with these B-25's. We didn't have an inkling that we were being trained to carry the planes for Jimmy Doolittle's raid. *(Doolittle's raid was one of the most renowned exploits of the entire war. With events in the Pacific looking bleak for the Americans, General Jimmy Doolittle led a perilous air attack on Tokyo designed to shock the Japanese and give a psychological boost to the Americans. The famous 1943 motion picture, "The Purple Heart" was loosely based on one of Doolittle's crews.)*

When we got to Alameda, California, we saw 16 B-25's on the dock waiting for us. We hoisted them aboard with cranes and left that same day. We had to leave these planes right on the flight deck because they were too big to bring down to the hangar deck. With Navy planes you could fold the wings and bring them down by elevator but the B-25's were just too big.

Once we had these planes on deck we were defenseless because if we were attacked we wouldn't be able to bring up our own fighter planes to protect us. We also couldn't send our scout planes ahead to see where the Japanese were. So when we were at sea we met up with the Enterprise and her task force. They would provide air cover for us until we got these planes up and off our deck. Each of us had a task force made up of two Light Cruisers, two heavy cruisers, and six destroyers.

As soon as we got out of sight of land our Captain Mark Mitscher got on the P.A. and told us exactly what we were supposed to do. I think he was the best commander in the entire Navy. He gave you so much confidence that if he told us we were going to Tokyo Bay we would've said, "Fine". We would have followed him. He told us that we were taking these bombers to within 200 miles of Japan to bomb it. It was really to lift morale back home and make the people feel like we were doing something good.

About 400 miles from Japan, we ran into a Japanese trawler. The Enterprise sunk it immediately, just blew right through it, but the commander of the Enterprise was afraid that the trawler was still able to get a message off to warn the Japanese about the bombers. So, instead of 200 miles out, the planes had to leave from there. This is why some of the planes didn't have enough fuel to make it back to China. Some just fell into the sea.

The day we launched the planes, April 18, 1942, was one of the roughest days we ever had at sea. Water was coming over the bow. The ship would go down into the trough of a wave and then back up again. The flight officer timed it so that the planes wouldn't take off until the ship was on the rise. The ship didn't have catapults or anything so they'd just rev up their engines and go.

After we launched the planes we headed north and then back down to Pearl Harbor. We were given strict orders not to discuss where we had been or what we had done. We didn't want the Japanese to know where the planes had come from. The Captain also told us that if the Japanese had found out which ship launched them they'd be out to hammer us. So, we all kept our mouths shut. By the time we got back to Pearl Harbor it was in the newspaper that the Japanese homeland had been bombed. I'll never forget it because when the reporters asked FDR where the planes came from, he said, "They came from Shangri-la". *(In June of 1942 the Hornet participated in the Battle of Midway. This great naval battle left the Japanese fleet badly damaged and reversed the tide of war in the Pacific.)*

We were there for the entire Battle of Midway. We carried 85 planes, a Fighter Squadron, a Dive Bomber Squadron, a Scout Squadron, and a Torpedo Squadron. Before the battle we went to sea and waited for the Japanese east and north of the island of Midway. They didn't even know that we were there. Then, the Enterprise and the Yorktown arrived and surprised the Japanese. They came to Midway as the Kings of the World and when they left they had nothing. We lost our entire Torpedo Squadron there but one pilot survived. His name was Ensign Gay and when he was shot down he was able to bail out. He floated in the water while the battle was going on all around him. When it was over a PBY picked him up.

When the Marines landed in Guadalcanal in August of 1942, we furnished the air cover. We supported the whole landing. A few weeks later, the Wasp, another carrier, was sent in from the Mediterranean to help out. In less than a month the Wasp was sunk by the Japanese and some of her planes had to land on our deck. I'll never forget this because I watched her burning as she got sunk. That left only the Enterprise, the Hornet, and the Saratoga there. Then the Enterprise and Saratoga got hit and at one point we were the only carrier at Guadalcanal. For about a month and a half we were alone there.

In all this time we never took a single hit on the ship. Nothing. I always felt that we'd go forever. Then, finally at the Battle of Santa Cruz, right off Guadalcanal, our luck ran out. The night before we got hit, one of our scout planes had located the Japanese carrier force but the Admiral of the Enterprise didn't want to launch a night attack. Our commander wanted to because at Midway we were successful against the Japanese at night.

So the next morning, by the time we launched our planes, it was too late.

They had already launched their planes to attack us. So we got hit with the entire attacking force, I think it was 64 planes. We had only 8 fighter planes to protect us and there wasn't much 8 planes could do against them. Even with all the firepower our task force had, we just couldn't stop all of them.

I was down in the fire room and I heard this big bang! The ship started listing toward the starboard side and I thought, "Holy Cripe, we must be making an emergency turn -But we were hit - I think by three torpedoes. The ship began to shake and pretty soon we were dead in the water. Then, the bombers came and dropped anti-personnel bombs on us and an entire gun crew on the port side were wiped out. We lost an entire Marine crew on 2 of the 5 inch guns and another bomb hit down in the engineer's mess hall and it wiped out an entire bomb crew there.

One of the kids with us in the fire room was yelling, "I don't want to die." I was yelling that we should cut off some of the burners but another guy was saying that we shouldn't. There were still no "abandon ship" orders so we had to stay down there. Finally, the lights went out and an officer told us to get out.

Two Japanese planes crashed into our ship during the first attack. One came into the #1 elevator pit and landed on the hangar deck and killed some of the officers. The other one crashed into the ship's "island", the place where the Captain navigates the ship.

Before 12:00 noon we got the order to "abandon ship" so they dropped these life rafts down that were made of balsa wood. They weren't lifeboats. They were just rafts that we could hang on to when we left the ship. Then, they rescinded the order because some Japanese high altitude bombers were coming in and the captain thought that we'd be in worse danger in the water. He thought that we'd be killed in the water by the concussion of the bombs. So there we were, on the flight deck, all bundled up trying to protect ourselves when the bombers came over. There were no direct hits and we were given the second order to abandon ship. But by now the life rafts were gone so all we had were our life jackets. The ship was listing badly now toward the starboard side so the port side was high out of the water. We couldn't jump because from that height the life jacket would break your neck when you hit the water. So we had to climb down by rope.

I had the young kid with me and an older guy about 50 years old. He was worried because he couldn't swim. I said, "You have a life jacket, you don't have to swim." We climbed down the knotted rope and were in the water. I don't know how long we were there but it seemed like forever. There was oil all over the water and most of us were covered with it. Some of the guys swallowed it and were vomiting.

Finally a destroyer came. I'll never forget it – The Mustin, DD413. They had cargo nets strung over the side to pick up guys and they also had guys on the bow who were throwing lines down to us. I grabbed one of the lines and was pulled on board. Eventually the young kid and older guy were rescued. The older guy was later reassigned to another ship that was sunk.

When they pulled me on board I scraped my arm up pretty bad but I was so happy I didn't even care. They took me to sick bay full of oil in my hair, eyes, face, and clothes. They took my clothes and cleaned me up. Now I had no clothes and all they had left were a pair of longjohns. So, for the next few days all I had were this pair of longjohns...and my shoes. I wouldn't let them take my shoes and I was lucky because the deck of the destroyer was like an oven.

After everyone was rescued, the Mustin and another destroyer fired on the Hornet and finally it capsized and sank. Finally, after a few days we met up with the task force and were transferred to a cruiser, the North Hampton. They gave us dungarees, a shirt, shoes, and socks. But the best part was being able to take a shower. We went to New Caledonia and waited to be reassigned.

I came back to the states on a 30 day leave and surprised my mother. She cried and asked me how I was doing and I said, "Fine." She told me that she had a bad dream and saw all these men floating in the water. I didn't tell her what happened to the Hornet. But later, after I left, it was in the newspaper and that's how she found out.

Finally, I was assigned to Coos Bay. Our job was to pick up pilots who were shot down. We must have picked up 100 pilots around Guadalcanal, Truk, Rabul, and Saipan. We had another near miss right before the end of the war. We had just left the Navy yard after an overhaul and we were escorting an ammunition ship in the Pacific. There was a merchant tug headed right toward us. It was really a stupid thing to happen in a big ocean like that but the tug headed up right toward us. And then, the tug ran right into the side of our ship and flooded the engine room. The tug skipper backed out and was going to leave when our Captain said, "If you leave, I'll turn the guns on you and sink you." So he waited until we made temporary repairs. Then we went back to Pearl Harbor.

When the war was over we ended up in Tokyo Bay and we were right there when MacArthur accepted the Japanese surrender.

Today, I consider myself a lucky man. Every day since October 26, 1942, has been gravy to me. It's like God gave me an extra 51 years.

I still have the life jacket that saved me. I keep it in the attic - oil stains and all. I went through a lot to save it but every time I look at it, it reminds me that I got a second life.

Feulner reenlisted in the Navy after the war and served for twenty years including two tours of duty on a destoyer during the Korean War. Upon his retirement from the service, he returned to Stamford where he worked for the Post Office for 25 years.

- TRAGEDY ON THE "QUINCY"-

In the battle for the Solomans in 1942, three American heavy cruisers were lost, the Vincennes, the Astora, and the Quincy. Two Stamford men, Daniel Callahan and Gustave Belasco ,were aboard the Quincy which sank a short time after it was hit. Neither man was found, and as Navy policy dictated, both men were declared dead one year and one day after being lost.

Belasco was a veteran of 4 wars, including Mexico, Haiti, and the First World War. From 1928 to 1939 he worked for the Post Office but reenlisted in the Navy when the Second World War broke out .

Belasco died on his 49th birthday. He left behind his wife and his ten year old daughter Frances.[2]

- A LONG WAIT -

James Dockery was an antiaircraft gunner aboard the USS Intrepid. Although at that time many Blacks were often relegated to the role of non-combatants, Dockery's crew in Gun Tub 10 were among the first all-Black combat units in the U.S. Navy.

A little before noon on October 29, 1944, just a few days after the climactic battle at Leyte, a Japanese suicide plane headed right for the starboard side of the aircraft carrier. As the plane bore down on Gun Tub 10, Dockery and the crew remained at their station and fired at the oncoming kamikaze until the fusilage and the bomb dropped harmlessly into the Pacific. But the wing hit Gun Tub 10, killing 9 of the crew instantly and wounding 6. Dockery was hit in the leg with shrapnel. The force of the impact hurled him into the side of the ship and he was knocked unconscious. The crew was credited with saving the Intrepid and, although some of them were promised the Navy Cross, they received the Bronze Star instead.

After the war, Dockery returned to Stamford and quietly pursued the matter, but time and time again he was rejected. He finally gave up hope. Then, in 1993, Dockery's friend and crewmate, Alonzo Swann of Indiana, gained nationwide attention when, after 49 years, he was awarded the Navy Cross.

The Stamford Advocate then located Dockery, the only other surviving member of the guncrew, and ran his story. When Congressman Christopher Shays was made aware of the situation, he began to work with the Navy Department on Dockery's behalf. Just two months later, in January of 1994, the long awaited announcement was made, Dockery would be awarded the Navy Cross.

At the time of the announcement, however, the 87 year old Dockery was seriously ill and in the hospital recovering from abdominal surgery. The ceremony would have to wait until he recovered which, up to the day of the ceremony, was in doubt.

Finally, on April 5, 1994, James Dockery received his Navy Cross aboard the Intrepid, the same ship where it was promised to him almost 50

years earlier. In an emotional ceremony attended by friends, family, and local school children, Rear Admiral David Goebel pinned the cross on Dockery adding that "This medal is a symbol of debt that can only be recognized, but never repaid".[3]

---

[1] "Stamford Men on Sunken Carrier". <u>Stamford Advocate,</u> October 25, 1944, December 22, 1944, p.1.

[2] "Belasco. Veteran of Four Wars MIA". <u>Stamford Advocate,</u> September 16, 1942, September 11, 1943.

[3] Karla Hudecek. "50 Years Later, Vet Receives Navy Cross". <u>Stamford Advocate,</u> April 6, 1994.

CHAPTER FOUR

SUBMARINES:

THE SILENT SERVICE

Submarines played a significant role in the US strategy in the Pacific. Prior to Pearl Harbor, submarines were used primarily to defend the coast of the US, the Philippines, and Hawaii. Once the US entered the war, however, they were forced into a more significant role.

During the first year of the war, unreliable torpedoes and inexperienced commanders made the submarines largely unproductive but by 1943 they began to hit their targets with more consistency.

The men of the "Silent Service" tolerated cramped spaces, the ever present residue of diesel oil on their clothing, and long periods of boredom punctuated by bursts of furious action. In the frightening depths of the Pacific they braved the threat of depth charges and the knowledge that any damage to their craft would result in certain death.

Between 1942 and 1945, the US lost 52 submarines and over 3,000 crewmen but by the end of the war they had inflicted a devastating toll on Japanese ships. Over 200 Japanese warships and 1113 merchant ships were sunk by US submarines, more damage than was inflicted by all of the other US forces combined.[1]

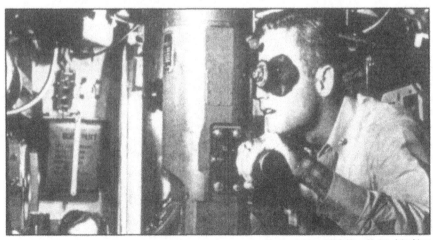

Photo courtesy of U.S. Navy National Archives

- JAMES RAYMOND -

When World War II broke out Jim Raymond was married and operating a Mobil Service Station in town. At age 28 he was drafted and later volunteered for the "silent service." After completing his training at the submarine School in New London, Connecticut, he was sent to Key West, then to Portsmouth, New Hampshire, where he was assigned to the newly built U.S.S. Sea Cat.

The following interview with Mr. Raymond was conducted in 1992 by Frank Derato

We left Portsmouth in June of 1944, and after visiting several east coast ports, headed through the Panama Canal into the Pacific Ocean.

Everyone on board got along well with each other and all ate well. The food was good, and you could eat all you wanted. We used to leave port with milk and fresh fruit and fresh meat. We even made our own ice cream from a powder. We made our own drinking water – we had evaporators. We would take sea water and make our own drinking water from that. Once we had an evaporator break down and the water got pretty lousy for a while.

The only problem was when you went from compartment to compartment you had to learn to duck. After all, I was 6' 2". After you hit your head a few times it wasn't any problem. A little guy could just step over and go from one compartment to another with no problem. We had half a dozen fellows on our boat who were tall. Our skipper was as tall as I am.

I was a machinist's mate. I worked in the after engine room, first as an oiler, then as an operator. My job was to run the diesel engines while the boat was under way. We started and stopped the engines, but they were controlled by the maneuvering room. We had four big Fairbanks Morse diesel engines, and if you needed more power, you started another one up. As soon as it got running, the maneuvering room would take over its control.

Once we had a major breakdown that put an engine out of commission. One of the driveshafts broke, and we had to get that fixed so we could get all four engines running again. We did that while we were submerged and while we were on a patrol operation, running on three engines. We had to work four hours on and four hours off. You got pretty tired after a few days of working like that.

We spent most of our time in the South China Sea and in the Sea of Japan where we made five war patrols. On one patrol, we sank a small freighter and picked up two Japanese survivors. When you take survivors like that, they have to come aboard with no clothes on. They were outfitted, and when they left the ship they looked like a couple of United States sailors – dungarees, shirts, sea bags, a lot of goodies. At the end of that patrol we were going back to Pearl Harbor for a major overhaul and we took them back with us. We had them aboard with us for about two weeks. They were friendly, and we were friendly towards them too. Of course they couldn't speak English but they learned how to smile and say thanks and goodbye.

On several occasions, the Sea Cat was depth charged. It was scary as hell. Like being in a closet with someone beating on the door at you, and you can't run. There were times the fellows would walk around with their bibles or pictures of their wives or girlfriends. Nobody made fun of them because everybody was scared. It wasn't like you were out in a field someplace and you could duck behind a tree and run – you just couldn't.

One time we developed a few water leaks from the concussion of the depth charges. A couple of our salt water lines broke in the after-engine room and we had to plug them up. Another time we were depth charged, we didn't have any major problems other than being held down for about 18 hours. That's quite a long time to be submerged. You start to run out of oxygen. You're quiet, and you just have to wait for your chance to get up and out of there. Usually that's at night. We couldn't sneak up otherwise.

We only received our mail when we went into port. That was also the only time when we could mail our letters. But it might take three or more weeks for a letter to reach home, and depending on our patrols, the letters might be months apart. Of course, we could never identify our location because the letters were all censored. All my wife Alice knew was that her husband was somewhere in the Pacific.

On our last war patrol, we were on our way to the Kuril Islands (*a string of islands between Russia and Japan*) to shell a radar installation, when we received word that the war was over. We sailed to Tokyo Bay and were there when the surrender was signed on the U.S.S. Missouri. We were there for almost a month and finally by December of 1945 I was back home.

We didn't have any really distinguished service. We didn't sink a whole bunch of ships but at least we were there doing what we were supposed to do. And we all got back safely.

When Jim Raymond returned to Stamford he opened up another Mobil station on Summer and 8th Streets. He expanded his operations to include two more stations on the Merritt Parkway in New Canaan. He and his wife are now retired and living in Florida.

The Sea Cat traveled a total of 130,000 nautical miles and made 739 dives. After the war it was used as a training ship until it was decommissioned in 1968.

- MAX MICHA -

It might be said that Max Micha defied the odds. In early 1943, the Machinist's Mate was reported missing in Action when his submarine, the Grampus, was sunk in the Solomons. It was revealed later, however, that Micha was on leave in Australia at the time the sub was lost. That same year Micha, who had earned a Commendation from the Commander of Submarines, and two commendations from the Commander of the Grampus, was assigned to a new sub, the Corvina. On November 16, 1943, the Corvena was sunk off Truk, in the Carolinas. This time Micha was on board.[2]

- HENRY SMITH -

Henry Smith joined the U.S. Navy in 1942 and was sent to torpedo school in Newport, Rhode Island. In 1944 he was stationed aboard the "Seahorse." Commissioned in 1943, the Seahorse became one of the most successful American submarines in the entire war. During 8 patrols in the Pacific, it is credited with sinking 20 Japanese vessels weighing over 72,000 tons.

I hooked up with the Seahorse at Pearl Harbor and made five patrols with it. The Skipper, during most of my patrols, was Slade Cutter. He was quite a guy. He single-handedly beat the Army football team in 1934 when he kicked a field goal for the Navy. He was also an intercollegiate boxing champion in the 1930's.

My first patrol was in the Marianas and it lasted about 60 days. That was about the average time you were out on patrol, but I do remember one time we were out for 105 days. Most of the time we traveled on the surface, but when we got to our area or "station" then we dove. If the skipper saw something through the periscope, we would surface then give chase. Occasionally I'd be on watch on the periscope for a half hour a day and believe me, it was very tough to handle. I'd be exhausted by the end of my watch.

I remember stopping at Johnson Island to refuel and the skipper telling us that the first thing we were going to find out was if the Japanese had good radar. They did, but we still got the best of them. We sank five ships on that patrol including one sub and one sub tender. We were depth charged a few times, but we made out all right.

The thing I remember the most was sinking that submarine. At the time, I was in the forward torpedo room making the #1 and #2 tubes ready. We fired at close range, maybe 500 or 600 yards. It took about 450 yards just to arm the torpedo. When we let it go, there was a big explosion. I was in my BVDs at the time and the concussion knocked me right down. I thought at first that we got hit. But when we asked the captain, he told us that we had just hit a sub. He said, "They were so close they were looking right at us." *(This incident is recorded in "Silent Victory" by Clay Blair, Sr.).*

We were always working blind. Most of the time, only the skipper saw what was going on. Sometimes after a hit, though, we would surface, and I would be able to see a ship going down or on fire. A lot of times after seeing a ship go down, I was happy to take my chances on a sub. It was probably safer under water.

But when we got depth charged, it was another story. The purpose of the depth charge was to force us up to the surface. When this happened, everything was turned off. The air conditioning was cut off, and we would sweat like pigs. Then the Captain sent everyone who wasn't on duty into the forward torpedo room to give us a down angle and keep us down. Then came the unnerving part, when we heard the pings of the Japanese sonar tracking us.

On the second patrol, up near the Philippines, we spotted the Japanese fleet, but one of our motors burned out so we couldn't pursue them. After this we came back to the states for an overhaul and then went back out on another patrol.

I think the worst patrol we made was in the Tsushima Straits between Korea and Japan. We were supposed to plot the mines there, but we got the hell kicked out of us. Sometimes when I was below, I could hear rocks scraping up against the outside of the sub. If we had even taken one hit, that would have been the end for us. We also got depth charged a lot up there, and if that wasn't bad enough, we even got strafed by one of our own planes.

Another time when we were in the Marshall Islands, we were bombed by one of our own planes, but we were not damaged. We had what were called, "safety lanes." Those were areas where American ships could pass safely. Well, we were late for a raid on the Marshalls, and to make up some time, the skipper left the safety lane. We were on the surface at the time and I was down below cleaning the bilges when all of a sudden, we get hit. The sub jerked and the handle of a torpedo door hit me right in the shoulder. I thought this was the end. It turned out that we got hit by a B-24. The sub was damaged, too.

Sometimes we'd draw lifeguard duty. That meant that we'd be assigned to pick up American pilots who were shot down in the Pacific. A few times we even picked up Japanese P.O.W.s. During one of the Philippine raids, a Japanese Betty was shot down. We picked up the radio man. He spoke English, too. He stayed with us for about 45 days until we got back to port. We got along very well with him. Some nights I'd be on the surface charging the batteries of the torpedoes and 'I'd be so tired that I'd doze off. He'd see the captain coming and say, "Smitty, wake up, number one man coming." He was petrified of the Marines though. We used to tease him about turning him over to the Marines. Then when we got back to Pearl Harbor, don't you know that this huge Marine comes to get him. He must have been at least 6' 4". About four years ago I got a call from one of my buddies on the sub who told me that he just read an article about the guy. He was now a very wealthy, successful Japanese business man. Another time we picked up two P.O.W.s, a young guy and an old one. The old guy was okay but the young guy was so violent that we had to lock him up.

The danger of all of this never dawned on me at first. But on my second or third patrol, I remember thinking, "Hey, a guy could get killed out here." And you were always alone out there with no one to protect you. There have been a lot of movies made about subs, but none of them could ever do this part of it any justice.

Henry Smith returned to work at Electrolux where he had been employed before the war. He worked there until his retirement in 1985. The Seahorse received the Presidential Unit Citation for its exemplary record in the war and was decommissioned in 1946. Slade Cutter was recognized as one of outstanding submarine commanders in the war and was awarded four Navy Crosses for sinking 19 Japanese ships. Only one American submarine commander in the war was credited with sinking more ships.

- TAKE HER DOWN -

One of the most legendary acts of heroism among submarines is that of Lieutenant Commander Howard Gillmore and his sub, the "Growler". While on the bridge, Gillmore was unable to avoid a collision with a Japanese provision boat. In order to save his own submarine, as the Japanese were firing down at the bridge, Gillmore assured his own death with his one last order to "take her down". Lt. Commander Arnold F. Schade, a Stamford High School graduate, reluctantly obeyed the order, closed the hatch, and took the submarine down. Gillmore was last seen clinging to the bridge as the ship submerged.

With the "Growler" badly damaged, it was now Schade's job to return the sub and his crew to safety. Although 18 feet of the bow was crushed, and water was seeping through bullet holes, the new skipper managed to get the sub back to Brisbane.

For sacrificing his life to save his sub from enemy fire, Gillmore was posthumously awarded the Congressional Medal of Honor. Lieutenant Arnold Schade of Stamford was awarded the Silver Star and the Navy Cross for the safe return of the "Growler" and its crew. He served the U.S. Navy for 42 years and retired as a Vice Admiral in 1971.[3]

Fred Freeman's painting depicting Gillmore's last moments.

1 Keith Wheeler. *War Under the Pacific.* (Alexandria, VA: Time Life Books, Inc., 1982), p.23.

2 "Max Micha". Stamford Advocate, December 15, 1943, December 16, 1944.

3 "Skipper Killed, Stamford Boy Brings Sub Home". Stamford Advocate, May 7, 1943.

CHAPTER FIVE

THE ISLANDS:

GUADALCANAL

Before August of 1942, few, if any, Americans had ever heard of Guadalcanal, yet the battle proved to be a decisive moment for the United States. It was the first American offensive of World War II.

Prior to the battle for Guadalcanal, the Japanese had overrun most of the Pacific. Although their Navy was defeated at Midway in 1942, the Japanese Army had defeated the Americans in the Philippines and the British in Burma, Malaysia, Singapore and Hong Kong. They now controlled the Pacific from Asia to the Solomon Islands. When they began to set up an air base at Guadalcanal, it became clear that Australia and even some of the other American islands were in jeopardy. The Allies decided to draw the line at Guadalcanal. They would stop the Japanese advance and attempt to make it one of the stepping stones to victory in the Pacific.

On August 7, 1942, the American offensive began when some 20,000 Marines landed at Guadalcanal. Over the next six months, the U.S. met the enemy head on. In these dense, humid jungles, the combat was ferocious and at times, hand to hand. Finally, on February 6, 1943, the Japanese were forced to evacuate what later became known as the "Island of Death."

The victory, however, came at great cost to both sides. Over 1600 Americans were killed, while the Japanese lost over 20,000. But, in the end, Guadalcanal proved to be a turning point for the U.S. and it was the first victory on the road to defeating the Japanese in the Pacific.[1]

Photo courtesy of World Wide Photos

- STEPHEN JOHN VITKA -

Stephen Vitka joined the Marines in 1926 at the age of 18. Over the next 30 years, he traveled all over the world, from the Orient to Central America. During this time, he participated in the incursion into Nicaragua, witnessed the Chinese Civil War and served in both the Second World War and Korea.

In August of 1942, as an Artillery Officer assigned to the famous 1st Marine Division, he was among the first soldiers to land in Guadalcanal. He remained there until December, when his entire division was evacuated.

Going in, I supported a company which was commanded by Captain Bill Hawkins from Stratford. In fact, I believe that I registered the very first artillery fired against the Japanese in World War II because I was assigned to fire first to establish a firing pattern.

We all knew that the war was coming, and we knew it would be against the Japanese because we were involved with them while we were in China during the later 1920s. We saw the Japanese first hand and knew them better than any of the other armed services.

In 1940, we were in Cuba trying to organize a division. Usually, a division has about 30,000 men; we had only 17,000. Later we made it up to about 35,000, but most of these were reserves. We trained in Cuba and later Camp Lejeune, and when Pearl Harbor was attacked, we were not surprised. We were almost expecting it.

In April of 1942, we were told that we would be going overseas. To show you how unprepared the country was, we didn't even have enough transports (ships) yet. When we went to the Kord Islands to make some practice landings, we weren't prepared. The landings were a disaster. The coral was so bad that it was shearing the bottoms of our boats. Then we had to get out of the boats about a mile from shore. We didn't have the right kind of boots, and the coral ruined those, too. We were the "guinea pigs." We learned the hard way. It's still amazing to me that we survived the real landing.

In August, we loaded in New Zealand and were ready to go. We didn't know where we were going, but we knew we were going into combat. The day before we landed, we were told that it was going to be Guadalcanal, but none of us had ever heard of it. Nobody even knew where we were except the navigator, and he had never even seen the place before.

We got there before dawn on August 7th. We opened up with the bombardment, and the planes went in and softened up some of the targets. When we were in the boats going in, it was still dark. I went in on a boat that was no larger than a rowboat. Thousands of us went in like that.

We were lucky though. We had very little resistance when we landed. We caught them so far off guard that their food was still warm when we got there. They retreated into the jungle, and on the first day, the beaches were ours. We were lucky because if Guadalcanal was defended like Tarawa, we would have been annihilated. The biggest obstacle was the Kunai grass. It grew as high as 8 feet, so you couldn't see a thing. You didn't know what to expect; you had to keep guessing.

Because we didn't have much initial contact with the Japanese, we were able to start unloading the supplies, and we got about one-third of it off the ships. The Japanese had also left so much behind that we were able to use their weapons, dried fish, rice saki and beer. That kept us happy.

But on the second day, all hell broke loose. Our ships were caught by the Japanese. That night, they sank four of our cruisers, and when we woke up the next morning, our ships were gone and we didn't even have enough supplies for two weeks. We went on two rations a day the first week and then down to one ration plus what we captured from the Japanese. I weighed about 180 pounds when I got to Guadalcanal, and when I left, I was down to about 135 pounds. It was that way with most of the men. Later I got malaria and so did about 75% of us. There were also other tropical diseases—dysentery, fevers, everything. But unless your fever went above 103, you had to stay on the line.

For two weeks, our ships were gone, and we didn't have air cover. So during that time, the story was mainly survival. We were getting hit from the air and from the Japanese ships. Then the Japanese would make landings at night, 200 or so of them at a time. That would keep us on our toes. This went on day after day, and we had four or five battles with them where we killed hundreds of them. Sometimes we would have to strip the dead for food, clothing, and weapons.

In October, reinforcements came, but most of the soldiers were from the National Guard and didn't have real jungle training. We worked with them because we'd already had combat experience. We had a nucleus of men who knew how to survive in the jungle.

I was an Artillery Fire Director. I would set up in the jungle between our front line and the rear battery. I had about five troops with me. The advancing troops would radio us and tell us where they wanted the artillery to land. I would then figure out the coordinates and call it in to the battery. I'd always try to fire the first one long because we didn't want to hit our own troops. After this, I could get an accurate reading and see if our maps were correct. In the jungle, sometimes it was hard to maintain contact, even with the radios. So we had sentry dogs—Dobermans and German Shepherds. They were especially good at night because they allowed us to get some sleep. If there was any problem, they would react. I can't say enough about them.

The Japanese were very deceptive. Some spoke English so well that many of our signs and countersigns were words that began with the letter "L." We were told that the Japanese had trouble pronouncing the letter "L." One time, we were cooking something for breakfast and a bullet hit the mess pan square. There was a Japanese soldier in a tree right above us.

Sometimes the younger troops were scared. They'd get shaky. We didn't have any psychiatrists or sociologists to calm these youngsters down. Because I was older, I would sometimes take a small group out with me and explain to them exactly what was going on. I always thought that a lot of their fear was because they were never told what was going on. I would try to give them the big picture, make them a part of it. Sometimes I would say, "Look I'm 35. I have a wife and two children. You watch me. If I get excited, you get excited.. If not, don't worry." A lot of times these young men would go back and talk to the others and be a good influence on them.

One time, our radio man turned around and said, "Sir, we're surrounded." There were only five of us, and about eight Japanese came right up from behind. They could have easily killed all of us, but they were surrendering. Their Lieutenant was a graduate of Princeton, and he had just about had it.

I think the worst thing that ever happened to me was one day when I was talking with my Commander. We were reviewing what was going on. All of a sudden we were strafed by a Japanese zero and a young kid who was my runner jumped into us and knocked us both down. His actions saved both of our lives, but he was killed when he was hit in the head. God love him. He was the finest young man I ever knew.

In 1978, I went back to Guadalcanal. They were commemorating the independence of the Solomon Islands, and I met two Japanese officers who were in the battle. We talked for a while, and one of them said to me, "The artillery was ferocious." I said, "I know, I directed it."

I very seldom think about the battle now. I've seen so much in my life. I've been through earthquakes, a locust plague, and I was even kidnapped in China, but Guadalcanal was the worst. But here I am now, at the age of 85, and when I think of all the youngsters that gave their lives out there, I wonder often why I'm here.

After the battle, Mr. Vitka was reunited with his family whom he had not seen in over two years. He served his country again, during the Korean War and moved to Stamford a few years later. He has been active in local politics and community activities, serving on the Fair Rent Commission and the Stamford Area Senior Citizens Alliance. He is a past president of the Stamford Veterans Council, Vice Commander of the D.A.V. and one of the founders of the Western Connecticut Retired Officers Association.

Mr. Vitka has also received the Presidential Unit Citation, two Battle Stars, the American Defense Ribbon, and the Yangtze Service Medal.

- LT. JOHN B. DOYLE, JR. -

John Doyle, Jr. distinguished himself at Stamford High School in both football and lacrosse. He went on to attend Boston College, where he was named to the All New England Lacrosse Team. After graduating in 1940, he attended the Harvard Graduate School for Business Administration, but left after one year to enter the Marines.

He was commissioned a Second Lieutenant in 1942 and sent to the Pacific. During the battle for Tulagi in the Solomons, with a squad of fewer than ten men, Doyle repelled a Japanese attack against his mortar observation post and succeeded in pushing the enemy "over the side of a precipice". On August 7, 1942, he was awarded the Silver Star.

The following year, while under intense enemy fire near the Matanikau River in Guadalcanal, Doyle "descended a steep wooded hill" to help evacuate the wounded. The enemy fire was so intense that at one point, "one of the wounded men he was trying to carry back was killed while in Lieutenant Doyle's hands". On that day, he saved the lives of at least three of his men.

For his heroism at Guadalcanal, Doyle was awarded his second Silver Star, which was presented to him by Admiral William "Bull" Halsey, Commander of the South Pacific Fleet. Later, in commenting on his actions at Guadalcanal, Doyle would only say that, "Anyone in my position would have acted in the same manner".[2]

TARAWA

Because it was believed to have a relatively small force of Japanese defenders, few American military planners believed that Tarawa, and its companion Makin in the Gilbert Islands, would be one of the bloodiest battles in Marine Corps history.

In November of 1943, after a furious air and sea bombardment, the assault on the Gilberts began. Although Makin fell in two days, the battle for Tarawa proved costly. The Japanese defenses withstood the savage bombing that preceded the invasion. In addition to this, the water around the island was not as deep as planners had thought and large coral reefs stopped the American landing craft hundreds of yards from shore. As the Marines advanced, the Japanese concentrated all of their fire power on the very narrow portion of shoreline that the Americans had to use as their landing site.

In the first hours of the invasion, the Marines suffered heavy losses, but finally after four days of savage fighting, Tarawa was taken. Of the estimated 4800 Japanese defenders, all but a few were killed. The Marines had lost over 1000 men with another 2000 wounded, but although it was a costly fight, the American planners would apply the lessons learned at Tarawa to future island campaigns.[3]

Photo courtesy of U.S. Marine Corps

- HAROLD YALE RODANSKY -

Harold Rodansky enlisted in the U.S. Navy in 1942, where he became a Pharmacist's Mate. Because they had no hospital corpsman of their own, Rodansky was assigned to the Marines during the initial assault on Tarawa. About 300 yards from shore, Rodansky left his landing vehicle and began tending to wounded Marines and bringing them to safety. He waded through the water three times to evacuate his comrades. On the third trip he himself was wounded by a Japanese shell that landed nearby. Rodansky was washed ashore, where he was finally evacuated.

The following is Rodansky's own account of the events at Tarawa as it was related to Joan Doman of the Stamford Advocate in 1944.

We were aboard our troop ship one day, when all the men were called into the officer's wardroom and given instructions for the coming invasion. Four days before D-Day, our warships were supposed to knock out all the (Japanese) gun positions, and our planes would drop 1000 lb. bombs. Most important of all, there was a coral reef around the island, but we thought our planes would take care of that. In short, we thought it would be a snap. We thought.

When D-Day came, we all went over the side, down the nets, into the boats that were waiting for us, and off toward Tarawa. When we got a half mile off the island, we waited for the set time. The planes were still bombing and we could see the huge fires they started. It really felt good to see our battleships let loose with their 16-inch guns. It seemed as if after four days of bombing and shelling, there should not be a live Jap left.

Then came word for us to rush in. Praying there would be holes in the coral so we could get through, we started forward. We got within about 300 yards of the beach, when our boat ran up on the coral. The coxswain tried his best to get over it, but all in vain. The Japs noticed by this time that the shelling had stopped and manned their guns. The coxswain swore and gave up, so over the side we went into chest high water.

Just as I hit the water, they opened up with everything they had. Lots of men never got out of their boats, they were blown up. We still had 300 yards of water to wade through to reach the shore...we were unable to fight back and they (Japanese) were in their fox holes just picking us off.

About 100 yards off shore, I met a pharmacist's mate from L Company dragging a man that was hit bad. His face was half gone. I went over and he asked me to take him to the boats that were waiting to carry the wounded back to the ship. I managed to get him aboard and started back toward the fight.

By this time, the bullets were coming from all directions. You have no idea what it feels like to be powerless to fight back. Keeping low and ducking the bullets which struck all around me, I made my way to within a hundred yards of the beach, when I saw a man groping around in the water. I went to see what was wrong, but he didn't have to tell me. His face was burned badly and he was crying that he was blind. I gave him a half grain of morphine and led him back to the boats though a rain of lead.

Once again, I made my way towards shore. What happened to me, I can't say. I must have gotten too near a shell that was meant for the boats...for it knocked me out like a light.

Someone must have dragged me onto the beach or the tide washed me ashore, because one of the men in the company saw me in the sand. Thinking I was dead, he passed me up to treat the wounded men. Eventually, someone noticed I was alive and put me on a track that was going to the ship.

That's about all that happened to me. I was discharged from the sick bay nine days later.

Four days after our part of the invasion, we raised our flag and the English flag over Tarawa. I guess you know how many Marines were buried there.

Tarawa, in the Gilberts, is another step closer to Japan and that day won't be far off now. I thought of mother while those Japs were taking shots at me, and did lots of praying. My prayers must have been answered.[4]

Rodansky recovered from his wounds and later saw action on Saipan and Tinian. For his courage at Tarawa, he received the Silver Star.

- LT. MYLES FOX -

On August 7, 1942, the first U.S. offensive of the war began with the attack on Tulagi and Guadalcanal. Lt. Myles Fox of Stamford gave his life during the bloody battle for Tulagi and was posthumously awarded the Navy Cross for extraordinary heroism.

Fox attended King School and Williams College, where he played baseball, football, hockey, and was named to the All New England Soccer Team. He was commissioned a Second Lieutenant in the Marines in 1940, and volunteered for the Marine Raider Battalion.

On the night of August 8, 1942, during the assault on Tulagi, a Japanese attack threatened to break a battalion line between two companies. During this engagement, Fox was wounded and died the following day. His Navy Cross Citation reads that Fox:

although mortally wounded, personally directed the deployment of personnel to cover the gap. As a result of his great personal valor...the enemy suffered heavy losses and their attack was repulsed. Fox, by his dauntless devotion to duty, upheld the highest traditions of the United States Naval Service.[5]

In January of 1944, the Navy launched a new destroyer, the U.S.S. Myles Fox, which was named in honor of Stamford's fallen hero.

THE MARIANAS

The Marianas served as a stage for some of the most bloody fighting in the entire Pacific War. The most significant fighting took place on the islands of Saipan, Guam, and Tinian.

In June of 1944, a combination of American air power, naval, and expeditionary forces assaulted the island of Saipan. Within days Guam and Tinian were also invaded. The battles for these rugged well-defended islands raged for weeks and at the end the cost was staggering.

Saipan was the largest and most important of the islands in this chain. It was the headquarters for both the Central Pacific Japanese fleet and the 31st Army. Of the 29,000 Japanese on the island over 27,000 were killed. This includes thousands of civilians who committed suicide rather than surrender to the Americans. The U.S. too, paid a heavy price. Over 16,000 men were either killed or wounded. Of them over 12,000 were Marines.

Guam was the next island to be invaded. Fighting there lasted longer than the other two Marianas and American losses were 405 killed and over 17,000 wounded. The Japanese lost over 17,000. Although the battle ended on August 10, 1944, survivors would continue to surface for years, the last one surrendering in 1972. Guam was the first American possession in the Pacific to be retaken.

The last of the islands to be invaded was Tinian, the smallest of the Marianas. The battle continued there until August 1, 1944, when fighting ceased. There the Japanese lost over 6,000 men with U.S. casualties totaling under 2,000.[6] One year later, Tinian served as the air base from which the atomic bomb missions against Hiroshima and Nagasaki were launched.

Photo courtesy of U.S. Marine Corps

- EDWARD MANJUCK -

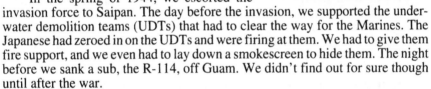

Ed Manjuck left high school during his Senior year to enlist in the U.S. Navy. As a Second Class Gunner's Mate aboard the U. S. destroyer Wadleigh, he saw action in the Marshall Islands, Marianas, and the Carolinas. In 1944, his ship supported the invasions of Saipan and Tinian.

I remember vividly the morning I left for the Navy. I got up around 3:00 a.m. to catch the train to New Haven. I had a paper bag sandwich bag with a comb, a toothbrush, and a tube of toothpaste—that was it. I didn't want to wake anyone, but my sister heard me leaving and said, "You're not going alone." So she walked me down to the train station.

In the spring of 1944, we escorted the invasion force to Saipan. The day before the invasion, we supported the underwater demolition teams (UDTs) that had to clear the way for the Marines. The Japanese had zeroed in on the UDTs and were firing at them. We had to give them fire support, and we even had to lay down a smokescreen to hide them. The night before we sank a sub, the R-114, off Guam. We didn't find out for sure though until after the war.

The day of the attack, we began the actual shore bombardment in support of the invasion of Saipan. At the time, I was the gun captain for the 40 mm guns. We went up and down the coast of Saipan and fired whenever we were called upon. We got in as close to the reefs as possible to try to back up the Marines. As the troops moved along the beaches, we would move with them. If they ran into a tank or a pill box, they'd call in for support and we would knock it out.

On two occasions we had to rescue pilots that were shot down. One time we had to go after a pilot in the channel between Saipan and Tinian, and we drew fire from both islands. We picked up the pilot, but he was badly burned. Later we found out that he had died. Another time, a pilot was shot down, and the Captain promised a case of beer to whoever spotted him first. We got him back safe and sound.

The coast of Saipan was loaded with caves. We had to open up on them throughout the battle. Sometimes we had to shoot snipers in the cliffs and caves. Some nights we had to fire star shells to illuminate the island. We were very effective and were considered specialists with the shore bombardment. *(In his book, "Saipan: The Beginning of the End", Major Carl Hoffman credits the Wadleigh with firing 4,598 rounds— the most of any ship in its class and over 1,100 more than its nearest competitor.)*

As a matter of fact, the Japanese gave us a lot of credit. They said that the bombardment hampered them, that they might have been able to hold out a lot longer.

Toward the latter part of the battle, the Japanese were being beat and were being pushed into the northern part of the island. It was inevitable that Saipan was going to fall. Early one morning, we were at the north end; one of the men yelled out that the Japanese were jumping off the cliffs (now called Banzai Cliff). I looked up and saw hundreds of people just jumping right into the ocean. They didn't have a chance. People were taking children and just hurling them out over the cliffs. It didn't look real, almost like dolls falling into the surf. There were bodies in the water for days. I remember particularly well, one beautiful morning, seeing a man in a khaki uniform floating face down. Along side him was a woman, bare breasted, and next to her a young boy with khaki shorts. It looked like a mother, father and son. That stands out in my mind. Soldiers jumped with the civilians here, but most of them jumped off another on the island (*now called Suicide Cliff*). There was almost no feeling, just a fascination that this could happen. A few days earlier, they were shooting at us.

People were trying to escape the island too. During the battle, some of the Japanese were trying to get to Tinian. In each case, we would launch a boat and try to get them to surrender. They rarely did, and we would have to fire on them. One day we picked up a Korean boy who was swimming. I don't know where he would have gone if we didn't pick him up. We picked up quite a few Koreans and Okinawan laborers but very few Japanese and no soldiers.

During the battle, you got very little sleep. If you got one or two hours in a stretch, you were lucky. We slept right at our guns. You couldn't sleep below. It was like being in a garbage can and having someone beating on it. We had one day when it seemed like everyone was firing at us—the Japanese shore battery, planes and even our own guns. *(The ship diary confirms that, in addition to avoiding enemy fire, the Wadleigh was mistaken for a low flying aircraft and fired on by the Americans.)*

During the Tinian invasion, we set up a dummy invasion that was designed to draw the Japanese to one side of the island. It worked, and while they were mobilizing at one end, the Marines attacked a very small section of beach on the other side of the island. Compared to Saipan, this invasion was almost unopposed.

Tinian was also littered with caves on the east coast. At one point, we had a Marine who could speak Japanese. He went on the P.A. and began telling the Japanese to surrender before we opened fire. A lot of soldiers surrendered, and that night we fired on the caves. There were a lot of suicides at Tinian, too. Not too many people know about that.

We were between Tinian and Saipan for about two and a half months. Then we went back to the Marshall Islands and were preparing to take part in the invasion of the Philippines. On our way, in a place called the Kassol Passage, near the island of Peleliu, we were sent out with a mine sweeper. The sweeper would cut the mines loose, and we would fire and detonate them. We removed 23 mines, but the 24th hit us. Three guys were killed, and we had a 40 x 50 foot hole. We were dead in the water. The Navy Department wanted us to scuttle the ship, but the Captain transferred most of the crew and sent some of us to try and salvage the ship. We worked in three shifts around the clock. While we were there, we were strafed by Japanese planes. They must have been the worst bombers they had, because they never hit us. Then one night, while we were listening to the radio, Tokyo Rose came on and said, "Tonight's songs are dedicated to those poor boys who are half sunk in the Kassol Passage." She did this for three nights. It didn't hurt morale. It made us feel important. She was talking about us.

The Wadleigh was patched up, and we got back to Pearl Harbor on Christmas Day 1944. I never went back to the Wadleigh because I was given a leave, then sent to Washington. The ship got back in the war, though, and was right next to

Manjuck (right) revisiting Suicide Cliff in 1991 with his brother

the Missouri when the Japanese surrendered. I wish I was there. In Washington I was sent to the Naval Gun Factory where I studied a few different guns. In fact, I was there when FDR died and saw the funeral. It was very sad because as a young boy, I shook FDR's hand when he was on his way through Stamford. Later when I was on the aircraft carrier U.S.S. Franklin D. Roosevelt when it was commissioned, I got to shake Harry Truman's hand. That's my claim to fame; I've shaken hands with two Presidents.

Anyway, the FDR never got into battle. The war ended and I was home by 1946. There is a lot of talk about heroes in the war. We weren't heroes. We never had time to think that way. To us it was a job, and we knew that the sooner we finished it the sooner we'd go home.

Ed received four Battle Stars for participating in three campaigns with the Wadleigh and sinking one submarine. The day he returned, he worked for his father's business, Bill's Auto Wrecking, and later opened the Stamford Driving School, which he operated for over thirty years. In April of 1994, Mr. Manjuck passed away.

- CHET BUTTERY -

Chet Buttery enlisted in the Marine Corps immediately after his graduation from high school in 1944. He arrived in Saipan in the spring of the following year and, as a member of the 5th Combat M.P. Battalion, was stationed there until 1946.

I originally wanted to enlist in the Marines after Pearl Harbor, but my father told me to finish high school first and then we'd talk about it. When I graduated two years later, I went for my physical, but because I was 17, I needed my father's signature. He wasn't too happy about it, but he signed the papers, and I was in.

After basic training on Paris Island at Camp Lejeune and antitank training at Camp Pendleton, we were shipped out to the Marianas, first to Guam and then to Saipan. We were only at Guam for about a week, but the first day there we were attacked by Japanese planes. While we were there, they were preparing to ship all of us to Okinawa, but at the last minute, they picked 500 of us out of 5000 to make up the 5th Combat M.P. Battalion. By luck of the draw, I was one of the 500. The rest of the guys went to Okinawa, and within a week, ended up with somewhere near a 90% casualty rate. I lost a lot of buddies up there. It was just dumb luck that I didn't end up at Okinawa.

We were shipped to Saipan where we were attached to the 2nd Marine Division and trained as combat M.P.s. We found out later that our Battalion was being trained to be on the beach before the first wave attack on Japan. Thank God for Harry Truman and the Atomic Bomb. That invasion would've been a nightmare.

In the meantime, there was still a lot of mopping up to do. There were still plenty of Japanese on the island and a lot of caves that had to be cleaned out. As a matter of fact, the first day one of the guys went across a road after some bananas, and he was shot and killed.

After we dropped the bomb, we were still mopping up. We would go out each afternoon and set up Fire Teams. Once it got dark, we'd be instructed to shoot at anything that moved. We'd do this every other night. It was amazing. The island was small, but there was still so much rough country left. We were still rounding up Japanese months after the war ended.

Once we went into a valley, and there were still hundreds of machine gun nests there. We also found the remains of bodies that were there since the time of the invasion. They were actually chained and padlocked to their guns.

Later, our outfit took control of the POW camp at Saipan. There were over 1500 Japanese prisoners there. We had to move the camp down from Mount Topatchau to one of the beaches. While the prisoners were digging fenceposts for the stockade, they began to unearth hundreds of bodies. Apparently this area was used as a mass grave. (The *beach referred to here was along Tanapag Harbor on Saipan, and it was indeed a mass grave. In July of 1945, it was the site of one of the largest "Banzai" attacks of the war. After two Japanese Commanders committed suicide, thousands of Japanese soldiers hurled themselves into the marine artillery positions. When the battle was over, more than 4300 Japanese had been killed.)*

Overall, the Japanese prisoners didn't give us a hard time. They did go on strike once. They refused to work. But in a short time, we were able to get them back to work. As far as the enlisted men were concerned, the war was over and that was it. It was the officers that gave us a hard time. They were very antagonistic and arrogant. They would never even deal with us; they would only deal with another officer. They were the elite.

I came home a year after the war ended. What we did was interesting at the time—it was real—and I was also very lucky.

> *When Chet returned to the States, he resumed his job at Cyanamid. Shortly after, he went to work for the phone company where he stayed for 35 years. Chet has also been a volunteer at Belltown Fire Department since 1951.*

- JACK GOLDEN -

After working at the Naval Air Station in Bermuda, Jack Golden returned to the states and enlisted in the Marine Corps in 1942. As part of the Third Marine Division, he served on Guadalcanal and participated in the landings at Bougainville, Guam, and Iwo Jima.

We arrived in Guadalcanal in November of 1943. By that time, the battle had been over for quite some time, but there was still plenty of mopping up to do. We were stationed at Henderson Field, and to protect it, we set up a perimeter each night and were instructed to shoot anything that moved.

Going into Bougainville, I was manning the 40 mm guns. Bright and early one morning, we were just scanning the skies when all of a sudden a Japanese airplane came in right along side of us and hit the ship right next to us. There must have been at least twenty LSTs, and we all opened fire on it at the same time and just destroyed it. It's amazing that with all of that fire, we didn't shoot each other. We spent about a month at Bougainville and were back in Guadalcanal by Christmas of 1943. We didn't know it at the time, but we began training for the invasion of Guam.

Before we went into Guam, we were at sea for 55 straight days. After a while, we used to joke that we were passing the same wave every day. It was unbelievable. Finally on July 21, D-Day, we went in. We got into the Higgins boats before dawn and were just floating around in the water for a few hours while they bombarded the island.

The beach landing was not the worst of it. The biggest problem was the tough resistance we met on the interior parts of the island. Our maps were wrong, too. We were told that the beach we were landing on had a huge trench surrounding it, but we never saw it.

Guam was hell. At one point, we were on the line for 16 straight days. You'd be in a ditch that was wet and humid, and you'd have to take turns sleeping at night. You never really slept soundly, though. Sometimes at night, the Japanese would scream to us, "Marine you die tonight." Other times, you'd hear noises and you didn't know if it was an animal or the enemy. Then if one guy fired his rife, ten more would. One time, three guys in a foxhole fell asleep. One of them must have had a nightmare and thought he was fighting the Japanese because the next thing you know, the three of them ended up in a big brawl right there in the foxhole.

An odd thing happened just before we landed at Guam. When we were on the LST, a friend of mine kept telling me he didn't want to go in because he had a premonition that he was going to get hit. Sure enough, when we were on the beach, he was shot in the side of the face. He must've had his mouth open because the bullet passed through one cheek and came out the other. It didn't touch a thing in between. Nothing. It was remarkable. If he had been an inch to either side, he probably would have been killed. But he was evacuated and turned out fine.

While I was in Guam, I met a couple of local guys who were in the Seabees, Billy Coughlin, Tony Good and Ralph Jessup. The Seabees had much better food than we did, so every once in a while the guys would sneak me in to eat with them.

After Guam, we left for Iwo Jima. We weren't scheduled for the initial assault, but were supposed to go in later. Three different times, we got into the Higgins boats for a landing, but all three times were called back. The beaches were so congested, we never made it in. So we got back on the transport and watched the battle from there. I'll never forget what happened later. When they began to take the wounded back to our ship, it was discovered that one of the kids who was badly wounded was the son of the ship's Captain. You could see that the Captain was torn apart emotionally. He wanted to be with his son, but he had to run the ship. His son later died on board.

In 1945, we began to train for the invasion of Japan. The 3rd Division was supposed to spearhead the assault, and I think they were going to use all of the divisions. We were told that it would be bloody, but then the Atomic bombs were dropped and the war ended.

I'm a believer in Providence. I was originally assigned to the 4th Marine Division, but I developed spinal meningitis at Camp LeJeune and was later reassigned. Who knows what would have happened if I hadn't gotten sick. The 4th took very heavy casualties. Maybe I wouldn't be here right now.

Overall, I don't regret a thing. But I do hope that my grandchildren never have to go to war and experience what we did.

Jack Golden returned to the states after the war was over. He was a plumber in Stamford for over 40 years.

- JACK PALMER -

Jack Palmer enlisted in the Marines in 1942 and never saw home again until the end of the war. In 1944, he participated in the battle for Peleliu which held the largest air base in the Palau Islands. Originally the island was supposed to be bypassed, but believing that it would only take three days, the decision was made to invade. Unbeknownst to the American attackers, the island contained a network of tunnels, caverns, and well protected artillery. Operation Stalemate, as it became known, dragged on four weeks and became one of the costliest battles in the Pacific.

When we left the states from Camp Pendelton (California), we were sent to the Samoas. They were already well developed, and it was a beautiful place. It was also the last time we would see a girl until the end of the war. From there we must have seen 10-15 islands, usually after they were secured.

When I went to Guadalcanal, the first thing I did was look for Carl Battinelli, who was one of my closest friends. I walked up to the first Marine I saw and said, "Do you know Carl Battinelli?" And the guy says to me, "Yes I do, but he just got transferred out yesterday." We were there a long time after the battle, but they were still mopping up. You could never completely clean out an island. It took forever.

The first two battles I saw were at Peleliu and Angaur. At first the Marines were sent to Peleliu, and I was sent to Angaur along with the Army. Angaur had so many flies that you had to wave your hand in front of your mouth as you were eating your K-rations. You still ate flies; I must have eaten a million of them.

I will never forget, as we were going toward Peleliu, you could see the battleships opening up on the islands. The big guns pounded it, one after another shells hitting the island. You're saying in your head, "When we get to shore, there won't be anything left. There is no way anyone can survive." But somehow they survived. They were there!

Then the Marines went in, and the first guys ashore got smeared. They were dropping like flies. The Japanese were dug in. The caves were so deep, I bet some of the guys are still there.

We must have been out in the water five or six days before we went in. When we finally got to the island there were a lot of dead bodies— a lot of Marines, a lot of Japanese. The thing that got you the worst was the death around you. Bodies in the water floating, bloated. If I had to go through that again today, I couldn't; but we were trained to expect this.

I was trained as a machine gunner. So when we went in, the first thing we did was dig a big foxhole and set up our machine gun. We each had an area. At night there would be gunfire, flares going up in the air, and the Japanese would be screaming at us "banzai." That would keep you awake all night. Sometimes they would attack and sometimes they wouldn't.

Believe it or not, one of the scariest times for me was when we had to climb up one of the volcanoes. We had all of our equipment, and because I'm afraid of heights, this was worse than anything for me. I'm still afraid of heights.

We were warned not to touch any of the dead because some of the bodies were booby trapped. But some guys were always looking for souvenirs and somebody would get killed. Once I saw a Japanese soldier's wallet, and I actually felt sorry. At the time we hated them, of course, but when I saw pictures of his family, I realized that his pictures were just like the ones we had. I mean, there he was, laying there dead; he didn't know what happened. He did what he was told just like we did.

I was out there about three or four months. The people back home probably knew a lot more about the war than we did. We didn't know anything. We couldn't even celebrate when an island was secured because there was nothing out there— no cities, no girls. We did get warm beer.

I don't think about the war too much anymore, except once a year on the Marine Corps Anniversary when a bunch of us get together for dinner. That's the only time we talk about it, and because I'm the oldest of the local boys, I get to cut the cake.

Jack returned to the U.S. and later operated a construction and excavation business in Stamford for many years. At present he owns and operates High Ridge Variety on High Ridge Road in Stamford.

New Guinea

    The Japanese captured New Guinea in 1942 and during the early years of the war, it became an important air base for Japanese bombers. But as the tide of war in the Pacific turned toward the Americans, the Japanese high command made a decision to defend New Guinea at all costs, and with 35,000 defenders, the task of capturing the jungle island seemed daunting.

    In April 1944, the American offensive began when forces under General MacArthur invaded the Northern coast of New Guinea at Aitape and Hollandia. The air, naval, and amphibious assault was successful and by the end of 1944, New Guinea was captured with relatively low casualties, while costing the Japanese over 15,000 men.[7]

Photo courtesy of U.S. Marine Corps

- EDWARD POLTRACK -

Edward Poltrack enlisted in the Army Air Corps after high school in 1940, with the dream of becoming a flyer. At the time, however, there was a college requirement for all pilots. When the war broke out in 1941, the college requirement was dropped, and at the age of 20, he became a B-25 pilot.

During the war, Poltrack flew 61 missions in the Southwest Pacific, most of them in New Guinea. On 15 of those flights, he served as the Squadron Commander.

I arrived in New Guinea in the fall of 1943. The temperature was always around 100 degrees, and the humidity was incredible. It was a fascinating place, like being taken back in time. There was a terrifically dense jungle, and the terrain went from sea level to 15,000 feet.

The Japanese still held northern New Guinea. To get there, we had to fly directly over steep mountains. Getting this huge plane with all of its weight over these mountains was always an experience. The plane would be chugging and shaking while it made the steep climb, and all the while you'd be practically touching the tree tops. Then, once you were over the mountains, you'd have to go into a straight dive down to the target. The weather was also a major factor. Sometimes everything would be fine, then suddenly you'd be in the middle of a thunderstorm.

The first mission turned out to be a pretty hot target. We were attacked by Japanese fighter bombers, and when we went low, we were fired on from the ground. I could see this guy on the ground firing a machine gun at us. We were going close to 200 miles per hour, and I probably only saw him for a split second, but I remember him very clearly. At one point, I broke formation, and the Flight Commander yelled at me to, "Get the hell back here." I never really felt the danger, though; I was busy looking for a target.

While we were in New Guinea, I met up with my cousin who was a First Sergeant with a photo outfit. He told me that my brother, Frank, was on one of the neighboring islands. It was Christmas, so I asked the Squad Commander if I could take a plane to look for him. My Commander took a big chance, but he actually let me do it. Sure enough, my cousin and I found Frank. He had just arrived from Guadalcanal and was preparing for another landing. I was so lucky to find him because we got to spend a few hours together.

Incidentally, the next day I actually flew a mission which supported his Marine Division as they invaded Cape Gloucester. As the plane peeled up, I could see the boats going in and it was like a scene from a John Wayne movie. Here I was flying a mission and down below, my brother was making the landing. We were supposed to fire our machine guns in bursts because the barrels got too hot and burned out. That day, I burned out all of my guns because I just kept firing.

Francis made it through the landing, and I visited him shortly after when they secured the islands, but this was the last time I saw him. Later he was killed during the invasion of Peleliu. I was up in the Philippines when I got the news. The next day, I received a letter he had written the day before he died.

Most of the time the weather was more dangerous than the Japanese. One time we were supposed to hit an area of flatland that was almost at sea level. It was a new target, and I was on the Flight Leader's wing. There was a bank of clouds straight ahead near the base of a mountain. I assumed that our Flight Leader would go above the clouds; instead he flew right into them. He must have had second thoughts because all of a sudden he went into a steep bank to lead us back out of it. I went full throttle to keep up with him, but suddenly I couldn't see him at all. I knew that there were mountains ahead, but I wasn't sure exactly where. Just as I pulled the plane up and out of the clouds, I saw Japanese fighter planes ahead. For a split second I thought, "Oh no, I'm alone here with these fighter planes." But then two more of our planes popped out of the clouds, and Lord knows where the others were. I signaled the others to get on my wing and follow me to the target. But I wasn't sure where the target was. We ended up joining another squadron and followed them to the target. The Japanese fighters were outnumbered and pulled away.

Just as we hit the target, I heard a large bang. A 20mm shell hit the armor plate on the front of the plane. The plane was clanking along, and I knew that I shouldn't attempt to climb over the mountains so we landed at an alternate base.

When we landed back at the home base, the Commanding Officer asked me what had happened. I told him, and he just mumbled and walked away. We later found out that our flight leader and the rest of the squadron had turned around and never got to the target. We were the only ones who completed the mission.

Probably the toughest mission we ever had was a 10-hour, round trip flight to Hollandia, which was at the far end of New Guinea. Of 127 planes that went out on that mission, only about half made it back. In fact, our plane was the only one in our squadron to land intact.

On the way back from Hollandia, there was a terrible storm. To get back to our base, we had to go through a cut in the mountains. But the visibility was so poor that I decided to follow the coast and try to land at an alternate base. The storm got worse, and we had to drop right to the deck (fly just above the trees). We could barely see enough of the coast to gauge where we were. Every once in a while, a plane would soar by, but not too many knew where they were going.

All of a sudden, there it was, the prettiest sight I'd ever seen—a little airstrip. It was one of those temporary runways which were made of metal matting. The metal runways were always short and didn't give you a lot of room to land. As we got closer, we could see damaged airplanes all around. One with blown tires, another that had gone right off the runway, and one with damaged landing gear. Fortunately, we landed safely and taxied to watch the other landings. Two planes collided on the runway and exploded into flames. Another plane came in and caught its wing on the wreckage and sheared it right off. We'd seen enough, and the

Edward Poltrack (right) visiting his brother Francis (center) on Christmas, 1943.

first thing we did was get ourselves a drink. This was probably the scariest day of the war for me.

We had limited contact with Japanese fighters, but I do remember one time we were attacked by one. I looked out and as plain as day, there was a fighter coming right at us. I could see the flashes of the machine gun firing right at our plane. "Hey this guy's for real," I thought. Luckily, one of our gunners got him, but it was nothing like in the movies when the crew is talking to each other over the intercoms. This was more like a baseball game with everyone shouting out directions at the same time.

My co-pilot eventually got his own plane and was lost at sea. We searched for him, but I remember thinking how impossible it would be to find him in such a vast ocean.

Then after my 61st mission, I was asked to volunteer for just one more. It was going to be an attack on the Japanese fleet. I had never been involved with a mission like this, so I was very reluctant to go. But I volunteered anyway. At the last minute though, some new hotshot colonel came in and wanted to fly, so I was bumped. It turned out to be a very tough mission, and the first three planes in the squadron were shot down. Once again, I was a very lucky man.

Mr. Poltrack returned to the U.S. in 1944, after his 61st mission, and supervised instrument flying requirements at Andrews Field in Washington, D.C. After the war, he married his sweetheart and went to Yale University to study Electrical Engineering. He worked for AMF, Barnes Engineering, Norden and Pitney Bowes until his retirement.

- FRANCIS POLTRACK -

Francis Poltrack, or Frank as he was known to his friends, was three years older than his brother Edward. After his graduation from SHS, he entered the Marines, where he became part of the famed First Division. He participated in the landings at Guadalcanal, New Guinea, and Peleliu.

In a letter to Edward on September 13, 1944, he reassured his brother, telling him, "don't fret...I'm still mentally tough."

Just two days later, Francis Poltrack was killed in the bloody assault on Peleliu. He was twenty four years old.

IWO JIMA

Iwo Jima was one of the epic battles of the war. The island was only eight miles square, made mostly of rock and ash, yet it proved critical to American strategy in the Pacific. Because it was only 600 miles from Tokyo and on a direct route from there to the Marianas, Iwo could serve as a fighter base for the big bombers on their way to the Japanese mainland.

The battle for the island turned out to be one of the bloodiest battles of the Pacific. By the time it had ended, the U.S. had lost over 7,000 men, with 20,000 wounded. Admiral Chester Nimitz later said of the battle: "On Iwo Island uncommon valor was a common virtue."[8]

- JOE SHAWINSKY -

Joe Shawinsky enlisted in the U.S. Navy and was a member of the "Sea Bees." He received marine training and was attached to the 4th Marine Division which participated in the initial invasion at "Yellow 2" beach in Iwo Jima. It was the first time that an entire battalion of "Sea Bees" took part in a Marine assault.

I don't know if people realize today that the only reason that they're breathing free air and expressing themselves as they wish is because some kid gave his life. There are a lot of my friends still out at Iwo Jima. They said that a lot of Congressional Medals of Honor were given there but as far as I'm concerned, they couldn't give enough medals.

We left Maui in December of 1944, and while we were out at sea for about two weeks before we landed, we were told that it would be Iwo Jima.

We were told that Iwo would be a 72 hour operation. In fact, we were already discussing our next landing in Japan. That's how much we knew.

We were supposed to land at "Yellow 2" on the northeastern part of the island. This beach was steeper than most and actually had terraces. For weeks the Navy threw everything it had at the island to soften it up for the invasion. As a result, by the time the landing took place, there was no greenery, just rock and sand. It looked like Dante's Inferno. What made it more eerie was that parts of the island were still cooling off and had sulfur fumes coming up. It stunk like hell, and it looked like hell.

The island was honeycombed with caves made by Korean laborers. Thousands of Japanese soldiers were dug in, and they had their big guns zeroed in on the beaches. No matter where we landed, the Japanese couldn't miss, so we knew it was going to be rough. I would like to have a talk with whoever it was that said it was going to be a 72 hour operation.

On the morning of February 19, 1945, at 2 a.m., we had what they called "dead man's chow." It was a steak dinner with all the trimmings and, for many of the guys, it would be their last meal. Then we got on gear, got ready, and entered the boats that would take us to shore.

It was a funny feeling. After sitting around the high seas for weeks and wondering, we were almost relieved when the moment finally came. There was the island; there was the enemy; this was going to be it. We bobbed around in the water until we were given a line of departure and a signal to make a run for the beach. The ramp went down, and we ran out onto the beach.

This is when I knew it was for real. I actually said to myself, "So this is where it's all going to end." The beach itself was terrible. You couldn't dig a hole because the sand was so fine. *(In one account, a private said, "It was like trying to dig a hole in a barrel of wheat."*[9]

It seemed like it took a half day just to dig a foxhole. Then we had to climb up a series of terraces. You'd take one terrace and then there was the next one.

Everything was frontal assault. What a mess. Some of the equipment got bogged down on the beach; guns and artillery were going off all around.

I was stuck in that shell hole for much of the first day. We were pinned down. That night we captured a block house just a few feet from the beach, and I helped a few of the guys set up communications.

As the marines moved off the beaches and further inland, our job was to build roads around the beaches and to the airfield. But because the sand was so bad, it took a long time, and the beach was my home for the next two months.

Shawinsky's photograph of the destruction at Nagasaki

After about three or four days, we could get some work done; it was always under fire. I remember one time I was preparing a foxhole for myself and a buddy was laughing at me. He said, "What are you doing that for? We're not getting shelled." I said, "You do what you have to and I'll do what I have to." A few minutes later an artillery shell went over our head, and who do you think jumped into the hole right on top of me?

After a few days on the beach, I heard a big cheer go up all along the beach area. They were all pointing to Mount Suribachi, and there was the flag flying. It was such an important moment for us, so symbolic. What a great feeling. We knew we still had four-fifths of the island left to go, but this was when we knew we were going to win this thing.

But, it was always scary. Something could always happen. There were guys who made it through the tough stuff and got killed after five weeks. Booby traps, snipers—there were always hazards. We were told not to go into the caves. Once, one of the guys went into one of the caves, probably looking for a flag, or a sword as a souvenir. The next minute he was killed.

You just never know how you are going to react. Some of the toughest-looking guys broke first, and some of the smallest guys became the heroes. Some of these poor guys took part in so many of these landings that they just finally had it. For so long they were waiting, thinking that soon it would be their turn to die.

And me? I never got a scratch? Why? Why wasn't I killed? Why was I spared and some other kid was not? I just have to believe that someone had other plans for me.

Joe Shawinsky's 133rd Sea Bee Battalion was dissolved and attached to the 31st NCB. However, it earned its place in history. It is believed that the first Black ashore at Iwo was Cleveland Washington of the 133rd. The battalion also suffered the heaviest casualties of any Sea Bee Battalion in the war.

Shawinsky came home to Stamford where he became a history teacher and principal in the Stamford Public Schools until his retirement in 1990.

- WILLARD WOODHALL -

On the night of February 24, 1945, during the battle for Iwo, Marine Sergeant Willard Woodhall awakened to the sound of enemy artillery fire close by. Woodhall left the safety of his shelter and found some of his own artillery crew pinned down and the acting section chief wounded. With Japanese 320 mm rockets bearing in on their position, Woodhall, on his hands and knees, began carrying ammunition to his loader, directed fire, and destroyed the enemy gun position. For his courage under fire, Woodhall, a veteran of the Saipan and Tinian invasions, was awarded the Bronze Star.[10]

- ARTHUR "JIM" TROWER -

Recruited out of Yale University, Jim Trower became a Marine Officer in 1944. As a Second Lieutenant in the Fifth Division, 27th Regiment he was in the first wave of Marines that hit the island of Iwo Jima on February 19, 1945. Trower's company landed at the south-ernmost point of the invasion, designated as the "Green" and "Red" beaches.

When we were out at sea we didn't know exactly where we were going but we had these sandbox models of the island. The only thing we knew was that it was shaped like a pork chop.

As we were going in we could see the island being bombarded by the Navy ships. Everyone figured that this couldn't last a long time. We thought, "This will be nothing." There was no way anything could live through that bombardment. But when we got there we found out otherwise.

Going in we were supposed to have our helmets on but I had mine strapped to my back. I was wearing only a campaign hat. Well, it didn't take long for me go get my helmet and put it where it belonged. It still amazes me that we got as many men ashore as well as we did. It was utter chaos.

The terrain on the beach was very strange, volcanic ash. But I think it might have been to our advantage because a lot of the Japanese shells coming in at us seemed to bury a little in the sand before they exploded. The shrapnel didn't fly as far. If the surface was harder I think the schrapnel would have been worse. But it was impossible to dig yourself in; you couldn't get a firm edge. In fact, I was buried a few times on the first day. There would be a loud explosion and the next thing you know you were covered with sand.

Most of our division was green but some of the guys were veterans of other island campaigns. One of our guys was "Manila" John Basilone who won the Congressional Medal of Honor at Guadalcanal. He didn't even have to be with us. He could have been back in the U.S. selling war bonds. He was killed on Iwo.

There were heavy casualties on that first day. I lost two of my friends who were with a rifle company, right there on the beach. In the first hour I was hit in the arm, but it wasn't so bad that I couldn't patch it up myself. Not too smart, huh? All you could think about was, "What am I doing here?" and hope it didn't last long.

I don't remember exactly what our first objective was but we did get off the beach and got to an airstrip by the end of the first day. (*The airstrip was probably Chidori on the south central part of the island.*) That night we dug in and first thing the next morning a round landed near us and I got buried again.

I don't remember the day to day things we did after that but we always kept moving. I remember trying to take one hill and being forced back a few times. Each time we did we'd pass the same dead Japanese soldier. (*This hill was most probably 362A which was taken by the 27th Regiment.*) We came in contact with cave after cave and we had to flush the Japanese out of each one. One day we heard a large explosion in one of the caves. They had blown themselves up.

One of our men, a forward observer, was evacuated off the island because he was suffering from shell shock. A few days later they brought him back and he was out there again. One day I was talking to him on the phone and all of a sudden the phone went dead. He had been shot right through the head.

I don't remember when we finally realized it was over but at the end I was the last original officer in the company. Of over 200 men who had started out, only 60 of us were still left.

After Iwo we were sent to Hawaii and were preparing for the assault on mainland Japan. We were supposed to hit the southwest coast of Kyushu. Then the war ended and I went in with the Occupational Force. When we got there we found out that there were more Japanese in our planned landing area alone than were thought to be on the whole island of Iwo. We would have been slaughtered if the Atomic bomb hadn't been dropped. I stayed in Sasebo until the Spring of 1946. We actually liked the Japanese people once we got through fighting with them. The kids were cute and we treated them nicely and gave them little treats.

In one little village I went into a house and saw a Singer sewing machine there. The only difference was that the woman pictured at the machine was Japanese instead of American.

I also got out to Nagasaki and was amazed that just one bomb could do all that damage. The city was just laid level.

Trower won two Purple Hearts and was one of a select few men who survived Iwo from D-Day to the end of the battle. After leaving the Corps be became a special agent with the FBI and stayed with the agency for the next twenty-six years. In 1973 he joined Mobil Oil Corporation as a security advisor for its international operations and later worked for the Stamford based Gleason Plant Security.

- TO THE SHORES OF IWO JIMA-

Prior to entering the Marines, Lt. Herbert Schlosberg of Stamford was an executive for Monogram Pictures, Inc. As a member of the Fourth Marine Division, he directed films on the battles for Kwajalien, Saipan, and Tinian. During the battle for Iwo Jima, Schlosberg filmed the Marine and Navy amphibious invasion which was later released by United Artists as the motion picture short "To the Shores of Iwo Jima". The film, which was in Technicolor, was shown at theaters across the country.[11]

- DAVID McKEITHEN -

David McKeithen joined the U.S. Army in 1940. He was one of 52 black recruits from Connecticut selected as cadre to train other black soldiers. When the war broke out he was a Second Lieutenant in an 81mm Mortar Platoon. He resigned his commissionwhen he was informed that ,as a black officer, he would not be allowed to serve overseas at that time. Influenced by his brother Angus, who was already a Marine, McKeithen, too, entered the Marines in 1943. In 1945 he was finally given the opportunity to fight for his country during the fateful battle of Iwo Jima.

We were called the "Gross 52 from Connecticut". First we were sent to Fort Devins, then to O.C.S. in Fort Benning, Georgia, then out to Fort Huachuacha, Arizona. I became an officer in the 92nd Buffalo Division. There, the black officers were not allowed to mix with white officers. We even had a segregated mess hall. One time a few black officers refused to sit at segregated tables and were thrown in jail. One of them was a guy from Stamford, William Nelson. He just went right up and sat at the Commanding Officer's table. After this incident, they sent the rest of the division on maneuvers, but took us 52 officers and sent us on a three day forced field march. The white officers rode in a jeep while we walked. Then at night they would go back to the main compound, while we would have to camp out. Well, the last night of the exercise we were taken to our bivouac area and told to bunk out for the night. That night we heard shells going off around us and a fire broke out just above us. When we got back to the compound I heard some white officers talking about the fire and how it forced them to cancel their drills. They were going to saturate the area with artillery. They could have killed all of us if that fire hadn't broken out. Later the Inspector General B.O. Davis came to investigate the incident. He told us, "I may be your color but I'm not your kind." Nothing ever came of this incident.

Later I was sent to the Presidio in San Francisco to teach bayonet and unarmed defense to other recruits. For long periods of time we had nothing to do. Unless new recruits came in we'd just sign in and sign out every day.

Then, I applied for overseas duty. A lot of black troops were being sent over to Europe but I was told that they weren't going to send any Black Army officers over at that time. Once I was told, I resigned my commission. My brother Angus was a Provost Marshall in the Marines and that convinced me I should join.

When I arrived at Marine boot camp I still had my Army officer's raincoat on. The Battery Sergeant picked me and another guy out of the group. I was the smallest guy in the group and the other guy had to be about 6'4". He took us into a room and worked us over real good. When he finished he said, "That's just to show you that nobody's too big and nobody's too small to follow orders." They were tough on us there but when we were finished, we were fit for combat.

At our graduation the Commandant said to us, "I've been all over the Pacific, to Guadalcanal, and I've seen men blown up, killed, destroyed. But when I came back here and saw you people in the Marine Corps uniform I knew we were at war". He didn't say it in a derogatory manner. That's just how it was.

We left Hawaii in January of 1945 and sailed all over the Pacific for 33 days. All the while we were hearing about how the U.S. was saturating this island with bombs. The day before we went in, we were finally told where we were going. We had maps and everything and were told that we would be landing on Blue 2 (a beach on the southeastern shore) of Iwo Jima. I was with the 34th Marine Depot attached to the 3rd Marines which was part of the Fifth Amphibious force. They told us that this would be a 72 hour operation and that it was just a "tune up" for the big invasion. Later I found out that they were talking about Okinawa.

When the first wave went in we were told that they didn't hit a lot of resistance. But later the Japanese opened up on them. Later that day when we went in we suffered our first casualties. A mortar came in and this kid from Brooklyn, Hank Deverny, got hit. He was wounded in the side and they had to take him out. Another kid was killed. It was too bad because he didn't even have to be there. Before we left Hawaii he had an infected foot and was not going to be sent along with us. But he was with us for a long time and wanted to stay with us.

Our bivouac area was in front of the howitzers. At night it would be quiet and all of a sudden the shelling would begin. The Japanese would always try to infiltrate at night. One particular night we were in a bunker and a shell came in right next to us. We decided we weren't going to stay there so we set up on the reverse side of a big mound. We were told that it would be a safer place. Then there was another blast and we got covered with sand. We moved again and crawled underneath a disabled 4x4 to try and get some sleep. A marine came up to us, a big tall skinny kid with red hair. He told us that his Amtrack had conked out on the beach and that it would be a better place to stay. It was nice and dry and it was probably safer there. So we got up again and weren't 50 yards away when the 4x4 took a direct hit. This must not have been our night to die because when we got to the Amtrack a short round from one of our own ships almost hit us. Finally, we said, "The hell with it". After a while you began to live like barbarians. You don't sleep that much, don't shave. Sometimes there were dead bodies all around you and it doesn't even affect you. At first you're scared but after a while you get numb.

We heard on the radio that we had secured the island, but I had to laugh because there was still fighting going on all around. There may not have been any organized resistance but the island was never safe. We'd be watching a movie at night and bang, a shot would go off. One morning in broad daylight we were going for chow when we heard a bunch of shots. A big Japanese Imperial Marine tried to get into the food line. He was wearing U.S. Marine dress greens too. The MPs shot him 15 times.

You could go from one end of that island to the other, underground. That's how many tunnels there were. Sometimes you'd go through a tiny entrance just big enough to squeeze into and you'd get inside and it would be big enough to fit 30 six-wheel trucks. There were also boxes and boxes of rice and dried fish. One day a Marine came out of one of the caves with a pair of woman's underwear and everybody started howling. One night, everybody was shooting their rifles up in the air and yelling. It was like the Fourth of July. That's when we found out that it was VE Day.

We were in Saipan Harbor headed for mainland Japan when we heard the news that the war had ended. We were scheduled to go into Sasebo with the Occupation Force. What still sticks out in my mind is that when we were in the Sea of Japan all you could see were mountains and cliffs with guns mounted on both sides. All I could think about was that if we had to invade here we would have been slaughtered. When I visited Nagasaki I said, "Oh God". There was nothing left. You have no idea of the damage that was done. I just couldn't believe that all that force could come from one bomb.

In Japan the people treated us well. In some cases they hated the white Marines so we were actually treated better. Sometimes at the Geisha houses they wouldn't even make us wait in lines. This had to be the only time that we were treated as superiors.

It still amazes me when I look back at Iwo Jima. The Japanese had forty years to prepare that island. They had pillboxes that could take a direct hit and guns built on rails so that they could retract. But in only a few days Uncle Sam took the whole thing apart. I still have some volcanic ash from Mt. Suribachi that I keep in a bottle. It is my little reminder of Iwo Jima.

When McKeithen returned to Stamford after the war he was among the first Black Police officers in the town. He later left the police Force and went to work for Pitney Bowes where he stayed until his retirement in 1986. Today he remains active in the Oldtimers Association and still works as an umpire at local softball games.

- JOE AIELLO: A MIRACULOUS FALL -

Joe Aiello joined the Marine Corps in 1938 and was among a select group of men chosen for the First Marine Parachute Regiment. Shortly after the U.S. entered the war, Aiello was sent to the Pacific and participated in the campaigns on Guadalcanal, Bougainville, and Vella LaVella. Shortly thereafter, his regiment returned home and was retrained as the Fifth Marine Paratroop. During one of the jumps, Aiello's parachute "dishragged", or failed to open, and he fell an estimated 500 feet to the ground. Although Aiello was badly injured, he survived the fall and recovered in time to participate in the battle for Iwo Jima. In fact, his story was so incredible that it appeared in "Ripley's Believe It Or Not".

After the war Aiello returned to Stamford where he was a Carpenter until his retirement. He now makes his home in Florida.

- CHARLES GUINTA -

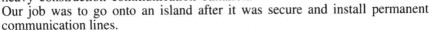

Charles Guinta graduated from Stamford High School in 1941. When he was finishing his first semester at the University of Connecticut, the draft age was lowered and he volunteered for the draft in 1942, and served with the Army Signal Corps until he was discharged in 1946.

I went through basic training with about 25 guys from Stamford. In fact 15 or 16 of us stayed together right through to the end of the war. One of these guys, Carmine Chicatelli, went all the way through school, training and the war with me and we remained close friends.

Initially we were trained for the Barage Balloon Battalion, but eventually we were switched over to the Signal Corps. We were a heavy construction communication battalion. Our job was to go onto an island after it was secure and install permanent communication lines.

The word we had going into Iwo Jima was that the Navy had pounded the island so hard for months that most of the heavy resistance was gone. We were told that the bombardment had softened up the Japanese so much that the battle would only last a few days.

Little did we know that when we landed the island was far from being secure. There was still plenty of fighting. It was a rude awakening. When we went ashore maybe one third of the island was secure. We were still lucky though. It could have been a lot worse. We didn't suffer nearly as much as the Marines and we never faced the heavy fighting that they had. But there was still plenty of mopping up.

For a long while we lived in holes or caves. We slept with our rifles because the Japs were always trying to penetrate our perimeter. At night they would try to sneak off Mount Suribachi to try and reach their front lines. For a while we slept with a wire strung across the opening that led into the mount. If someone tried to exit at night they would trip the wire and a flare would go off and light the area. One night the wire was tripped, the flare went off, and everybody came out firing. But the Japanese had sent a cat out to trip the wire. They tried this a few times but never fooled us again.

There were still many Japanese holed up in Mount Suribachi. Our base camp was there and each day we'd move out and string our telephone lines but we always had to have our rifles ready. There was nowhere to hide since there was no vegetation. That's what made it so tough for the Marines.

We did lose a few men from our unit. One of my closest friends (Darryl Feeney, from Maine) was killed one of the first nights we were there.

We did a lot of work around Airfield #1. There were planes taking off and landing even as the fighting was going on. A lot of times we saw crippled aircraft coming in with one or two engines out. One time we saw a B-29 that couldn't make it land right out in the ocean near shore. The plane must have hit a sandbar because it landed perfectly. It didn't break up or anything and eventually all of the men were taken out safely.

Stamford men on Iwo Jima: The 49th Signal Battalion. (Bottom L to R), Al Kelly, Howard Anderson, John Kosinski, Jerry Sotille, Ed Burke. Middle Row: Fred Santagata, John Bova, Howard Gilvear. Top: Tony Altimoro, Charles Guinta, Carmine Chicatelli, Dan Remling, Al "Buck" Celotto

I met another kid from Stamford there who was a fighter pilot. He was young. Could have only been 18 or 19 and he looked even younger. He showed us an empty bunk on each side of his and told us that they belonged to two of his buddies that didn't make it. I tried to look him up after the war but I never could find him. He was from Springdale–his name was Joe.

One day around May or June, two B-29 pilots were taking bets on when the war would end. They kept betting everyone that it would end in August. They wouldn't tell us how they knew but they were sure it would all be over in August. Now, of course, we know why. In August we were on our way to Okinawa to prepare for the invasion of Japan, when we heard the news that the war was over. So instead we went to Saipan.

One day I saw this big Marine walking down the road and I thought "I know this guy". He walked up to me and said, "I hear there's some guys from Stamford here". The Marine was Chet Buttery.

The war itself seemed so unreal. You're there but you're not there. If you had talked to me 45 years ago I would have been climbing the walls telling you how unbelievable this whole thing was. But over all these years you develop a different perspective on it. We were young. We took chances but we had jobs to do and we wanted to do it as it well as we could. We knew some of us wouldn't come back. But that was the game we were in.

Charlie returned to Stamford and worked at Waldenbooks. In 1990 he retired as its Senior Vice President. He remains active in the community, most notably, with the Ferguson Library and in 1992 he was honored as Stamford's "Citizen of the Year".

SIX KILLED ON IWO

The battle for Iwo Jima claimed 6 Stamford men. George Roth, believed to be among the first to reach the shore, was in the U.S. Army. Richard Von Egidy, William Malezewski, Robert Rotunno, William White, and George Hyland, who died several months after the battle, were all Marines.[12]

OKINAWA

As the U.S. began to grind the Japanese war machine down and advance toward the mainland, one more significant objective remained. Okinawa, one of the largest of the Pacific islands to be invaded, was only 300 miles from Japan and would make a fine base from which the final assault on Japan could be launched.

On April 1, 1945, Easter Sunday, the invasion began. By the end of the first day, thousands of Americans reached the island with relatively few casualties. Within a few days it appeared as though the American attackers had advanced virtually without opposition. What the Americans did not know, however, was that the Japanese had conceded northern Okinawa and were preparing to make their stand at the central and southern regions of the island. Furthermore, American intelligence estimated that the island held approximately 75,000 defenders when, in fact, the Japanese had over 100,000 troops. The island, which appeared so docile at first, would become one of the bloodiest battlegrounds of World War II.

As the Americans advanced to the more rocky mountainous south, they were met by a fierce and well entrenched enemy. Using everything at their disposal including flamethrowers and tanks and supported by a formidable armada of air and seacraft, it took the Americans over three months to secure the island.

In the Okinawa campaign the Americans suffered almost 50,000 casualties. In addition to this, over 700 aircraft were lost and over 400 ships sunk or disabled, many in kamikaze attacks. For the Japanese, the toll was much worse, one from which they could not recover. It is estimated that they lost over 100,000 men and 8000 aircraft, almost 1500 in the kamikaze attacks alone. Sixteen ships were sunk with 4 damaged.[13]

Okinawa proved to be the most costly battle of the entire Pacific War, but when it was over, the defeat of Japan was at hand.

Photos courtesy of U.S. Marine Corps

- TONY DiPRETA -

Tony DiPreta was the sixth of the seven brothers to enter the service. He was among many Stamford High School boys who were given early graduation in March of 1943 to join the war effort. Aboard the AK Cargo Ship the USS Appanoose, he saw action in the Pacific including three months at Okinawa.

After boot camp I was stationed in Washington, D.C., and we were part of a communications outfit. I could have stayed there until the end of the war but in the back of my head I had this feeling that I should be out at sea. I didn't want to sit the war out in Washington, D.C. When my brother Jimmy was killed I wanted a transfer and I volunteered for sea duty.

Jimmy was really a Gung-Ho Marine. He was a very special guy. He was a few years older than me and he was my hero. He was very popular, good looking and had lots of friends. When I got to high school it was very intimidating to me because everyone liked him so much. I was shy and in a lot of ways I didn't measure up. He was always upbeat, had a terrific sense of humor and was the family favorite. He loved the Marines and was so proud to be one. Just before he died, he was in a newsreel done a day or two before the invasion of Tarawa. They showed some of the guys at mass before they boarded the ship. The film showed Jimmy receiving Communion.

After Washington, D.C., the first place we went was to the Philippines. We weren't involved in the invasion but we came in afterward. We were carrying the Sea Bees and these big square blocks that they were going to use to make wharves, piers, barges, and that sort of thing.

On Christmas Eve of 1944, a friend and I were sitting on deck, lamenting about our sad state and thinking about our families back home. Pretty soon we heard an airplane flying overhead and the two of us were trying to figure out what kind it was - a PBS, - a Corsair? All of a sudden the plane shuts off its engine and drops a torpedo. We stood there mesmerized, watching the wake of the torpedo go right across our bow and smack into the ship right next to us. The instant the torpedo hit, we saw white hot and then red hot flames. It blew a hole as big as this room. That was our first taste of action.

I guess the pilot bailed out and in the confusion someone called out for a lifejacket and one of our crew threw one overboard. It was pretty embarrassing because later they found the pilot on the island of Samar and he was wearing a lifejacket with our name stenciled right on it.

The main danger for us was always kamikazes. Later when we were sent to Okinawa right after the original invasion, it was the height of the kamikaze planes. *(At this point in the war, with their resources dwindling and a shortage of experienced pilots, the Japanese decided on a great kamikaze offensive to be used against the American fleet at Okinawa. This offensive was named "Ton-Go", which translated means Heavenly Operation.)* We lived day after day under the threat of kamikaze attack. You'd see a ship in front of you hit, to the left of you get hit, behind you get hit. One day I was up on the bridge with the Captain. I was the "Captain's talker" which meant that I communicated his orders to the rest of the ship. We saw the plane coming right at us – and he missed us. The pilot had to be inexperienced because he was so bad he just plain missed us. At Okinawa we got to the point where we said, "What's the point of brushing our teeth, we're all going to die tomorrow." And that's just how you felt because they were relentless.

We were at Okinawa for over 90 days and we spent most of these days anchored in the same spot. This is when you were in the greatest danger. The only time we moved was if a ship was headed back for the states, we would go over to get their fresh fruit and food. The Japanese not only had kamikaze planes but we were told that they had kamikaze boats and kamikaze swimmers too. The swimmers were the most frightening because you had no warning. We were told that they'd climb on board a ship at night, get into the sleeping quarters, slit a man's throat, and then leave. This never happened on our ship but you can imagine the psychological impact that these stories had on the men. So we had guard duty every night and walked around with Thompson Sub Machine Guns. If you saw anything you shot. Well, most of us had no experience with machine guns. What the hell did we know? We were sailors. Every once in a while a guy would think he spotted something and start shooting. Before you knew it everyone was shooting, and it sounded like the fourth of July.

The suicide boats were barges loaded with dynamite. One of these barges hit our ammunition ship and sunk it. We couldn't even see it because at the time, we had laid out a smokescreen.

The only time we got a real break from the kamikazes was when a typhoon was coming, because then they made us go out to sea. We had three typhoons at Okinawa and sometimes you'd see an entire ship disappear under the waves. It was probably for only three or four seconds but it seemed like these big ships were just being swallowed up. One time I was in the flying bridge, the uppermost part of the bridge. At one point the ship turned and it was almost touching the water. Fortunately, at the age of 19 you don't have any fear.

Once we had these guys come aboard and tell us how we had it made, how we got hot food and could shower every day. But we said, "At least you guys have somewhere to hide." Later we got a prolonged kamikaze attack and these guys couldn't get off the ship fast enough.

Once there was a destroyer about a half mile away. On the stern of the deck they carried depth charges. A kamikaze came in and slammed right into the deck and the depth charges. You could see the entire ship lift out of the water and only half of it came down. No one who was on that half could have survived. We were so lucky because we were one of the few ships out there that didn't get hit. I still say that if the Japanese had started earlier and had more skilled pilots, it would've been a longer war.

Later, when we docked in Saipan I asked the Commanding Officer if I could go ashore and try to find my brother Nick, who was there. He said yes and so a friend and I got off the ship. We weren't too far away when I noticed that the ship was underway. It was leaving! We raced to catch up with the ship and they threw us down a Jacob's ladder and we climbed back on. I never did get to see my brother. And he was less than a quarter mile away.

When the war was over I went to the Hollywood Canteen and they had a register book. I signed in. I looked at the list from the day before and I saw the name Nick DiPreta. I missed him by one day.

Once we were out at sea and I saw an LST. I knew by the number that I had a friend on board. So I signaled over to them. "Is Larry Nemchek aboard?" They answered affirmative and about an hour later he came aboard and we laughed and had a nice little visit. Of course it wasn't the best place in the world to meet.

Toward the end of the war I transferred off our ship and ended up on a new carrier "The U.S.S. Tarawa". I specifically requested this ship because of my brother. I was on that ship until the end of the war.

Tony returned to Stamford in 1946. He worked for AMF in Stamford and later for the Lifesaver Company in Port Chester where he worked until his retirement.

- THE FIGHTING DiPRETAS -

While many have heard of the five "Fighting Sullivan Brothers", it was a Stamford family that sent an unprecedented seven boys overseas to fight in the Second World War.*

Vincent and Concetta DiPreta of Avery Street raised twelve children, ten boys and two girls. When Mrs. DiPreta died in 1936 the family had to pull together and most of the responsibilities of caring for the family fell, first, to Palma, the oldest daughter, and later, to her younger sister Mary.

After Pearl Harbor, the lives of each family member were touched in some way by the war. The three oldest sons and their father were employed in vital defense industries. Alfred worked at Luders Boatyard in Stamford which manufactured PT Boats. Frank made fuses for bomb sites at a plant in Massachusetts and both Joseph and father Vincent worked at Yale & Towne. Palma and Mary had to bid farewell to seven brothers as they were called to serve their country.

Victor, who enlisted in the Army was the first to go overseas. His work with the Coast Artillery brought him to Iceland and Europe. Tom also entered the Army and served with an anti-aircraft battalion in Hawaii and Okinawa. Nick, a US Marine, and Dominick, who joined the Coast Guard, were both stationed in Saipan and Okinawa. Anthony served in the Navy as the quartermaster of a cargo ship and saw action at Okinawa. John, the youngest of the boys, served in Italy in 1945. Jimmy entered into the Marines and was sent to the Pacific. In November of 1943 he was killed in the assault on the island of Tarawa. When the war was over he was the first Connecticut boy to be brought home for burial. One by one the other boys returned home from the war, married local girls and resumed their lives in Stamford.[14]

At present only three of the original twelve DiPreta children remain. Frank lives in New Canaan. Tony is retired and lives in Darien and Florida for part of the year. John, the youngest in the family lives in Norwalk. Mary (Ienner), who resided in Stamford, passed away in 1995.

In the 1970's under Mayor Julius Wilensky, the town dedicated a small park in the Cove to the memory of James DiPreta. The park also serves, in some small measure, as a permanent tribute to the family that sent seven of its boys off to war.

Five of the seven DePreta brothers (l to r) Dominick, Thomas, Tony, Nicholas and John. The pictures on the table are those of their other two brothers, James and Victor (from an Advocate Photo, 1964)

* An article in the Stamford Advocate by Shirley Haner (November 28, 1964) states that the Kjera family of Minnesota also sent seven sons into World War II; however, not all served overseas.

- FRED JOHNSON -

Fred Johnson entered the U.S. Navy in 1943. After working at the the Naval Communication school in Darien, CT, he was sent to Virginia where he was given training on amphibious craft. He was assigned to an LST (Landing Ship Tank) and participated in the assaults on Iwo Jima and Okinawa.

From day one when I was shipped to Staten Island Blacks were segregated. From here I was stationed at the Old Soldier's Home in Darien. The Navy had taken over that building and also Wee Burn Country Club which was being used as a communications school. There were 12 of us colored sailors altogether. Eleven of them were classified as Stewards. I was the only one classified as a Seaman. We were part of the work detail there.

The discrimination part, right there even at this early time, hit me the wrong way. At the Old Soldier's Home they must have had 300 empty sacks (beds); I mean empty! But instead of letting us sleep there they put us on the second floor of a house that was there on the property. I used to sit there and wonder why we were on the second floor of a house instead of in the empty barracks.

Then it really hit home one day when two fellows walked in with their sea bags. They were both motor machinists and they happened to be colored boys. Later that day the personnel department called over and said that a receiving ship needed two motor macs. So they sent these two guys. Sure enough the two guys were sent back. I guess they weren't exactly what the ship was looking for.

One day at Wee Burn I needed to use the phone so to get to it I walked through what they called "officer's country". Later my commanding officer called me over and said, "Johnson, you can't do that again." I said, "You mean I can't walk across this floor anymore." And he said, "No, next time go downstairs and use the back stairway." Little incidents like this would happen and I'd always speak out. It just hit me the wrong way. I wanted to serve my country, maybe make things a little better for my own people but I kept seeing things that weren't right and I just couldn't buy it. If something was on my mind I'd say it. And a lot of times I paid for doing this.

Once, the Commander of the Post was making a general inspection. I was standing at my post at attention and he came up to me and said, "You've done a good job." So he turns to my commander and says "These men are supposed to be made Seamen Second Class–so we'll make them Steward 2nd Class." This was the same money but not the same rank. If you were a Steward, all you could do was cook or clean. In other words, be a servant. I couldn't be a Gunner's Mate or a Radio Operator no matter what I did. So, I said, "Sir, that's not right". He said, "It's the same money." And I said, "I know sir, but it's not right." He looked at me, mumbled something, and walked away.

Later I was transferred to Camp Bradford in Little Creek, Virginia. It was a big amphibious post. Over 200,000 men were there. We couldn't eat in the same mess hall or sleep in the same barracks. I wanted to take the test for the motor pool but they wouldn't let me and again I spoke up. I had more arguments than you could shake a stick at. And I'd usually end up in the brig for it and three days of bread and water. We used to call it "the days of cake and wine." Another time a captain was giving me a hard time and he said something like, "Your country is at war." And I got so mad I said, "No captain, your country is at war". I was so mad it came out. I was sent to the brig for that, too.

I always took the punishment because I thought I had a good cause. And one thing about the brig, it wasn't segregated! We all slept together, ate together and used the same bathroom. In the brig eveyone was equal, you were all in it together.

When we first got to Bradford the first thing I did was get in the chow line. I was tired and hungry. A bunch of us had just traveled all night on a "smoke train" (coal burning). We tried to get some food in Cape May but no place would feed us. It was heartbreaking. You just didn't want to believe it. I knew stuff like this happened in civilian life in some of the cities but now the country was at war. We were all supposed to be hanging together. Anyway, I got in the chow line at Bradford, got some food, and sat down. I noticed that one of the guys was staring at me. Finally he came up and said, "You can't sit here." I was so tired and mad that I told him that I was going to sit there until I finished eating.

At one point they kept sending me for these tests. I think they were IQ tests. I think they were trying to find out if I was nuts or just plain stupid. The fifth time they sent me the Commander called me in and said, "Jesus Christ - There's nothing wrong with you; I wish everyone here had your IQ. I'm going to stop this foolishness right now." And he did.

Finally in 1944, I was assigned to an LST. We carried troops, tanks, shells, bombs, and everything needed for the amphibious landings. There were only 4 Blacks on the ship and, again, we were segregated. Because I had time and seniority, the captain put me in charge of the others. He also called me in one day after he looked at my records and he said, "What have you been doing?" And I said, "Just what it says there." He told me that there was no reason we couldn't get along.

When we got our General Quarters assignments all 4 of us colored fellows were assigned to hoist ammunition. This was 3 decks down. Then we ran into some action off of Saipan and lost one of our ships. This shook me up so I got the men together and told them I didn't think that it was fair that all four of us were 3 decks down. If something happened to the ship we had no chance of surviving. I said to the guys, "Look if we get hit we bleed red just like everyone else and we could die just like everyone. I'm going to see the Gunnery Officer and ask for our positions to be changed." So I went to see the Gunney–his name was Mr. Dunnegan. I told him how I felt. I told him that at least the other guys on the second deck or quarter deck had a chance to get off the ship if something happened. For us there was no way out. With all of the ammunition around us we didn't have a chance. So Mr. Dunnegan listened, then he took a chart out, made some scribbles and said "Ok Johnson, this is what I'm going to do;" and he moved all of us around, one guy to the bow, two to the quarter deck and one near the 50 mm gun. In fact one of the guys was assisting on the 50mm when we shot down our first Japanese plane.

We did our jobs and expected to be treated like human beings. Most of the time things were fine but we had a few run-ins. One time we were on a beach it was hot and we were drinking beer that was hot. One of the guys was drunk and every other word out of his mouth was "nigger." Finally I went over and said, "I don't know if you're talking to me or your grandfather but we're going to have a problem if you keep it up." His friend settled him down and after a while we reached a happy medium. We'd say "hello" to each other but not much more.

We took part in two campaigns, Iwo Jima and Okinawa. At Iwo Jima we were part of the 2nd Marines. Our job was to bring in tanks and 105's. Each time we'd go ashore, drop our ramps and unload our cargo. Then we'd go back 3 to 4 miles, load up again, and bring it ashore. While we were on the beach we felt like sitting ducks. The Japanese were dropping mortars all around and we could hear them whistling by our heads. What I'll never forget is that trenches were dug right on the beach and corpses were dogtagged and dropped right in. That was the hard part.

Because the LST had a flat bottom it could get right up to the beach. Before you went in you'd drop a stern anchor out in the water so that if you hit the beach too hard and got stuck, you could use the anchor like a winch to tow yourself off. One time we hit the beach and got stuck there. The stern anchor couldn't pull us off so we sat there for hours, right out there on that beach. We just had to wait until the tide changed.

It wasn't until Okinawa that it dawned on me that I could die. We were part of Task Force 38 and our flotilla went in as a decoy. But some Japanese planes got through and one of the kamikazes hit the side of our ship and exploded. His engine ended up on our quarterdeck.

I don't know what the story was with those kamikazes. I don't know if they were dedicated or drugged but you'd see them fly right in the middle of 100 ships with all the guns firing at them. Sometimes, you couldn't believe it but they'd make one pass and not get hit. They'd just crank right back up and make another pass to see if they could make a direct hit.

I have to say, though, that the scariest time of all was when we ran into the typhoon off of Okinawa. That's when it dawned on you just how powerful water really is. You'd look out and see steel beams bending and making a dinging sound practically singing to you. The only thing the captain could do was head right into the storm. I saw big ships, APAs, and tankers flipping on their sides like a can of sardines. This part was worse than getting hit by the kamikazes.

On the way back we stopped at Saipan and were told that we were preparing for the invasion of Japan itself. About this time I started to worry. I figured we made it through two of these things. Maybe the third one might be it. But fortunately for us the war ended.

As far as I'm concerned the war was a great experience...in a hard way. I wouldn't sell it but to be honest with you I don't know if I would go through it again.

Johnson was discharged in December, 1945, and received two Battle Stars for Iwo Jima and Okinawa. He settled in Stamford, raised a family there, and worked for the Stamford Fire Department until his retirement. He presently serves on the Board of Representatives for the 10th District.

- CARL BATTINELLI -

As a teenager, Carl Battinelli distinguished himself as a fine swimmer and diver. When he turned 18, he joined the Marines. As part of the 14th Defense Battalion and later the 2nd Marine Division, he was assigned to Guadalcanal, Guam, Saipan, Tinian, Tulagi, and participated in the invasion of Okinawa.

Guadalcanal was probably the most beautiful beach I saw on any island in the Pacific. They could have made a resort out of it. But all of the islands were beautiful. You'd have papaya trees, coconut trees, and banana trees all around you. It's just too bad that so many people had to get killed to take them back. The thing that got me the most was guard duty. You were always assigned guard duty alphabetically and according to rank. With my last name, I always drew the crap detail, the outer perimeter. There was the camp detail. Then about 100 yards outside of that you had the inner perimeter. Then about another 75 or 100 yards outside of that there was the outer perimeter. That's where I was on every island. A little before dark, you would be given your post and you would have to stay out there in the boondocks until morning. You would do this every night until the island was secure.

At Guadalcanal, we were there for mop up, but there I was, a young kid, scared, out there alone in the jungle. You didn't know a thing about it. You would be sitting out there and you weren't supposed to move. On a bright night you would have to make sure that you weren't silhouetted against anything. You were not supposed to give away your position by firing a shot, so if anyone got close to you, you were told to use your bayonet. It was scary, but every morning when the sun came up, it was a new day.

Some nights your imagination would run away from you. Sometimes I'd see the whole Japanese army coming at me. One night, it was pitch black. I heard this noise and thought, "This is it, here they come". I got my rifle ready, and all of a sudden I felt something was on my leg. I was sure it was a hand, but it was one of those damn blow frogs. It jumped off or I probably would have blown my leg off. Yet, I'll never forget guard duty. Alphabetically, according to rank.

Then, after the Canal, we went to Guam. We guarded the Orote airstrip there. Not much happened there, but next we went to Saipan where all those Japanese civilians were jumping off the cliffs. We did everything we could to stop it, but they did it anyway. It was sad, even to me as a kid. At one point, I got so mad I said, "Go ahead and jump you sons of bitches," but then you'd see a woman holding a baby and you knew how sad it was.

The only time you ever felt safe was when you were on ship, because you were surrounded by all your buddies. Then on our way into Okinawa, we got hit by a kamikaze. We intercepted a few, but this one hit the front of the ship and knocked out a couple of 20mm guns. We were lucky that was it, because we had a lot of ammunition on board. Some of the air raids we saw at night on the ships were just spectacular, like the Fourth of July. You'd see tracer rounds all across the sky. The dog fights were just like watching a football game. You would just pray it was one of them that went down and not one of our own.

When we got to Okinawa, we were supposed to be involved in the initial assault on the southern tip. We spent five days on the water in an LCI just trying to draw fire from the Japanese. I guess they were trying to bring all the Japanese to the southern tip of the island. We would start in toward the island then circle back. We did this every day for five days. Then finally, on Easter Sunday morning, we got orders. In layman's terms it was, "Don't circle back. Just keep going."

Before this, all we were doing was teasing them. They would fire at us, but I guess the sailor on back knew exactly how far their guns could reach. The entire time, we would have to keep our helmet on, shoes untied, back pack unbuttoned. All so that if the boat was sunk, you could get all of your equipment off quickly. After a few days of this, we were tired and sea sick. After a while I just prayed we would get sunk and get it over with.

All the while, planes were bombing the island and the ships were out there lobbing in everything they had. Airplanes were flying by and strafing the beaches. We just stood out there and figured, "That's it. There can't be anything left on that island." The hell there wasn't!

On Easter Sunday, when we got to the beach, all I was concerned about was sticking with my platoon and finding cover. You were on your own until you could regroup and reorganize. The adrenalin is pumping and the survival instinct takes over. The movies make it all look so good—like everyone knows exactly where they are going. But you are just trying to stay low and find a rock, a tree, anything for cover. We were lucky. The Japanese weren't close to the beach. There was no hand to hand or anything like that. But we still got the hell beat out of us. I think that in 14 days, we only moved something like 1400 yards.

The Japanese tried to work on your mind. On the radio, Tokyo Rose would be asking us if we knew what our girlfriends back home were doing. And then, there was Piss-Call Pete. That's what we called him. At night, he would fly over in a small plane just to aggravate us. Everything would be nice and quiet and then he'd come in and we'd have to call an air raid. He couldn't really hurt us. He didn't even have any bombs. He just kept us from resting. We got very little sleep for a few weeks. But who the hell wanted to sleep? You were too scared. Finally they pulled us off the island because we had about 50% casualties. We went back to Pearl Harbor and then headed back for Japan. We were supposed to be in on the initial assault at Nagasaki Harbor. We were on our way when the war ended. It's a good thing Truman made the decision he did because we would have never made it to shore. Believe me, a mosquito would not have been able to get through that harbor. They had guns pinpointed on every square inch of it. And there were cliffs on both sides. When we got into Nagasaki, I saw one huge area that was just leveled. All that was standing were a few chimneys and a few pipes sticking up. There was nothing else left.

Once we got there, we had to round up all the guns and ammo we could. A lot of the civilians were hiding in the hills. Interpreters kept telling them on loudspeakers, "We are not going to hurt you. We're here to help you." Finally, after three or four days, people started coming out of the hills. That's when we saw a lot of the burn victims. It was a shame, especially when you saw some of the kids.

The people weren't rebellious. They were more scared than anything. Most of the time, we'd go to their homes and tell them to surrender their weapons, and they did. They weren't belligerent. A lot of the time we'd work side by side with them. There were no problems.

Finally, in January of 1946, we headed for home on an LST. We were at sea for over 30 days. About 3 days out of San Francisco, we ran out of food and had to break into the supplies in the lifeboats. But we made it home, and I got to see so much—all before I was 21 years old.

> *Carl Battinelli returned to Stamford and became a carpenter. Before long, he formed his own business, Carl Battinelli Builders.*

- *FOUR KILLED ON OKINAWA* -

Four Stamford men were killed at Okinawa. The first reported to be killed was Vincent Tripodi, US Navy, who was killed in the Naval battle around Okinawa in April of 1945. The following month, two more local men, David DeFelice and Oswald Fabrizio, both Marines, were killed. The last reported local man to die in the bloody struggle for Okinawa was William Skura, also a Marine.

[1] Lt. Col. Eddie Bauer. The Marshall Cavendish Illustrated Encyclopedia of World War II. (NY: Marshall Cavendish Corp.), Vol.5, p.1295.

[2] "Lt. Doyle Receives Medal for Heroism". Stamford Advocate, August 12, 1943.

[3] Bauer, Vol. 9, p.2334.

[4] "Thought Dead at Tarawa, Rodansky Resumes Fight". Stamford Advocate, February 19, 1944.

[5] "Navy Cross Posthumously for Lt. Myles Fox". Stamford Advocate, September 21, 1943.

[6] Bauer, Vol. 8, pp.2283-2295.

[7] Bauer, Vol. 9, p.2309.

[8] Keith Wheeler. The Road to Tokyo. (Alexandria, VA: Time Life Books, Inc., 1979), p.57.

[9] Ibid, p.47.

[10] "Stamford G.I. Wins Award for Heroic Feat on Iwo". Stamford Advocate, September 21, 1945.

[11] Stamford Advocate, April-July 1945.

[12] Stamford Advocate, April-June 1945.

[13] Wheeler, p.193.

[14] Shirley Haner. "Seven Stamford Brothers Overseas in World War II". Stamford Advocate, November 28, 1964.

[15] Stamford Advocate, April-July 1945.

CHAPTER SIX

RETURN TO THE PHILIPPINES

In the early dark days of the war, the American forces were driven from the Philippines by the Japanese, and General MacArthur, although forced to evacuate the islands in disgrace, made a solemn promise to return.

As U.S. forces crippled the Japanese navy and "leapfrogged" across several chains of islands in the Pacific, the time was ripe for an assault on the Philippines. On October 20, 1944, the American invasion of the Philippines began and MacArthur triumphantly announced, "People of the Philippines, I have returned." The Japanese, however, were not ready to concede defeat. Over the next few weeks, they launched a series of Naval battles known as the Battle of Leyte, and although their naval capabilities had been smashed, the combat which took place on the islands was savage.

The bloody battle for the Philippines would last for over six months, but when it was over the Americans had cut off the Japanese shipping lanes to Southeast Asia and established a staging area for the invasion of mainland Japan.

- FLAVIO FOGIO -

Flavio was drafted in 1941 and served the 192nd Field Artillery Battalion. This unit included scores of Stamford boys because it was originally a branch of the National Guard which was called into service when the U.S. entered the war. The 192nd was attached to the 43rd Division Artillery which saw action in the Pacific including Guadalcanal and the Philippines.

Our job was to act as support for the infantry. We operated 155 mm howitzers which shot a 96 lb. projectile. It had a range of about 7 miles and would sometimes leave a crater 35 feet in diameter. Under the right conditions, we were extremely accurate...maybe within 20 yards. The Navy would bring us in and we would set up right on the beach.

I first saw action in February 1943 at Guadalcanal. Our job was mostly mopping up, but that's where we got our first taste of aerial bombing. One night when we were on the beach, the Japanese bombed us. Guys were digging holes in the beach with their helmets and their hands. That's how scared we were. Antiaircraft, search lights, guns going off all around us—you've never seen such a spectacle.

Once we were on this island, Koka Rona, in July 1943. It wasn't occupied by the Japanese. We were only supposed to protect the Sea Bees while they built an airfield. All of a sudden, a squadron of Japanese bombers came in. I don't know how many there were, but what a sight! We were not prepared for them. We didn't even have our antiaircraft in place yet. They must have killed about 100 Sea Bees...it was terrible. Over the next few days, we got our equipment in place. Then, on July 4th, I'll never forget it, this big squadron of Japanese planes came back for the kill. They were flying low. They probably thought they'd hurt us again. But this time our antiaircraft batteries just threw everything at them. There were 28 or 30 bombers, and we shot down every one of them. Not one of them got back home to tell what had happened.

They were in such close formation that one would explode and take another down with it. We talked about that July 4th for quite some time. We also saw a lot of fighting at Munda, in the Solomons. *(This is an understatement. The War Department later said that at Munda, the 43rd "assured its place as one of the great fighting divisions of the U.S.")*

Sometimes the enemy was malaria. We were given a drug to take, but the rumor went around that it made you sterile so a lot of guys wouldn't take it.

Usually we set up on the beach well after the infantry went in, but at the Lingayen Gulf in the Philippines, we landed only a half hour after H-hour. We ended up pinned down on that beach for 9 days. I didn't take my boots off for 9 days.

There is no doubt that our toughest fighting came during our assault in the Philippines. Every night, we had to fight like the infantry because the Japanese would try to infiltrate. One night, the Japanese rolled grenades down at us from a hill. The order at night was to shoot anything that moved. One night one of our own guys was killed. He went to get something from one of our trucks that was outside the perimeter. The next thing you know, he was shot.

The following night we set up our perimeter, and I was laying down near a stone wall close to the perimeter. I shouldn't have been there, but it was a quiet night. All of a sudden, I hear a noise, and I got up and saw a figure walking down a dirt path. I drew a bead on this guy. I should have shot him, but the only thing I could think about was what happened to our guy the night before. I couldn't quite make out the figure, but he was walking so nonchalantly. A few seconds later, there was a burst of fire. Sure enough, it was a Japanese soldier with five grenades. He was probably trying to sabotage one of the howitzers.

After a while you wouldn't believe how proficient the gun crews got with the artillery. It was supposed to be an eight man job, but sometimes we had to do it with five— especially when you were going 24 hours at a time. One time, the antiaircraft shot down a Japanese plane made by Mitsubishi. When we looked at the wreck, we saw that the ball bearings were made by Norma Hoffman in Stamford.

I had enough points to be discharged, so in August of 1945, I was on my way home. I was on the high seas when the war ended. I heard that we dropped the Atomic Bomb, and my first reaction is, "What the hell is the Atomic Bomb?"

We did lose two Stamford guys in our division, George Fielding III and John Mownn. John was a forward observer. He used to go out into the jungle for three days at a time. John's three days were up, but he stayed three more. While he was out there he was killed by a mortar. When I got home, I went to see his father. They had a big farm on High Ridge Road. His father was wearing John's watch. He said to me, "Whether this watch works or not, I'll wear it till I'm dead." I felt so sorry; I wished I had never gone to see him.

Flavio, a friend Charlie Santasiero and "Night Fighter" their good luck charm.

When I came home, we didn't have psychiatrists or anything. The thing that surprised me was that nobody asked us anything. The people back home must have been told, "Let them forget about it." Nobody asked you anything. It was like you never left home.

I will say one thing, though, everybody has high points and low points in their life. I've had a good life, but thinking back on it—if it wasn't for my war experience, I just don't think my life would have been as important.

Flavio left the war as a First Sergeant. In March of 1945, he was awarded the Bronze Star for "remaining cool under hazardous conditions and inspiring men under him" during the invasion of the Philippines.

- 192nd FIELD INFANTRY -

During the Second World War hundreds of Stamford boys fought with the 192nd Field Artillery Battalion. The unit, originally founded in Stamford in the late 1600's, was involved in every military engagement from colonial times right on through World War II.

The 192nd served with distinction in the Pacific most notably in the Philippines and Solomon Islands. The unit also played a critical role in rescuing a young Navy officer, John F. Kennedy, after his PT Boat was split in two by a Japanese destroyer. When Kennedy carved his help message into a coconut shell, he gave it to a native who in turn brought it to Everett Robinson, a resident of Greenwich, and member of the 192nd. The rest, is still history.

The unit was headquartered in Stamford until 1971 when it moved to Norwalk. Due to military downsizing, and the newer self-propelled artillery units, the need for the 192nd was greatly diminished.

Finally, in 1933, after over 300 years of service to this nation, the 192nd was deactivated. It remains however, the nation's oldest field artillery unit in continuous service and one of the oldest regiments in the U.S. Army.[1]

JAMES ALBERT WINSLOW

When a Kamikaze crashed in to the U.S.S. Intrepid on October 29, 1944 part of the plane hit Gun Tub 10, a deadly fire ensued. Rushing to help some of the trapped crewmen was James Albert Winslow, a 20 year old Pharmacist's Mate. Without regard for his own safety, Winslow rushed through the flames and helped to pull some of the gunners out of the burning tub. Among those in the tub that day was James Dockery, also of Stamford, who was a member of the all Black crew which shot the Kamikaze from the air. For his heroism on that day, Winslow was awarded the Navy Cross.

Less than one month later, during the battle for the Philippines, the Intrepid was hit by two more Kamikazes. This time Winslow was close to the huge explosion. Although several of the Pharmacist's Mates worked furiously to save their heroic friend, Winslow died along with 68 other crewmen.

In addition to the Navy Cross, Winslow had also received the Purple Heart and the Silver Star.

- DR. KARL BLUME -

Dr. Blume was raised in a suburb of Munich, Germany. In 1937, at the age of 16, he left his mother and brother to live with his father in Stamford. After attending Dartmouth for three years, he left to work for Yale and Towne. When the U.S. entered the war, he enlisted in the U.S. Army.

The people at Yale and Towne gave me a huge farewell party before I left for the service, but when I got to Fort Devins, I was told that I was not on their list and they wouldn't accept me. I was furious and embarrassed. After all, these people gave me a big party and said goodbye to me. Now I would have to go back and tell them that I wasn't even accepted into the Army.

I still can't believe what I did next. I called the Pentagon and demanded to talk to the Adjutant General. I was so persistent that some VIP finally came to the phone and agreed to straighten out the mix-up. He did, and soon I was on my way to California to join the 87th Mountain Infantry Regiment for which I had originally enlisted. *(This elite force was trained in skiing and mountaineering at Paradise Inn on Mount Rainier and Ft. Lewis, Washington.)*

We eventually made a landing at Kisca and Attu (in the Aleutians), and it was a disaster. We were supposed to attack the Japanese who had a base camp. But when we got there, the weather was so bad that we did not know that the Japanese had already cleared out and, in the confusion, many Americans were killed by friendly fire.

We were sent back to the states, and all of my friends were signing up for Officers Candidate School. I did, too, but every time I applied, I was always transferred out because of my German background. No company commander would stick his neck out to recommend me for O.C.S. I was assigned to six or eight branches of the Army and was stationed in at least a dozen different camps all over the country.

They really didn't know what to do with me. Because I was from Germany, they really didn't want me as an officer. They just kept shipping me out, to Texas, Louisiana, California, Arizona, and many places I can't even remember.

Finally, in 1944, it looked like I'd be going to Europe with the 90th Division. But a few days before departure, the order came that all Axis born non- citizens had to be transferred to the Pacific.

Back we went to Fort Ord in California. Three days later I was a citizen, and I was headed for Australia. It took almost 30 days to get there, and while I was aboard the ship, I was once again reclassified from combat soldier to clerk/typist.

Later, when we landed in New Guinea, they needed a clerk typist for the 6th Army Headquarters, and I volunteered. Oddly enough, I was assigned as a flunkey to General Walter Kruger, who was also a German himself. In fact, he served in the Kaiser's Army during World War I. This was a fantastic job because as a buck private, I was keeping the G-2 situation map for him. I got to travel all over the Pacific with him—to Australia, Biak, Morotai, and later the Philippines. I had a dream job. I also got to see some of the dark side of the bureaucracy, too. Some officers would recommend each other for questionable medals and I saw, first hand, in all its manifestations, what was meant by "pulling rank."

In October of 1944, our headquarters went from New Guinea directly to Leyte in the Philippines. We went ashore on D-Day under constant bombardment. Our ship wasn't hit, but ships on both sides of us were hit. But by the afternoon of D-Day plus three, the beaches were secure.

From there we landed at Lingayen Gulf on Luzon in January of 1945 and fought our way down to Pampangua River. We set up our headquarters at San Fernando Pampangua while the troops went on to conquer Manila. Here the fighting was fierce, and when the battle was over, the bodies were piled up like cordwood. Some of the Japanese were holed up in buildings that were shelled, and it would simply collapse on them. It was a gruesome sight.

At the time, I was a driver for a Staff Artillery Officer who I think was medal crazy. For days on end he would "reconnoiter" enemy positions in Manila, get lost, ambushed, and rescued. We had no business being there! The guy wanted to get shot at to earn the Purple Heart to add to his collection.

Once Manila was secure, we immediately began to prepare for the invasion of Japan. Our landing was planned for Kyushu. We were expecting at least a 50% casualty rate. It would have been an absolute slaughter. Our land-based planes from the Philippines would only have enough fuel for about 15 minutes over the target.

I still remember the exact beach we were scheduled to land on. It was called Aritaki Wan, and each day, I had to plan the position of every LST and transport. I was with the Transportation Corps, so my job was to figure out the exact load for each ship, how many men and how many supplies each ship would take. We were always short of ships and space, so I was always cutting here and there. I'd assign three days of supplies instead of four, 800 rounds of ammo instead of 1000. There were lots of details. I had blueprints, guides, and even little models to work with so it wasn't exactly a haphazard operation, but as I look back on it today, it was a tremendous responsibility. Imagine me, an amateur doing this; and I was still a Buck Private! I had done some of this work for the invasions of Yap and Okinawa, but this time, it was scary. Thank God it never came off.

We were out at sea for almost two months on our way to Aritaki Wan when the war ended. Then the 6th Army was sent to Kyoto, one of the few cities that had not been bombed. Nagoya, a neighboring town was devastated. We also had the chance to see Hiroshima. It was frightening, absolutely frightening.

The Japanese treated us well. If you had something to trade, you were treated like a king. Some of our interpreters at headquarters were university professors. If you had a pack of cigarettes, you could spend a weekend at one of their country estates and you'd be well fed.

As soon as the war ended with Germany, I was promoted to Staff Sergeant. Looking at it now, the fact that I never became an officer probably spared me a lot of trouble. At the time, I was angry because I was looking for action. In hindsight, I was very fortunate.

My brother in Germany was not so lucky. When he turned 16 in 1944, he was drafted into the German Army and sent to the Russian front. He was captured and remained a P.O.W. for 9 years. When the Russians finally did release him in 1953, he was wounded and sick. He just never had the opportunities that I did. I left

Germany just a few weeks before my 17th birthday. If I hadn't gotten out when I did, I could have ended up worse.

When Dr. Blume left the service, he finished his undergraduate degree at Columbia University and went on to the University of Pennsylvania to study dentistry. He has been practicing in Stamford for over 40 years.

- BOBBY WASSERMAN -

Before he entered the Army in 1943, Bobby Wasserman had a promising tennis career ahead of him. A 1940 graduate of Stamford High School, Wasserman held numerous titles including the New York State Amateur Championship. At the time of his induction, he was the 19th seeded amateur in the nation.

On Mother's Day, 1945, his mother, Mrs. Isidore Wasserman, received an orchid from Bobby who had been stationed in the Pacific. Along with the orchid was a note with the tragic news that her son had been killed some three weeks earlier in Luzon.[2]

- ANGELO CARELLA -

Angelo Carella was one of three brothers to serve in the war. He enlisted in the Army Air Corps at age 17 in hopes of becoming a pilot but after completing aviation training was reassigned to the infantry and sent to the Philippines in 1945. With the First Cavalry, he participated in the "mop up" of the Philippines and was stationed there until they were given their independence in 1946.

I was an aviation cadet at Kelly Field in Texas and had three months of pre-flight training. But when the war ended in Germany, they ceased all training for cadets with less than one year of training. That put all of us on hold. They told us that they were going to "wash out" 10,000 of us. Every week they'd post a list on the bulletin board of those that were washed out. I made it through all this but then right at the end I got caught in the "trickle washout". It was heartbreaking.

I was sent to Camp Croft, South Carolina, for 90 days of Infantry training, then to California, then out to the Philippines. When we left San Francisco, there was a great big sign saying, "Golden Gate in 48". We figured we'd be out there for two or three more years. It took us about 35 days to get there. That's when I saw Guam for the first time. It looked like a big piece of coal in the ocean. Everything was black and the trees looked like burned sticks in the ground.

Later we landed in Luzon and they began to prepare us for the invasion of Japan. Manila, which was called the "Pearl of the Pacific", was the orientation point. Every day thousands of 17 and 18 year old kids prepared for the invasion. Troops, ammunition, and supplies came in day and night. Twice a day we were put on Higgins boats and had to land on beaches, simulated to look like the coast of Japan. Half the kids didn't even know how to carry a rifle. In training, they told us that only 2 out of 10 would make it. Eight out of 10 would be killed. I think they were just trying to motivate us to train harder. You'd look out on the horizon of the Lingayen Gulf and all you could see from one end to the other were ships, every kind you could think of. Then, one morning we woke up and it looked like somebody raised the curtain. There wasn't a single ship out there. Then, it must have been two or three days later that we read in the paper "Yank" that the U.S. was shelling the Japanese shore. We thought this was it. We were ready to go. Then, one day the paper said, "Two Japanese Cities Missing". This is when we found out that the war was over. We had no idea what the Atomic Bomb was. We thought that a bunch of B-24s bombed them. In retrospect, it's a good thing that we didn't have to invade Japan. It would have been a massacre. We were all so green, just a bunch of kids. To show you how scared you get, one night, when I first got there, I went to go to the bathroom. I heard this kind of a hissing sound and something fell right over my head. They warned us about bombing, so I just dove to the ground and then I heard something hit the ground next to me. I waited for the explosion. I just stayed there on the ground and didn't move. As it started to get light I found out what it was ... a coconut.

The war was over, but there were still Japanese out there and they were dangerous. We slept in these huge canvas tents at night and every once in a while a Japanese sniper would fire into the tent and it would vibrate like a drum. I remember going out one night into the hills and putting out speakers and running the wires back to the staging area. The next morning a Japanese interpreter would get on the loud speaker and tell them that "the war was over, come on in". They would come in by the hundreds. They had to come in on a prescribed route and stripped from the waist up. We'd take them prisoner and bring them to the stockade. Some of them thought they had won the war. Once they were brought to the stockade, they were guarded by GIs but they did all of the cooking and cleaning themselves. They were well fed and had excellent care. But there were still lots of Japanese out there. At dark, when we got into the chow line, you'd have to hold the guy in front of you by the collar, because we heard that the Japanese were getting into the chow line and escaping into the jungle. The reason why prisoners were brought in along a prescribed path and given a sequence of things to do, was because some of them would come in armed and try to kill you. After a while the Marines took over the prisoners. So one day I was out in an area where the Japanese would come in and I was just watching. Three Japanese soldiers came in and the Marine guard was talking to them through an interpreter. One of them had a bandana around his chest. All of a sudden he dropped to his knees and another guy grabbed a gun that was in the bandana. The Japanese were all killed but not until they had killed the guard and the interpreter.

Once the Japanese were taken prisoner they were easy to work with. They were good workers, polite and didn't curse and talk in a vulgar way like the GIs. Every day they saw you, they'd bow. They were very respectful. But the prisoners that really scared me were the Imperial Marines. They were all big, over 6 feet tall and mean. Once we had twelve of them in a stockade. They were guarded closely and not allowed any privileges. All they did was curse at us in English. I was scared just looking at them.

Many of the Japanese hid in the trees. They'd fire at us, maybe only one round a day. Everyone would just fire back at the trees. At night they'd call out to us, "Hey Joe from Minnesota". It was scary. Sometimes at night you'd hear "Hey Joe, see you tomorrow". After a while some died up there and the stench was terrible. The Sea Bees would come in and bump the tree with a bulldozer to shake the body out of there. They were out there months after the war ended.

Once they were captured, though, they were lambs. Quite frankly, we had a harder time with the Filipinos. They were so hungry and desperate that they were stealing the eyes out of us. You'd go to bed at night and you'd wake up and your shoes were gone, or your pants. They even had these small boats and at night they'd go under the docks to steal food or supplies. Once I pulled a guy over and he had fifteen pairs of GI underwear stuffed into his clothes. Another time, it was Parker pens. Once we boarded a small boat that had four big drums on it. When I opened them up they were filled with rice. The officer with me told me to dig down with my hands and sure enough, underneath the rice they were all filled with American cigarettes.

From the start Manila was clear of Japanese. It was the outlying areas, the villages and the islands that had to be cleaned up. They'd send kids like us to clean them up. There were still a lot of pillboxes and when you came across one you had to go up about 25 feet from the opening and just start shooting at it. Then two guys with a flamethrower would move in, put it in the opening, and give it a blast. Then the See Bees would come in and bulldoze it. We couldn't do it any other way. When we'd bomb them by air nothing would happen to them. That's why they had to be destroyed from the ground.

Once the islands were cleared up, they put me in Recovery Personnel. Because I had flight training, I was picked for a unit that flew some of the Japanese POWs to the war crime trials in Manila. My best memory was of a Japanese officer. He was well dressed, clean, and in a full dress uniform. His name was Yamashita. We weren't supposed to talk to the prisoners but he spoke English and kept talking to us. He told us that he was going to jump out of the plane and that if something happened to him we'd have to serve his sentence. He said, "You boys are young. You'll never see your parents again". He talked a mile a minute and it was a three hour flight. He asked me where I was from but I wouldn't answer. He was very demanding and wanted to be treated like an officer. He scorched the hell out of us. Every five minutes he would ask for something–water, a biscuit, etc. At this point we were wondering if we really won the war. I'll never forget this guy. I can still picture him. He was shaped like a pear. *(General Tomoyuki Yamashita was the commander of the retreating Japanese forces in Manila at the end of the war. During this time thousands of Filipino civilians were murdered. Although he denied involvement and there was no direct evidence linking him to the atrocities, he was convicted at the War Crime Trials in Manila. His conviction was upheld by the U.S. Supreme Court and on Feburary 23, 1946, he was hanged in the town of Los Banos which was located just south of Manila).*[3]

One of the things you never read about is the living conditions over there. Malaria, no milk, everything powdered. You went to the bathroom in a trench and sometimes you were shot at. One time our captain was going and he got shot at. He was hit and fell right into the trench. We thought he was dead but it turned out

he was slightly wounded. When he recovered and was set to go home he called for a general inspection. As the guys lined up a few of them started laughing and were making sniffing sounds. You could see him steaming and finally he looked around and said, "The hell with you guys, I'm going home".

We had to take a big yellow pill for malaria - Adebrin. It made your complexion yellow and gave you a jaundiced look. When I got home, my mother took one look at me and cried. A year later I went to give blood for a friend of mine and they rejected me. The Adebrin was still in my bloodstream.

Nobody would believe how we showered. A truck would pull up with three compartments. You'd go through each, water,

General Tomoyuki Yamashita

soap, towel and then come out the other side.

there when the Philippines were given their independence in 1946. There were parades through the streets and the Filipino Army lined the roads to protect the government from the "Hucks". They were the guerrillas who were fighting the new government. When they introduced the new President of the Philippines there was loud applause and cheering. But when they introduced General MacArthur, the place went wild. He was like a god to them. He was there with his wife and son. A big truck full of photographers pulled up and they all got out. I was only a few feet away and the minute those photographers pulled up he went into his pose. He was a real showman.

Carella returned home in 1946. He became an engineer for Pitney Bowes and has worked there for over 40 years.

WARREN CORBIN

When the American forces landed on Luzon, there were still thousands of American prisoners that had been interned in Manila by the Japanese since 1942. On February 1, 1945, General MacArthur gave the order to drive to Manila and free the prisoners.

Over the next few days, American forces advanced over 70 miles to Manila. Instrumental in supporting this drive was Staff Sergeant Warren J. Corbin of the 21st Infantry Cannon Company. On the road to Manila, Corbin's self propelled gun crew was credited with destroying 50 Japanese gun emplacements, saving two important bridges before the enemy could destroy them and spearheading the infan-  *try company's attack to free over 2200 prisoners from the infamous Los Banos Prison Camp.*

Corbin repeatedly exposed himself to heavy enemy artillery mortar and rifle fire and ultimately, he would lose a leg as a result of the wounds he suffered in combat. In addition to the Purple Heart, the Combat Infantry Badge and the Presidential Unit Citation, he was awarded the Bronze Star, and a Silver Star.

In 1979 he died at the age of 60.

---

[1] Madeline Barillo. "Venerable Artillery Battalion Joins Ghosts of History". Stamford Advocate, May 16, 1993, p.1.

[2] "Noted Tennis Star Dies in Pacific". Stamford Advocate, May 17, 1945, p.1.

[3] Rafael Steinberg. Return to the Phillipines. (Alexandria, VA: Time Life Books, Inc., 1979), p.192.

CHAPTER SEVEN

CHINA - BURMA - INDIA

By the time the US entered the war, Japan had already been at war with China sporadically for almost a decade. Now they controlled Manchuria; Peking, Shanghai, and several other major Chinese cities. Soon after Pearl Harbor, the Japanese extended their conquests to include the Philippines, New Guinea, Borneo, French Indochina, Thailand, and Singapore. Now, they turned their attention toward Burma and by early 1942 the Japanese had captured its port of Rangoon.

Anxious to stem the tide of Japanese aggression, the allies formed the ABDA command (American, British, Dutch, Australian) to fight the Japanese in the area, defend India, assist China, and keep it in the war. A China-Burma-India Theater was established which included the remainder of China which was not in Japanese hands and stretched from the Arabian Sea to the Pacific Ocean.

- DR. JAMES CRANE -

*After completing his medical degree at
the University of Vermont, Dr. Crane enlisted in the Army Air Corps with dreams of
becoming a flyer. Instead he was assigned
to General Patton's Second Armor Division
at Fort Benning, Georgia. Eventually, however, he was reassigned to the School of
Aviation Medicine and just prior to U.S.
entry into the war was sent overseas with the
Atlantic Division of the Ferry Command.
Ultimately, Dr. Crane traveled across Europe, Africa, and Asia before arriving in the
Pacific Theater of action.*

When I first arrived in Europe, I was what you would call a combat observer.
I traveled around in Europe, and my job was to gather information on the location
of military installations, hospitals, and other facilities. I traveled in uniform and
in civilian clothes.

I was in Egypt on December 7, 1941 when the U.S. entered the war. I was
there alone so the first thing I did was go to the U.S. Embassy in Cairo to find out
what I should do next. Rommel was only 80 miles away, and he was closing in
fast. While I was at the Embassy, purely by chance, I ran into General George
Brett. He told me that he needed a doctor and that I could travel with him as an
aide. He was on his way to China to meet with Chiang Kai-Shek.

On December 13, we flew to India, Burma, and finally to Chung King,
China. Brett's mission was to formulate war plans with the Chinese, to see how
we could help them against the Japanese. We were joined there by General Claire
Chennault. *(Chennault led the American Volunteer Group which assisted China
in the air war against Japan. Later known as the Flying Tigers, they were credited
with destroying a total of 299 Japanese planes before they were disbanded in
1942.)*

We stayed right in Chiang's home and had dinner with him. I also got to meet
Madame Chiang. She was educated in the U.S. and spoke English fluently. She
asked me where I had gone to college and kidded me that she had gone to
Dartmouth. She was a beautiful and charming woman.

We stayed at Chiang's home until Christmas of 1941 when we left for
Burma. We were supposed to land in Rangoon but must have gotten lost because
just as we were about to land, I looked down and noticed that the airfield was
loaded with Japanese planes. I yelled to the pilot, "Get the hell out of here." We
already had the landing gear down, but we pulled up and got out of there in a hurry.
It turned out that we were off by almost 200 miles and were running out of fuel.
We finally landed in the last satellite field in southern Burma.

From there I went to Singapore, Australia, and then Java. While I was there,
the Japanese invaded Java. I had about 40 wounded men from a B-17 squadron
with me, and I received a call from General Brett instructing me to take the
wounded men to a place called Milan where we would all be evacuated. But by
the time we arrived there, the planes had already left. We were stranded. Finally
we went to a placed called Tsilijap where we hooked up with a Dutch freighter.
We boarded it and joined an Allied convoy, but we left the convoy because it was

moving too slowly. The next day the convoy was attacked and almost every ship was sunk. Finally, about five days later, we arrived in southwest Australia and had to travel across the country by train.

I arrived in Melbourne and reported to headquarters. I was told that I had to return to Washington, D.C., to report my experiences. I got back to D.C. a few weeks later and was interrogated. Then I was promoted to Major immediately to command the 801st Air Evacuation Squadron. The idea was that we were going to evacuate the wounded by air. We were part of the 13th Air Force in New Caledonia under Admiral Halsey. We had five flight surgeons and twenty-five nurses and started flying into Guadalcanal. We would fly supplies in and take the wounded out. I did this for about six months. Sometimes I can't believe some of the terrible things I saw.

There was still a lot of action on Guadalcanal so when we went in, we were escorted by a group of fighter planes. We'd land, unload, pick up the wounded and get the hell out of there, all in about twenty minutes. We usually had a lot of serious head and chest wounds. The pilot would ask me how serious things were, and I'd have to tell him how high to fly. The more serious the wounds, the lower we'd have to fly. The higher the altitude, the less oxygen and more potential danger there was to the wounded. I used to feel so bad for those Marines out there. The risks from malaria alone were enough to worry about.

After Guadalcanal, I was reassigned to New Zealand where I was the head doctor at an R & R hospital for pilots, bombardiers, and navigators. I'd screen them for combat fatigue and determine when and if they were able to fly again. I did this for about a year until I was sent back to the U.S. I wound up as the Chief Flight Surgeon at Fort Logan in Denver, Colorado. We had about 1,000 American POW's who were liberated in Europe by General Patton and the others. It was mostly psychiatric work. They were all gunners and navigators, mostly from the Eighth and Ninth Air Force. Some had been in prison camps for a couple of years.

I wanted to get back overseas again so I called General Brett. He told me to sit tight because the war was going to be over very soon. He knew about the

Dr. Crane (standing 5th from right) in Chung King China with Chiang Kai-shek and Mme Chiang (center seated). Aslo in the picture, American Far East Expert, Owen Latimore (standing 2nd from left) and Gen. Brett (seated left rear of Chiang).

Atomic Bomb. So I stayed in Denver and ended up meeting the General and Mrs. Doolittle, whom I was friendly with until his death.

While I was working with P.O.W.'s, a young man came in to see me. He was from Stamford. He told me that he wanted to go home and see his family. I cut through all of the paper work and sent him right home. Later, when I inquired about him, I found out that he had a very interesting background. Before the war, he had been in and out of jail and had been involved with some mobsters. When the war broke out, he wanted to enlist, but nobody would take him. So he went to a gunnery school in Texas and became so proficient that he was finally accepted into the Army Air Corps. He flew twenty-five missions and received the Distinguished Flying Cross.

When he came back to Denver, we had a chance to talk. He told me that before the war, he was nothing but a bum. He said, "Those first twenty-five missions were to repay my debt to society. The next twenty-five are for me." He went on to fly twenty-five more missions. After the war, I tried to look him up, but I could not find him. I always wanted to know how his life turned out.

Twenty-five years later I got a phone call. The voice on the phone said, "Major?" I knew immediately who it was. His life was going well and he was living in Pennsylvania, but he was having medical problems. I told him to come back immediately. I checked him into St. Joseph Hospital, and it turned out that he was diabetic. One day he brought me an English walking stick. He told me that it was his good luck charm. After every mission, he would take the stick and go for a long walk with his dog. He wanted me to have it because I would know what the stick meant to him. He died a few years ago in New Jersey, but by all accounts, he had lived a good life and was a fine citizen.

> *Dr. Crane returned to Stamford in 1946. He worked at Belleview Hospital for a few years before opening up his own local practice. He is an F.A.A. Flight Surgeon and deals primarily in Aerospace Medicine. In addition to this, Dr. Crane is the founder of the International Order of Characters which has included Jimmy Doolittle, Igor Sikorsky, and Walter Schirra as its members.*

- ROBERT MACDONALD -

Robert MacDonald was inducted into the Army in 1942 and was assigned to the 45th Quartermasters Trucking Regiment along with 26 other local men. He served in the China Burma India theater and worked along the Burma-Ledo Road for over two years.

When the war broke out I was working at the Alcoa Aluminum Company in Fairfield making parts for airplanes. I could've gotten a deferment, but all of my friends went into the Army, so I decided to go in with them.

We arrived in Calcutta, then went to Bombay, to Ceylon, and then by train and ferry to Osam, India. Malaria was the biggest threat and we had to take Adebrine every morning at chow. Some guys refused to take it, but I made sure I took mine.

The first thing you noticed in India was how poor it was. People were dying of a rice famine, 1500 of them a day. Some babies were born in the streets and died in the streets, never had a home. One day a lady came up to me and asked me for a handout. I gave her 16 cents and she handed me a baby. I didn't know what the hell to do with it so I went up to an Indian policeman and gave it to him.

The Indians were so poor that they could save their money for a lifetime and never even have enough to buy a bike. They could never even imagine that a working man like myself in America could own an automobile. In Calcutta, when people died in the street, they didn't bury them right away. They put a tin cup near the head of the body and when there was enough money in the cup, they would haul the body away to be burned. People were starving, but they'd allow a cow to walk around and eat right off a vegetable stand. Sometimes a bunch of American soldiers would go out and trap a cow, bring it back, slaughter it and eat it before the officers could find out. That's how efficient they were. Before we left India, some guys were practically herding cows.

I used to tease some of the Indian workers, but one day they reversed it on me. I was loading bags of barley onto a truck and was in a hurry because I wanted to get it done before chow. The Indians were stalling and messing around, so I teased one of the guys and said, "Hey Charlie, tell these Coolies to get going." And he said to me, "Hell, you're nothing but an American Coolie."

We had a lot of contact with the British, but they were so stiff. We thought nothing of talking with our officers or asking them for a smoke, but the British would never do that. One of them said, "You Americans don't have a god-damned army, you have a mob." And I said, "Yeah, but we know how to win."

The Burma Road was 1100 miles long and went all the way to Kumming, China. The trip took 11 days if the weather was good. But you could fly all the way back in four hours and ever since then I love airplanes. Your biggest enemy was the rain. One time I spent four days in the same place because the road was washed out behind us and in front of us. At the time, the Japanese were only 60 miles away.

The Burma Road

We saw Lord Mountbatten there. He came in to give us a hellfire pep talk. He said, "We have the Japanese right where we want them, right in the open." The next damn thing you know, the Japanese were 15 minutes away from us setting the elephant grass on fire. Mountbatten got all the fighting he wanted.

We took everything down the road, ammunition, bombs, men, dynamite, gasoline, rice, and every type of vehicle you could name. You'd go to the motor pool and they'd give you a piece of paper with a number on it. Then you'd look for a vehicle with that number stenciled on it, and that's what you had to drive, whether you were trained on it or not. I drove a British Laurie with the steering wheel on the right side and had to shift with my left hand. Another time I drove a Diamond T (truck) with a 13 ton tank on it. The Chinese were running the tanks off the road, so we had to take the tanks all the way up to the front for them.

There were mile markers all along the road, some I'll never forget. Ledo was the zero mark. "Hell Gate" was at 30 miles. Logali was 56, "The Gap" was at 90 miles, and Shimuang was at 126 miles. To go from 33 to 56 it took a full day, all uphill. Imagine a full day to go 23 miles. Some of the turns were so sharp you had to back up to go around them. Then, coming out of a mountain, you'd make one turn, then another, and if you made one wrong move, it was all over. There was nothing to stop you once you went off the road. Many a time we were so high up that a C-47 would fly by and it would be below us. On top of one of the mountains a chaplain put a sign, "All things pass. May God be with you." Then there was the Swailing Bridge in Burma. It was a rope bridge and only one truck at a time could cross.

All along the road you'd see trucks that didn't make it. During the rainy season it was the worst. From November to April it would rain inches every day and you'd be knee deep in mud. Then it would stop, the sun would come out, and it would go up to 120 degrees. But Burma was beautiful. Acres and acres of coconut, pineapple, and banana trees.

The Chinese had never seen any black people before, so when we went into a village, little kids would run up to us, rub our skin and feel our hair, but we weren't bothered by it. I suppose it would be like if a green person walked down the street right now. One of the things I admired about them was that they could name their family members all the way back 3000 years. I couldn't even name my great-grandfather.

We had white officers, but they treated us O.K. Once the Inspector General came out to see us and he asked us if we were being treated all right. I said, "Yes, but I wish I could join an infantry outfit." And he said, "Well, I would too, but instead they have me in this damn fool job asking these damn fool questions."

But overall, it was a great experience and at the end of the war, all of us were back in Stamford. All 26 of us went in together, and all 26 came back safely.

Mr. MacDonald returned home and went to work at Rolling Mills. A few years later he went into business for himself and opened, "Joy's Snack Bar" which operated in town for over 20 years.

- AFRICAN AMERICANS -

During World War II approximately one million Black soldiers fought in the US armed forces. Although their treatment on the whole, was slightly better than in World War I, they were nonetheless segregated and denied the opportunities available to other GI's.

African Americans served in every branch of service and distinguished themselves in every theater of the war. Dorie Miller, who shot down four Japanese planes at Pearl Harbor, won the Navy Cross. In the air, over 80 Black pilots won the Distinguished Flying Cross. And, in the steaming jungles and treacherous mountains of the China-Burma-India Theater, Black engineers helped to construct the famed Ledo Road which kept vital supplies flowing to China.

After the war President Truman recommended the elimination of racial barriers in the armed forces and by the Korean War, Americans fought together, regardless of race.

- EUGENE HART -

Gene Hart enlisted in the US Army in 1942, and was assigned to the 45th Quarter- masters Unit in Pittsfield, California which was made up entirely of African Americans. Two years later the unit was shipped out to the China-Burma-India Theater where they were assigned to transport supplies along the famous Burma-Lido Road. This route, later known as the Stillwell Road wound through dense jungle, across gorges, and up and down steep cliffs. When its construction was finally completed, the road stretched from India to China and served as a lifeline to the American and Allied Chinese Armies.

When we were shipping out of Fort Devins (Mass.) to various companies, the white sol- diers would go into one line and we would go into another. The peculiar thing is that all of the Portuguese kids from Massachusetts and Rhode Island were considered Black and came with us. One guy who was white according to his birth certificate refused to go with the whites and he came with us.

In California our main job was transporting Japanese POW's to prison camps. We were there until 1944 when we were shipped out. We were on the water for over 60 days on the USS George Washington. We went straight down to Tasmania, across the International Date Line, and back up into Bombay. This was our first stop but then we got right back on a British transport and were taken to Calcutta. From there we ended up on Ledo (India). While we were on the British transport we saw segregation first hand. Our sergeants didn't stay with us. They slept on a different part of the ship. They also confiscated all of our rifles when we boarded. The British treated the Indians like dirt, too, and we didn't like that because we felt that the Indians were like us. Later on, we were not allowed to eat in British camps.

We spent the rest of the war there, transporting goods down the Burma road as far as it was completed. By the end of the war, we were making runs all the way through to Kumming, China dropping trucks off to the Chinese Army.

We kept feeding the road as it went. We'd truck materials in to the engineers or food or medical supplies. We even supplied Merrill's Marauders for a while. Sometimes we would get to a part of the road that would be washed out during monsoon season. We'd just have to stay there until the engineers repaired it or built a log road. Sometimes a bulldozer would have to tow the trucks one at a time across a section. If we were traveling across a mountain road and it was raining, the mud would wash right down across the road and if you got caught in one of those mudslides you were gone.

You never knew how long a run would take either. It depended on the weather and the condition of the road. Sometimes it would take you a half day just to climb a few miles up a mountain road. Then it would only take twenty minutes to go down on the other side. You'd be looking straight down a cliff the whole time. Once we passed a column of Chinese soldiers with ponies. One of our drivers swerved to avoid hitting one of them and he went off the road and the truck began to roll very slowly down the hill. All we could do was watch as this truck kept on rolling. We lost a guy once when he accidentally put a jeep in reverse and went right off the road and down the mountain.

In Burma, when the road was washed out we would camp around and go hunting and fishing. We always made sure we slept in the truck and used our jungle hammocks. The mosquitoes, leeches, ticks, and malaria were always a problem. You'd never sleep on the ground because of the "minute snakes." That's what we called them because if they bit you, you were dead in a minute. If you were in the jungle after monsoon season when everything was wet, you would feel something on you and it would be a leech. Some of the leeches went right through your clothing and you didn't even know it. It was so hot your clothes would be soggy all the time. I can remember constantly being dripping wet. And all of your water had to be boiled or you had to use little tablets. If you got caught drinking water from the mountains you were in trouble.

The jungle was so thick that I can see why we couldn't win the Vietnam War. The Japanese were able to tunnel through trees and swamps. They had bunkers set up everywhere. We rarely had contact with them even when we went into a combat area to supply Merrill's Marauders.

At times when we were stopped along the road we would have contact with some of the Burmese natives. A lot of them chewed "beetle nut" and their teeth would be red from it. They also had something called "gunya" which was like a very potent marijuana. They would pack it into a tube of bamboo and try to sell it to us. But most of them were afraid of us and when they saw us they would just disappear into the jungle.

Along the road we had a lot of contact with Indian laborers. These were the "coolies" who built the road. The British paid them next to nothing for a day's work and they would be contracted to work for six months at a time. The Americans paid them more and also gave them food and medical care.

In China, we once went into a village and saw the strangest thing. All of the women had their feet taped. The story was that the village prince married a woman with big feet and ordered all of the women to tape their feet to keep them from growing.

Toward the end of the war we were going all the way to Kumming taking trucks to the Chinese. Once we got there we had to fly back to India through "The Hump." You would be up in that place and you'd hit an airpocket and some of the guys would scream. It was like your seat was there one minute and the next minute there was nothing under you. *("The Hump" refers to the flight back to India through the Himalayas. The combination of empty places, erratic weather, and dangerously high winds made this an extremely dangerous air route. Over 1000 men and 600 planes were lost going through "The Hump.)[1]*

I'll never forget one very sad day when we were all ordered to watch an execution. One of the soldiers, a black kid from Philadelphia, shot and killed an officer. A few days later, the British caught him and returned him to camp, and he was hanged. It was one of the stillest moments I remember in the Army.

We were at a checkpoint in China when we heard that the war was over. We started dismantling immediately. We went around to different storage areas to pick up supplies. Then we'd bring them to an area and light them on fire. Clothes, ammunition, everything. The biggest waste I saw in my life. The best thing about going overseas was that a great deal of the time rank didn't matter. You all worked together because there was a job to do.

Mr. Hart returned to Stamford after the war and attended trade school under the G.I. Bill. He became a machinist and worked for Pitney Bowes before setting up his own business.

- WINSTON STATEWHITE -

One of the more popular members of the Black community was Winston Statewhite. A friendly, outgoing young man, he left his job at Sabini Furniture and entered the Army in 1942 at the age of 37. Shortly

after, he was sent to the China Burma India Theater and, as a member of the 1883 Engineers, worked along the famed Burma Road. He also acted as a big brother to many of the local men who were assigned to his unit.

On December 14, 1944, Statewhite was killed in a huge explosion caused when 200 cases of dynamite were accidentally detonated. He was 39 years old at the time of his death.

After the war, Statewhite Street in the downtown section of Stamford was named in his honor, but the street was taken during urban redevelopment in the 1960's. Today, however, VFW Post 10446 bears the name of Winston Statewhite, one of the first local Blacks to die in the Second World War.

- LEO BARAN -

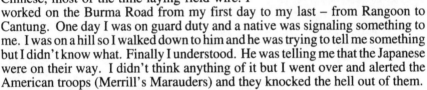

Before the war, Leo Baran distinguished himself as a fine athlete competing in baseball, basketball, and golf. In 1943, he left his new bride and headed for the China Burma India Theater. As a member of the 92nd Signal Batallion he worked along the Burma Road setting up communication lines.

While we were on our way overseas a Japanese bomber was coming right for us but he dropped his bomb off course and the ship in front of us was hit. There were men in the water and I can still see the propellers of the boats cutting them up. There was nothing we could do but keep on going.

Once we got over there I worked with the Chinese, most of the time laying field wire. I worked on the Burma Road from my first day to my last – from Rangoon to Cantung. One day I was on guard duty and a native was signaling something to me. I was on a hill so I walked down to him and he was trying to tell me something but I didn't know what. Finally I understood. He was telling me that the Japanese were on their way. I didn't think anything of it but I went over and alerted the American troops (Merrill's Marauders) and they knocked the hell out of them.

In Burma it was so hot and humid. It would rain for five months at a time. The rain wouldn't stop so you had to go out and do your work anyway. You were always wet. Then sometimes you'd walk through the mud and it would suck your boots right off your feet. During monsoon season everything would be flooded. We used to bathe in the streams but I'll tell you the Irrawaddy River was dangerous! Once this guy Johnson from Pittsburgh was with me and he jumped in the water and it just took him away. He never came up. The snakes were huge. You had to be careful because they'd be up in the trees ready to pounce. There were other wild animals, too. Once I was laying field wire near the Irrawaddy River and I took a walk downstream. There was a big water buffalo and when he saw me he started to charge. I ran like hell.

The leeches and the ticks were the worst. They'd take the blood right out of you. I got very sick over there. I had post-typhus. I was in a Bashi (hospital) for three months and nobody could see me. I was all by myself except when they came to give me these shots right in the chest. I lost my hearing in one ear and thought they'd give me a medical discharge but I stayed in and here I am. When I was discharged I got out on a 40% disability.

The Chinese were always good to me. They were all my friends and they were hard workers. Once they gave me a big dinner–almost twenty courses. Later they gave me two beautiful swords. The way they built the Burma road was amazing. They went right through the mountains. It was dangerous though, especially during monsoon season. You'd be going down the road and boulders would be rolling off the hills – mudslides too.

It was a rough few years, boiling our water before we drank it, nothing to keep the bugs away, fighting the weather and the Japanese. But I wouldn't trade the experience.

Leo came home in 1945 and was reunited with his wife, raised a family, resumed his golf game, and became the WSTC City Amateur Golf Champion in 1949. In addition to three Battle Stars he also received the "High Honor of the Cloud and Banner" from the Chinese Government. He worked for Conde Nast and Olin Corporation until his retirement.

Mr. Baran passed away in April of 1994.

Several Stamford companies received the Army-Navy E-Award. Among them were American Cyanamid, Machlett Labs, Yale & Towne, and Norma-Hoffman Ball Bearing Plant. Pictured above is Pitney-Bowes which won the award in 1943.

- HERB KOHN -

Herb Kohn left Ohio University during his sophomore year to enlist in the Army Air Corps. He was trained as a Cryptographer and spent almost two years in India.

Once the war broke out, school slowed up dramatically and interest in a formal education dwindled to almost nothing. Everyone wanted to get into the war. We were concerned about the future of the country and what was happening overseas.

The Air Corps was looking for college men, so I left school and went to New York to take all of the tests. They accepted me, sent me back to school, and about three weeks later, I was called up. In fact, I left school after a basketball game and everybody came down to wave goodbye. My biggest thrill was when a guy who used to hustle me regularly at the pool hall, came down to the train station to see me off. He bought me a pillow for 35 cents and told the Pullman Conductor to take good care of me.

I reported to Atlantic City wearing an "Alligator" raincoat and my brown and white saddle shoes, and I was herded in with a lot of other young men. We stayed at the Senator Hotel right on the Boardwalk. After we completed basic training there, I was sent to Colby College in Waterville, Maine, as part of a College Training Detachment. I had gone in with the intention of being a pilot and had some flight training up there, but it turned out that I was a lousy one, so it wasn't meant to be. I was at Colby for about a year and travelled a lot with the Army baseball team. *(Kohn was named to the "All-Army of the U.S." team as a shortstop).*

One of the commanders told me that they were looking for people in cryptography, so I was sent to Chicago to Chanute Field where I took an intensive, almost round-the-clock, training for 21 days. From there I was sent to Mitchell Field in New York City. My assignment was as an instructor, teaching cryptography to officers in the First Air Force. I was attached to a radar station which was commanded out of the Bell Telephone building on 7th Avenue and 17th Street that controlled the New York Fighter Wing. I taught the officers how to use a Cigaba, which was a machine that looked almost like a typewriter. It was a pretty complex decoding device in those days, but by today's standards, probably very simple. I also taught Field Operating Devices. The codes were changed regularly, and the machines had little rotors that were also changed.

I was on the east coast for about a year when I was sent to Newport News, Virginia, for debarking for points unknown. We were part of a big troop movement that went through the Panama Canal, to Australia, then finally to India. We were at sea for 47 days, and when we landed in Bombay, I never felt so glad to get a foot on the ground. From there we were marched out to a Tent City and in the heat after 47 days at sea, men were collapsing all around.

The Medical Officer called us all together, welcomed us to India, and warned us not to drink anything that didn't come out of our lister bags or unless it was bottled in the U.S.A. He also told us to make sure we slept with a mosquito net. Then, he told us about snakes. In particular, one called a krait. This was the most deadly snake and we were told that if we were bitten, there was little they could do for us. He told us to check our shoes each morning because they loved to curl up in a warm, dark place. Well, you could have heard a pin drop. We were all just looking at each other and nobody slept well for the first few nights. But it wasn't long before you lost all that fear.

Then we took a train right across India from Bombay to Calcutta and there is just no way to describe it. It took days and the train was packed. You slept anywhere you could except on the floor because of these huge cockroaches. The lavatories were crazy, too. You'd walk in and there would be an imprint of two feet on the floor to show you where to stand. And then there was just a hole in the floor. Guys would walk in and you'd hear them laughing.

When we arrived in Calcutta, I was stationed at the headquarters at Hastings Air Base on the Houghly River. General Stratemeyer was our commander and from time to time Claire Chennault would stop in and get everyone excited. I was attached to the signal center there and was one of those in charge of encoding and decoding all of the messages that came through there. We worked in a converted jute mill. There were about 10 of us there and we would receive transmissions all day. They usually came in blocks of 5 letters and by lining them up according to the code of the day you translated the message. There was no glamour or no romance to what we were doing. It was just a tedious job. We didn't know the significance of most of the messages we were receiving, but we knew in general what was going on. But even amongst ourselves we didn't divulge information. When you knew that other people's lives depended on you, you learned to keep everything to yourself.

I never saw combat and I have to admit it was frustrating. I was very lucky, but you knew that others were getting killed and there was a tendency to pooh-pooh our own participation in the war. I'd get a letter from a friend of mine who was in Europe or the Pacific and sometimes it would be difficult to respond.

But I did have the opportunity to witness some great sights while I was there. This was during Gandhi's time and on occasion I'd go into Calcutta and be able to see him. I have never seen such a crowd in my life. We go to a football game and think it's a crowd, but, there it was, millions of people. You were not in control of your own body. Wherever the crowd goes, you go. I also had occasion to see the Indians strike out against the British.

What struck me the most when I was there though, was the caste system. Whatever you were, you had no hope of changing. The villages were so poor that the people would take any work. Most of us had "bearers" or manservants who would take care of us from morning till night. They'd help us with our personal things, even light our cigarettes for us.

Some of the sights there were unbelievable. I remember that each day in Calcutta the water would be turned on and it would run down the streets. People would be lined up. Some bathing, some washing dishes, and some washing clothes. I also saw the burning ghat, which was where they piled wood and other combustibles to burn bodies.

The people there were wonderful, especially the kids. We used to play a lot of baseball there and sports was a vehicle for getting to know the people. One time the kids asked me to teach them baseball. I told them that I would show up on Sunday morning to teach them and when I showed up that day, it looked like the entire village was there. There must have been a couple of hundred kids waiting. I had to go back to the base and wake up the rest of the team to come and help me. But it was so rewarding. People would invite me over for dinner and the kids would all greet me each day when I went into town.

I stayed in India until 1946, and when we returned on a troop ship, we were told to expect big crowds to greet us. But the war had been over for quite some time and when we docked in Seattle, there were only a handful of people there. When they dropped the gangplank, a few guys ran to their waiting families and embraced. There were about 6,000 of us on that troop ship and I'll bet every one of us cried.

> *Herb returned home, married his sweetheart, and a few years, later he established KOMAR furniture which operated in Stamford for over 40 years. He was also active in city government serving on the Police Commission, Planning and Zoning, and Environment Protection Board. He was named the "Citizen of the Year" in 1967 and remains active in Twilight League Baseball.*

Don Moser. China Burma India. (Alexandria, VA: Time Life Books, Inc., 1974), p.80.

CHAPTER EIGHT

WOMEN, FAMILIES,

and

THE HOMEFRONT

More than in any previous war, women played a significant role in the war effort, both at home and abroad. With so many men overseas, women kept the homefront machinery running smoothly and fed the ever growing demand for new defense industries.

As factories experienced an ever rising shortage of manpower, the burden of domestic production fell squarely upon the shoulders of women. Traditional conceptions about women were replaced by the image of "Rosie the Riveter." Whether it was working for aircraft plants or ammunition factories, women became a significant force in the workplace, and by 1943, they made up one-third of the labor force.

In addition to working in the factories, hundreds of thousands of women answered the call to serve with the Army, Navy, Marines, and Coast Guard. The largest of the women's services was the WAC's or Women's Army Corps. The WAC's served at home and abroad in several capacities from clerical work to repairing trucks. The WAVES, Women Accepted for Volunteer Emergency Services, although not allowed to go overseas until 1944, also served as cryptographers, medical personnel, and even as gunnery instructors for men. Even the Army Air Force, which was initially reluctant to enlist women, created the WAFS, the Women's Auxiliary Ferrying Squadron, the Women's Marines, the Coast Guard, and SPURS, who performed the vital tasks which would free the men for combat duty.

As in every other American war, women continued to serve as nurses, both here, at home and in every corner of the world. Working as hospital nurses or surgical nurses, sometimes very close to the battle lines, these women often provided the only comfort to wounded service men who were alone, thousands of miles from home.

Whether it was in the factories, in civil defense, or with the military, the women in World War II changed forever, the nation's perception of females and their standing in society. They laid the groundwork for the drastic changes in women's roles that would occur in later years.

- ALICE WESTERBERG -

Before the U.S. entered the War, Alice Westerberg was working with the Stamford Visiting Nurses Association. After Pearl Harbor, the call went out for nurses and in February of 1942, she entered the U.S. Army Nursing Corps and spent three years overseas treating American soldiers in England and France.

I think I was always fated to be a nurse. As a young girl in New York City, I remember going to a lot of parades during World War I and the patriotic music inspired me. I remember the posters and the pamphlets calling for nurses and particularly the song, "The Rose of No Man's Land" which glorified the Red Cross nurse. *("It's the one red rose the soldier knows. It's the work of the Master's hand. Mid the War's great curse stands the Red Cross nurse. She's the Rose of No Man's Land").* Then in high school I volunteered during my unassigned time to work in the infirmary. By 1932, I had graduated the Long Island College Hospital School for Nurses.

Before the war broke out, I was a Public Health nurse in Stamford. Because I had just taken a maternity course, I was assigned the job of forming a "Mother's Club," which would have classes on prenatal care. At the time I had only 2 women join, but today all women take these classes.

When the war broke out in Europe and U.S. boys were beginning to get drafted, the government was requesting that any medical personnel volunteer for one year of service. I received a letter from a recruiter which said that, because I was involved in a "Vital Service", I wouldn't be expected to join. But shortly after that, I got a letter from a Captain Taylor in Boston, with a set of orders to report to Camp Edwards. But at the time I was taking a nursing course and talked her into delaying my entry until January of 1942. But before that happened, Pearl Harbor was attacked and now instead of serving one year, I knew I'd be in for the duration.

I reported to Camp Edwards in February, and about five months later my name was posted on a bulletin board for overseas duty. I told the chief nurse that I didn't want to go, and she told me that if I found a replacement, I wouldn't have to go. But then it occurred to me that I couldn't let someone else substitute for me, so I was definitely going overseas. An entire medical contingent was being formed at Camp Edwards with people from all over the country, and by September of 1942, I was on a troop ship headed for Europe.

We finally arrived in Tauton, England. I was assigned to the Third Station Hospital in Tidworth-Salisbury, along with four other nurses. The five of us were assigned to a damp, sweaty room with black curtains covering the windows. What a horrible place. But when I was able to get around and become active in the community life and meet the people of the village, these turned out to be the happiest two years of my life. I developed a lot of close ties and corresponded with many of these people for years.

Next I was assigned to the Isolation Hospital. I worked mostly with men who had communicable diseases. Some of the men were being brought over from Africa with malaria, but the others had everything from measles to syphilis. One night while I was on duty, I met a Chaplain who was with the 29th Division. He invited me to a Sunday service at his chapel, and that's how I met a lot of people in the village.

While I was there, there was an epidemic of spinal meningitis among some of the men in the 29th Division. These boys would come in delirious, some of them out of their minds. They would be thrashing about, and sometimes it would take six of us to hold them down so we could give them an I.V. of Sulfonamide. All of them recovered except one boy who we lost because we didn't catch it early enough.

A few of us also became close to a British Paratroop Officer's group who were part of the 6th Division. We'd invite them to an Officer's Club near the hospital and my friend would play the piano and we'd sing for them. We'd meet with them once a week for dances or other socials, and they were wonderful people.

Then one night I heard a rumble, and when I looked out at the sky, it was black with planes. When I found out that this was D-Day, I knew that all of the wonderful boys that I cared for, both British and American, were going off to fight. One of the boys that I was particularly close with was Charlie Bliss. He was a British paratrooper and participated in the D-Day invasion. I wrote to him and never got a reply. Later, when I was in France, I ran into one of his friends who told me that Charlie survived the D-Day jump, but was killed the following month in France. He also told me that Charlie was planning to ask me to marry him. I was shocked. I never knew he felt that way about me.

After Tidworth, I was assigned to a POW Hospital. My first reaction when I got there was, "Am I supposed to care for these guys?" But I knew that a nurse is a nurse is a nurse, so I did my job. One of the German officers I cared for told me, "You Americans are wonderful. I can't thank you enough." But some of the others were hostile. Once I assigned one of the young soldiers some chores. We did this once they were up and around. He looked at me and said, "I will not," but one of the officers yelled at him in German and laid him out in lavender, so he did what I asked.

I could have stayed there, but I wanted to get over to the continent, so in September of 1944, I was sent to France. It actually took us five days in a troop ship to make it across the English Channel. Once I was there, I was assigned to the 217th General Hospital in Paris. The worst we saw was the Battle of the Bulge. During one period, there were 1000 admissions every 24 hours. The battle casualties were pouring in. One of the young lieutenants we cared for was from the 29th Division. He told me that one of my close friends from England who was a doctor was killed before he even made it ashore on D-Day.

As patients kept coming in we'd sort them out. The serious wounds got immediate attention. The most serious were flown back to England. We saw every type of injury while we were there. I was working in this huge, medieval type ward with maybe hundreds of men in it. One night, when I went to turn off the lights, I said, what I always said, "Good night Children". Well this Irishman there said "Goodnight Mom", but then when I turned out the lights he started singing. The Chaplain walked in and I thought I was in big trouble, but instead he said, "Nurse, I have never heard anything more beautiful".

There are a lot of other men I'll never forget. One of them, a Cossack Dancer who performed in New York City, lost his leg. Another was a 17 year old who was seriously wounded in his lower back and had a cast going all the way up to his waist. I used to care for him every day. Some of the days he'd have his eyes closed, and when I asked him why, he said, "Because it doesn't hurt so much when my eyes are closed." Well, later he was sent to England and a few weeks later, I got a short note from him. It said, "Dear Mom, these nurses are nice but there's nobody here like you".

Alice Westerberg remained with the Army until April of 1946. She remained active in the Army Reserve for the next 20 years and worked as a Public Health Nurse and as a Teacher of Nurses for the New York City Board of Education until her retirement in 1969.

- THE VICTORY GARDEN -

In addition to War Bond Drives and Scrap Metal Drives, the town also participated in the Victory Garden program which was designed to encourage the local citizens to produce their own food and ease the demand created by the war effort.

In early 1943, Mayor Charles Moore was given the authority to use any vacant city land for use as Victory Gardens. Plots of land, 30 feet by 75 feet, would be granted to any citizens who pledged to use the land for growing food for their families. The first plot of land designated as a Victory Garden was a small field near the center of town, which was enough to supply 16 gardens.

A committee then named John C. Latham to be the War Gardens Director. Latham was a natural choice for the job. In addition to being a

professional gardener and florist, he was a World War I veteran and winner of the Distinguished Service Cross, the British D.C.M., the French Medaille Militaire, and the Congressional Medal of Honor. Latham carried out his duties with conviction and enthusiasm, encouraging the local citizenry to plant in their yards and reminding them that half of the country's output of vegetables was needed to feed the Armed Forces. When the need for the Victory Gardens was finished, Latham resigned as director and continued to operate his florist shop in town until his death.[1]

Today, across the street from where his shop once stood, and close to the location of the very first Victory Gardens, a park bears the name of John Latham, one of the town's most respected citizens.

- JANE BUCKLEY JACKSON -

Jane Buckley graduated Stamford High School in 1941 and joined the WAVES shortly after the U.S. entered the war. She was in the first class of non-commissioned WAVES and from 1943 to 1945, she was assigned to Naval Communications in Washington D.C. where she worked as a cryptographer.

I think I joined the WAVES because we were a very patriotic family. My mother's first husband was killed in World War I. He was with the Fighting 69th of New York and my mother's whole family was in that Division.

I'm sure this was an influence in my volunteering for the WAVES. My brother had extremely bad eyesight which kept him from being accepted into the service. It was his father, whom he never saw, that was killed in France during the first World War. I think it was my brother's support and cooperation that facilitated my being in the first class of non-commissioned WAVES.

It would be fun to have recorded our trip from New York to Iowa where we had our basic training. Meeting so many girls, going into the unknown with excitement and enthusiasm, it didn't take me long to realize that I had made the right decision.

Basic training was interesting. I've never forgotten the history and geography I was taught in just three months. However, we all thought it strange that we spent so much time learning the nomenclature of ships and aircraft, since we were not allowed to serve aboard a ship outside of the U.S. until after the war.

After basic training in Iowas, I spent another three months in Milligeville, Georgia fine tuning my skills. Then came our assignments. I was to report to Naval Communications in Washington, D.C. where I would spend the rest of my three year service. Many changes took place in these three years. The hardest was adjusting to working around the clock with the shifts being from 8:00 am to 4:00pm, 4:00pm to 12:00am and 12:00am to 8:00am. I never did adjust.

Life in D.C. was exciting. So many of my high school graduating class of 41 went through Washington and gave me a call. I never refused an invitation to meet them at Union Street for a hello and a goodbye -- never knowing if this visit would be their last.

Celebrating VE and VJ days were so memorable. Thousands of uniforms in front of the White House - tears, laughs, hats in the air. I still react emotionally when I recall those two days.

Having tea with Eleanor Roosevelt was another great day. She was absolutely charming and a real lady. I feel I started growing up after listening to her. She was a woman ahead of her time and she gave me so much food for thought - the meaning of life, the fact that one person can make a difference, being true to your beliefs, speaking out for what's right. She shaped a good deal of my philosophy.

In Naval Communications we were trained to work on the Japanese code. I'll never forget the pride all of my coworkers had in the work we did. We were part of a large team, working on a small part in communication. You were never to speak about what you did. In fact until recently, none of my many friends discussed our own work. We took our job seriously and knew that there was a world crisis.

My roommate of three years worked in the same building as I and she never knew that I was working on decoding Japanese messages nor did I know that she was working on Russian communication. We were just a small link in a very big chain. We were told nothing relating to the messages we decoded until Yamamoto was shot down. (*Admiral Isoruko Yamaoto was Commander in Chief of Japan's navy. In April of 1943, US intelligence intercepted a message with the date and time of his impending flight to Bougainville. On April 18, 1943, sixteen American P-38's were waiting for him and shot down his plane, killing him.*) We were told then that Naval Communications played a part in that historic event.

Jane was discharged from the WAVES in 1945 and went to work with Fidelity Bank. In 1949, she married Lewis Jackson and they raised five children in Stamford. In April of 1946, she was awarded a Ribbon Bar from the United States Communications Intelligence Organization. Accompanying the Ribbon was a letter which concluded by saying that " It is directed that because of the nature of the services of this unit, no publicity to be given to your receipt of this award."

- *THE WOMAN WITH THE BUDDY BAGS* -

While most people at home contributed in some way to the war effort, none had a more personal impact on the soldiers than Marian Plotnick. Throughout the war, and for many years afterward, Mrs. Plotnick was the driving force behind the "Buddy Bags."

Sponsored originally by the B'Nai Brith, "Buddy Bags" were small canvas bags filled with personal items for the local boys as they left Stamford for military service. Mrs. Plotnick was committed to making sure that each and every one of the boys received one and throughout the war she was responsible for assembling thousands of them. After soliciting donations from local merchants such as Syl Mays and the Phillips Company, she would fill each bag with as many as 15 different items including gum, cigarettes, razors, soap, toothpaste, playing cards, stationery, and even flashlights.

Throughout the war years, the Plotnick home became a virtual Buddy Bag factory and on any given day from 20 to 100 bags would have to be assembled, for the soldiers that were scheduled to depart. Any neighbor might be enlisted to help, but most of the work was done by Mrs. Plotnick and her two sons, Robert and Mark. "We'd come home from school, finish our homework, and then we'd have to start putting the bags together. The worst part was that we had to assemble each and every flashlight" remembers son Robert.

Whether two soldiers or twenty were scheduled to leave on a particular day, she was there, often arriving at the Railroad Station at 4:00 a.m. to see them off. To many of these youngsters, the last memory

they had of their hometown was the kindly woman with the Buddy Bag.

Mrs. Plotnick's commitment continued after the war and throughout the Korean War, a decade later. In subsequent years, she was remembered by every area veteran's group. She was named Grand Marshal of the Veteran's Day Parade, honored with a huge testimonial dinner, and even commended by Senators Ribicoff and Dodd. But according to her son Robert, she was not fazed by these honors. "She never thought of what she did as anything great. It was just something she felt she had to do."

- RUTH MAURER MILLER -

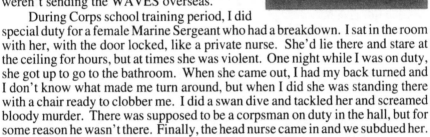

Ruth Maurer graduated from Stamford High School in 1939 and went to work as an artist for Conde Nast. After Pearl Harbor, she joined the WAVES and served with the Hospital Corps in Oklahoma, Tennessee, and New Orleans.

I did my basic training at Hunter College in the Bronx, and then we were sent down to Corps school in Hadnot Point which was attached to Camp LeJeune. In fact, we went through a little commando training while we were down there. I guess they figured that if push came to shove and something happened, we would be able to take care of ourselves because at that time they weren't sending the WAVES overseas.

During Corps school training period, I did special duty for a female Marine Sergeant who had a breakdown. I sat in the room with her, with the door locked, like a private nurse. She'd lie there and stare at the ceiling for hours, but at times she was violent. One night while I was on duty, she got up to go to the bathroom. When she came out, I had my back turned and I don't know what made me turn around, but when I did she was standing there with a chair ready to clobber me. I did a swan dive and tackled her and screamed bloody murder. There was supposed to be a corpsman on duty in the hall, but for some reason he wasn't there. Finally, the head nurse came in and we subdued her.

From there I went out to Norman, Oklahoma. When we got there, no one warned us about the water. It was filled with Epsom salts; you could taste it. Well, those latrines got quite a work out the first few weeks we were there. After that we drank Coke. The Coke machine was always empty because as soon as the guy came to refill it, we'd line up and start buying it. To keep it cool, we used to store it between the windows and the screens of our barracks. One night a few of the bottles froze and started popping and we thought people were shooting at us.

Norman, Oklahoma was a hospital discharge center. For a while I was assigned to the quarantine ward where there was an outbreak of spinal meningitis and scarlet fever. Then, I was assigned to Ward 8. That was for fellows who came back from the war mentally shattered. It was horrible...padded cells, the works. The only thing I'll talk about was this one case where a Marine had combat fatigue and he thought he was Jesus. His father came to visit him and I was absolutely horrified when his father reamed this boy out. He was probably only 17 or 18 years old and the father called him a coward and told him that he was not a patriot and on and on. I finally had to call a doctor. When the doctor got there he told the father to get out and never, ever come back. I don't know what happened to this kid, or any of the others. I don't know if they recovered or not. But I won't talk about the other things I saw there. It was just such a shame that such young boys came back with no minds.

In Norman, all you saw were these big oil rigs all over the place. Even the state capital building had one on the lawn. Out there the cities were dry. No alcohol was allowed. It was tough for sailors to sneak alcohol back to the base because they were searched as they came back. But the guards never bothered us so we used to bring it back for the sailors. We'd go into town and make friends with the bellhops because they'd always be able to get "white lightning" for you. We used to wear our long overcoats and fill up the inside pockets with pints or half-pints. The shore patrol never searched us, but one of them used to joke with us and say, "I've never seen so many thin women come back to the base so fat."

After Oklahoma, I was sent to New Orleans. Because our barracks weren't finished yet, we stayed right in dorms at the Air Station down there. It was a fascinating city with lots of history. I was stationed at the Naval Hospital there. We had a couple of pilots who were burned very badly and I hope I never have to see anything like it again.

Segregation was also very bad down there. If you got on a bus and there were no more seats, one of the Blacks would have to get up and give you their seat. Here I was, about 20 years old and I thought I knew everything. Boy, did this really open my eyes. Once I wanted to have the handle on my suitcase fixed, so I brought it to a man who used to fix the ambulances on the base. He could fix anything. When he gave it back, I thanked him and offered him some money, but his boss, a white guy said, "You don't have to give that Negra anything." I was shocked and said, "Well that's the way I was brought up." I offered the money again but he wouldn't take it.

I finally ended up in Memphis, Tennessee, at the Millington Air Station where I did dispensary (infirmary) duties. Again, there, Blacks were segregated even in the dispensaries. I was there when the war ended.

Overall, it was a very rewarding experience and I'd recommend it to any young woman. It was enlightening and I did some things I never thought I could do. But there was a war on and you rose to the occasion. You did what had to be done.

Ruth returned to Stamford in 1945, married and raised 3 boys. Along with her husband, she operated "Bob's Diner" which was a fixture in Glenbrook for over thirty years.

- BRUNO GIORDANO -
THE BEST SALESMAN IN TOWN

The top salesman of War Bonds and War Stamps was Bruno Giordano. By the age of 13, the Stamford Advocate newsboy and Boy Scout had sold close to $11,000 in Securities. The local newspaper attributed his success to

"a friendly smile and youthful energetic personality".[2] Bruno, however, may have been driven by another factor. Three of his brothers were already in the armed service and by 1944, five of his six brothers would be in the service. He himself would later serve in the Air Force from 1952-1955.

Bruno's drive and determination would serve him well in later years. In college, he captained both the Track and Cross Country teams and in 1951 he was named an All-American. In 1967, at the age of 35, he became the youngest mayor in the city's history.

124

Families

Three families in Stamford suffered the loss of more than one son. Mrs. Anna Kijek was the first to lose two boys in the war. Bronislas "Benny" was killed when his ship, the Juneau, was sunk in the Pacific in 1942. Less than five months later, his brother Frank was killed when his ship went down in the Atlantic.

Mr. and Mrs. Frederick Loveland lost Frederick, the first of their two sons in October of 1942 at Guadalcanal. Edred was killed at Luzon in March of 1945.

Mrs. Laura Austin lost her son, Albert, in the Italian compaign in 1943, and her second son, Arthur, was killed in the Pacific in 1945.

- NELLY KIJEK EKSTOWICZ-

The Kijeks were the first of three local families to lose two sons in the war. Bronislas "Benny" Kijek and his brother Frank both left high school to enlist in the U.S. Navy. Both were killed when their ships were sunk by the enemy. This interview was done with Nelly Ekstowicz, the sister of Benny and Frank.

We were a big family. There were twelve of us, six boys and six girls. We were all very close. You had to be back then because there wasn't much room for all of us at our house. It ·wasn't like today where everyone has their own room.

Five of my brothers served in the war. Joe was in Italy. John was a cook, and Benny, Frank, and Chester were in the Navy. Benny was the first to go in 1940. My mother was so proud.

They were all good boys, never in any trouble. Benny, my older brother, was always good to me. In fact, when I graduated from high school and needed to pay for my class ring, it was Benny who sent the money for it. Frankie was quite a fellow, too. My youngest brother, Chester, and he were very close. When they were little, Chester used to tail Frankie everywhere he went. Chester later named his oldest son after Frank.

In November of 1942, we got a telegram. It said that Benny was missing at sea. He was in the Pacific on the U.S.S. Juneau, and it was sunk during the battle for Guadalcanal. This was the same ship that carried the Sullivan Brothers. *(The Juneau was a light cruiser that was sunk by a Japanese sub on November 13, 1942. Among the 687 crew members only eleven survived. All 5 Sullivan Brothers were killed.)*

For months we received no other word from the goverment about Benny. I don't even remember when we finally did get word that he was actually declared dead. But we always kept the hope that somehow he had survived.

That April (1943), my sister Tessie got married. My brother Frank came home for the wedding. He didn't tell any of us this but he pulled aside my fiance and told him that he was due to ship out right after the wedding. We all said goodbye to Frankie, but we never knew that it would be the last time we'd see him.

Less than two months later a telegram came to the house. It was a Wednesday, my day off. I remember running to the door thinking, "Oh good, they

Benny Kijek

Frank Kijek

must have found Benny." I was sure that it was good news. Instead it was a letter telling us that Frankie was lost at sea. His transport went down in the Atlantic. That's all we ever found out. He was only eighteen years old. He was a baby. He shouldn't have even been there.

So, in less than four months, I lost two brothers. My mother lost two sons. She was distraught. The hardest thing is to lose a child and I don't think she ever got over it. Later, she got to christen a ship, the U.S.S. Norma. I knew she was very proud that day, but it could never make up for her loss. My mother lived to be 90 years old, and her sons died so young.

The war hit our family and our neighborhood very hard. On our block alone, 4 boys were killed in the war, 3 died in one year. Benny, Frankie, and John Lapinski died in 1943. Then we lost Joe Grabowski in 1944. All these boys grew up on Ludlow Street and South Pacific Street.

About ten years ago, I went to Hawaii. While I was at Pearl Harbor, I visited the Punch Bowl cemetery. They had a monument there, and on it was a map of the Pacific showing the different naval battles of the war. Right near Guadalcanal they had a spot marked where the Juneau went down. I can't explain it, but when I saw it there in front of me, I felt a sense of relief. It meant a lot to me to know that this would always be remembered.

Of the 12 Kijek children, there are seven that still remain. John, Chester, Tessie, Josephine, and Frances have moved out of town. Nellie and Jean still reside in Stamford. Today, Kijek Street, which is on the eastern side of High Ridge Road, reminds us of their brothers Benny and Frank Kijek who gave their lives in the Second World War.

- *FOR BOTH SONS* -

In June of 1944, Mrs. Anna Kijek, mother of Benny and Frank, was given the honor of christening the U.S. cargo ship, "Norma," in Camden, New Jersey. She was joined by her oldest son, six daughters, two granddaughters, and Stamford Mayor, Charles Moore.

When Mrs. Kijek smashed the first bottle of champagne prematurely, she was given a second bottle, which she broke across the bow of the ship. As the "Norma" slid down the ramp and into the Delaware River, Mrs. Kijek was heard to say, "One bottle for each of my sons."[3]

Gold Star Mother Christens Ship

Mrs. Anna Kijek, mother of two sons who died in action in the Navy, breaks bottle of champagne against the bow of the U. S. S. Norma, cargo vessel, at launching ceremonies where high tribute was paid to the Stamford woman.

–HOMER LEE WISE–
and the
MEDAL OF HONOR

Few who met Homer Lee Wise would ever suspect that this mild mannered soft-spoken gentleman was the recipient of the Congressional Medal of Honor. Yet this humble, self-effacing man was the epitome of the quiet American hero.

A native of Baton Rouge, Louisiana, Wise entered the U.S. Army in 1939. After our entry into the Second World War, he served in North Africa and was one of the first men to land at Salerno in 1943. Over the next nine months, Wise repeatedly distinguished himself in combat and earned the Bronze Star, the Silver Star, and the Purple Heart with two Oak Leaf Clusters. But it was on June 6, 1944, in a battle at Magliano, Italy, that Wise assumed his place in history.

With his platoon pinned down, and one man wounded, Wise and three other soldiers carried the wounded man 100 yards through fierce enemy fire to where he could receive medical treatment. Returning to the battle zone, Wise stopped an enemy flanking maneuver, rushing three heavily armed German soldiers and stopping them. He then fired a rifle grenade launcher and broke up the enemy position.

Next, Sergeant Wise grabbed an automatic rifle and, walking directly into heavy fire, captured an enemy gun crew. As an American tank advanced to support the platoon, Wise again risked his life by jumping onto the buttoned up tank, clearing a jam and firing over 750 rounds at the paralyzed enemy, allowing his battalion to take their objective.

On November 28, 1944, Homer Lee Wise was presented with the Congressional Medal of Honor by Lieutenant General Alexander Patch. "Let's give this man a salute," said Patch to the five other Generals in attendance. "I wish we had an army full of soldiers like you."

- MADOLYN DISESA WISE-

Madolyn DiSesa was born and raised in Stamford. She met Homer Lee Wise in 1942 and the two were married in 1945.

Homer Lee Wise and Madolyn

I met H.L. in Hyannis while I was on vacation. At that time he was in the army stationed at Fort Edward. We went out later that week and then he asked me if he could visit me in Stamford. Frankly I didn't think my mother would want him to, but when I asked her she said "Yes".

To tell you the truth, I liked him from the beginning and we became close friends. He visited me several times and met my parents. He would take the train down and if he couldn't get a seat he'd stand the entire way. He spent all of his vacations with us and got to know my entire family. They all loved him. Then, before he went overseas, we were engaged. He wouldn't get married before he left because he said that if he got crippled over there, he would never come back. So we were engaged for two years.

After he left for Africa I heard from him every single day, sometimes twice a day. The postman used to joke with me about it and would say, "When does he have time to fight the war?" He was not allowed to write where he was but before he left we made up symbols for different places and in each letter he would write down the symbol and I would know exactly where he was.

I worried every single day he was overseas. He was involved in four major battles and was wounded three times. The third time he was wounded my brother said to me "Tell him to stay behind a tree instead of sticking his head up." I got a big kick out of that one.

(In June of 1944 Homer Lee Wise was awarded the Medal of Honor.) The way I found out that he had won the Medal of Honor was when a reporter from the "Advocate" called and said, "Do you know an H. L. Wise?" When I said "yes" they told me that he won the "C.M.H." I really didn't know what it was and when they explained it to me I said something like, "Oh, that's nice". I didn't understand how important it was. Then the reporter told me that the reason he called me was that when H. L. was awarded the medal, they asked him where he would most like to go. He told them that he wanted to go see Madolyn DiSesa in Stamford so that he could get married. I was surprised to hear that. Then my brother called me very excited and asked if I had heard the news.

When he was awarded the medal he was offered a Captaincy right in the field if he would stay but he said no. He had been wounded so many times that he said he'd rather be a live Sergeant than a dead Captain. He came home in January, 1945 and we were married the following month. We stayed in Stamford the next twelve years because I didn't want to leave my parents. He was the local recruiter. But then he got orders to go to Germany and lived there for two years. We came home after that and then he was sent to LeRochelle, France for three years. We spent two more years back here at Fort Devins, then we were sent to Vicenza,

Italy. I loved it there. I was the perfect army wife because I loved to travel. H. L. used to tell me that I should have joined the army. We finally came back to Stamford for good in 1967 after he retired from the army.

He was somewhat of a celebrity but he was never comfortable with it. He was a quiet man. He never, never talked about the medal. In fact, while we were in Europe, and our son Jeff was in school there, one of the other boys, a Captain's son, said to him, "Your father won the Medal of Honor." Jeff had no idea of what he was talking about so when he came home he asked me about it. I told him, "It was just an award that your daddy got." Later the boy's mother, who was a friend of mine asked me why I never told Jeff about his father. I told her that we had never discussed it at home. It just never seemed important to H. L. Now I think back on it and realize that he never mentioned it. He just never said a word about it. My brother used to make a big deal of it but not H. L. In fact, he didn't even want to talk about the war. Never. People would come up and ask him how many men he had killed. He'd joke, "All of them." But he'd never want to discuss it.

He used to supplement his income as a waiter at the Greenwich Country Club. One of the people he waited on, a very wealthy man, found out about him and asked H. L. to sit with him. H. L. refused to sit. He said that he couldn't, he was working. So the man went up to the head waiter and said, "I'd like this man to sit at my table. I don't want him waiting on me." I thought this was awfully nice of the man but my husband was horribly embarrassed. Later when we went to one of the Presidential inaugurations this man insisted that H. L. get a first class car on the train. He actually met us at the station and had already gotten us the first class car. Later I met the man's family. They invited us to the house several times and were extremely nice to us.

My husband was a quiet and gentle man. He loved my brothers and they loved him so he never had a desire to go back to Baton Rouge. He died in 1974 when he was only 55 years old. He was a wonderful husband and a wonderful father and we got along beautifully. Everyone used to make fun of us and call us the "perfect couple" but honestly we were. I guess it was too good to last.

In 1976 a park on the corner of Bedford and Chester Streets was dedicated to Homer Lee Wise. Mrs. Wise remains a resident of Stamford.

[1] "Common Council Aid for Victory Garden." Stamford Advocate, March 16, 1943, April 8, 1943.

[2] "Advocate Newsie is Top Salesman." Stamford Advocate, May 25, 1942, April 18, 1943.

[3] "Anne Kijek Christmas Ship." Stamford Advocate, June 5, 1944.

CHAPTER NINE

SOUTHERN EUROPE

Once the U.S. entered the war FDR and the Allies decided to delay the Pacific offensive in favor of a "Hitler First" strategy. The plan was to initiate the offensive against the Axis forces in North Africa which were commanded by the legendary Erwin Rommel and his Africa Corps. In July of 1942, the Allies landed in Africa and within a year had driven the enemy off the continent. The tide of war was beginning to turn.

Once the war in Africa was won, however, the Allies debated about where to hit the Axis next. Although the USSR was pressuring for a second front to be opened with the invasion of France, the Allies decided, instead, to attack at Sicily and Italy.

On July 10, 1943, American and British forces invaded Sicily. At that time it was the largest amphibious assault in history. After slugging it out across the rugged mountainous terrain, the battle for Sicily was won.. The 39 day battle had cost the Americans over 7,000 casualties and the British over 11,000. The Germans suffered 12,000 and the Italians 145,000.[1]

Next the Allies prepared for the invasion of Italy. In September 1943, the assault began with the brunt of the attack coming at Salerno. The government quickly collapsed and an armistice between Italy and the Allies was signed. The German forces remained, however, and the battle for Italy raged on for almost two more years. On June 4, 1944, the Allies entered Rome but German forces managed to fight on until the end of the war in 1945.

The U.S. paid a high price for Italy. Over 70,000 Americans were killed but Hitler's war machine had been irreparably damaged.

- STANLEY KASLIKOWSKI -

The Kaslikowski family sent four of its boys off to war. Coincidentally, two of them, Stanley and his younger brother John, became paratroopers in the 82nd Airborne. Both boys also ended up in the 504th Parachute Infantry nicknamed the "Devils in Baggy Pants." Stanley had 3 combat jumps and took part in the invasions of Salerno, Anzio, and Holland as well as the Battle of the Bulge. His first jump, however, was during the invasion of Sicily in 1943.

In training I never saw John, but when I was at Fort Bragg I was doing a parachute jump and got stuck in a tree. Someone landed near me and when he heard all the thrashing, came over to help. It was my brother. He just started laughing when he saw it was me. We went overseas together and ended up in the same battles.

My brother and I were not supposed to be together as paratroopers. The army did not like two brothers in the same outfit. We did our training in French Morocco. We had sand models of the drop zone that we'd been studying. It was so hot there that most of our training was done at night — except the jumps. They considered it too risky to practice those at night. But our commander Lt. Mills pulled some strings so we both ended up together.

I'll never forget Sicily. It was July 11, 1943, my birthday. I was 27 years old that night. We left from French Morocco and were in the plane 3 or 4 hours. When we got near Sicily the antiaircraft opened up. I think it knocked down over 20 of our planes. *(In this tragic incident at Gela, 27 American planes were shot down, most of them by U.S. Navy ships.)*

The pilots wanted to drop us as soon as possible. We were supposed to be dropped near a beach but were nowhere near it.

When I jumped I couldn't see that well. I couldn't see the ground so I came down hard on a railroad track. I didn't feel it though because your system is like a boxer's. Your adrenalin is pumping. You are tense. Then I heard some rustling but I didn't know who it was. We all had a certain code word to use when we landed so I yelled out, "Apple". Luckily it was another guy from my outfit. Pretty soon about ten of us got together, including Lt. Mills. We started walking down a road. We kept hearing this noise. I could swear it was an enemy tank but I didn't say anything. So we kept on going until we got to this bridge that went over a small valley. We hit the bridge and were almost at the end when we met the Germans. I think that Lt. Mills fired first. I didn't even have a chance to get my rifle. There was a quick fight. I dove off the side of the bridge and that's when I got captured.

The Germans got us into a group and a soldier had his rifle pointed right at my head. I thought he was going to shoot. Finally I just made a run for it. Another shell came in and that's when I got hit. The guy next to me got his arm blown off. Lt. Mills also got hit pretty badly. All the while the Germans were yelling in English "Halt." I was hit in the arm and the leg but managed to get away. That night, in all the confusion, I dug a foxhole to protect myself. I had to do it with one arm. I was very lucky it was only for one night. The next morning the Americans came in and rescued us.

I was taken to a First Aid Station and who did I run into? Leon Dzilinski. We were neighbors down in the South End. We only lived a block from each other. He told me our plane was lucky because it was our men that were firing at us. About a half hour earlier there was a German raid and the Navy antiaircraft thought that we were the Germans coming back. I was also lucky when I was captured because it was a U.S. Navy shell that came in and allowed me to escape. I still have a souvenir inside my leg to prove it. After the First Aid Station I was taken to Africa and was in the hospital for six weeks.

The next jump we made was at Salerno. They had us jump there to help out some of our troops that were being pushed back to the water by the Germans. The jump itself was not so bad. It was during the day and we didn't have too much action. But later, when we fought in the mountains near Cassino we had it rough. It was very cold and we had to carry so much equipment. I was in charge of the 30mm machine gun. It only weighed 30 pounds but you had to carry that with all of your other stuff. And we were climbing up mountains the whole time. In combat you never walked around something. You had to go through it. We walked through everything — creeks, lakes, everything. You'd be wet up to your waist and it was miserable. We had to be careful about mines too. And after all this, you'd dig a foxhole and have to sleep in it at night. You were lucky to get 2 or 3 hours sleep.

We did all of this climbing while we were fighting the Germans. One night we overran an enemy position and during the fight I jumped into a foxhole and there were two dead Germans in it. I had to stay there all night with them. We were under fire and it was cold. You had to get used to things like that. We fought in Sicily for about six months and then in January 1944, we hit Anzio.

At Anzio I got hit again. We were fighting at a place called Mussolini's Canal. We were on one side and the Germans were on the other. They had some houses and buildings on their side and were protected. We weren't. We were out in an open field. German planes were coming over and hitting us and all we could do was stay in our holes. Our own planes were not able to support us because of the weather.

The Germans had these mortars set up behind the houses and they were firing on us. One of the shells came in and made a direct hit on a foxhole right next to me. It blew the guy's body to bits. The shells just kept coming and finally a few of us decided to make a getaway . That's when I was hit in the leg. I was lucky again because the poor fella next to me lost his leg. I just ended up with shrapnel.

They took me to the hospital and four days later they brought my brother Jack in. So here I was in one bed and my brother in the one next to me. Jack was hit in the foot but was lucky too. It wasn't bad. *(This incident was reported in the Stamford Advocate but incorrectly had Jack as the first brother wounded.)*

You know, in a way, sometimes you were better off once you got hit. You got to rest up. It was like heaven. You were in a bed, you had clean white sheets. Nurses taking care of you. When you were out fighting you were in these mud holes, cold all the time and you couldn't even leave the foxhole to go to the bathroom.

(In September of 1944 the 504th was called upon to make a jump into Holland. Their mission was to occupy bridges which spanned the large rivers of central and southern Holland.)

After I recovered I made the jump in Holland. We were supposed to be reinforcements for some British and Polish paratroopers who were dropped miles from their zone. They were slaughtered. We were supposed to take a bridge. The Germans controlled one side of the bridge so we had to cross the river and fight them on the other side. Rubber boats were dropped in and we crossed. We were loaded with equipment and if anything happened to our boat we wouldn't be able to swim. We were under fire but our boat made it across without too much trouble. By the time we got across it was getting dark and we fought most of the night. *(This incident took place at a bridge across the Waal River in Nijmegen. Of the 26 boats that made the initial trip across the river, only eleven were able to transport succeeding waves of paratroopers.)*

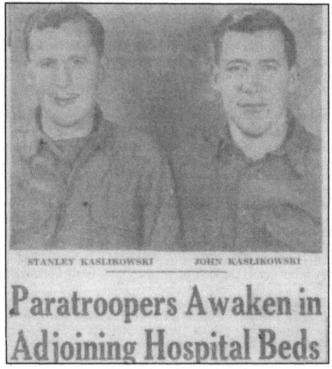

STANLEY KASLIKOWSKI   JOHN KASLIKOWSKI

Paratroopers Awaken in Adjoining Hospital Beds

Stamford Advocate, March 4, 1944.

On the other side of the river we were dug in. A few of us were in a foxhole all night. About ten feet away we heard movement all night and I figured it had to be one of us. When light came the next morning we went over and there was a young fella, maybe 18 or 19 years old. He was Polish but fighting for the Germans. I spoke Polish so I talked to him. I asked him why he was fighting for the Germans. He said, "Look, I'm a prisoner. I was forced to do this." He could have easily thrown a grenade into our hole during the night but thank God he didn't. We finally pushed the Germans back and took the bridge.

My last battle was during the Bulge. We had been fighting for months and were due for a rest. Instead while we were in France, the Germans made their breakthrough. So late on a Sunday night we were told that we had to go back to the front. We were hauled out and made about an eight hour drive to Belgium, outside a town called Cheneux. The Germans held part of the town and we had to cross a wide open field with barbed wire. We had to crawl like snails. It was cold and there was snow on the ground. Some of the guys would straighten up to climb over the barbed wire and were shot immediately. I was able to crawl over to a small group of trees. It was at night and we could hear the enemy but couldn't see them. They had these big flak wagons and were opening fire on us. We fired back but with one machine gun we really couldn't do that much damage. Then, a round came in, hit a tree and part of the shell got me right in the chest. It felt like I got hit with a sledgehammer. I fell down to my hands and knees and that was it for me.

(The combat record of the 504th indicates that the men had to cross a 400 yard field that had barbed wire placed at 15 yard intervals. Little cover was available and enemy fire was the heaviest ever faced by this unit. Despite these conditions the Americans succeeded in taking Cheneux by the following day.)

I was in the hospital for over a month and I couldn't use my left arm for a while. Because I was wounded so many times they decided to send me home. I came home in a hospital ship. That's when it finally got to me. My nerves were shot.

I don't regret joining the service even with all of my injuries. But I have to tell you that I could never do that again. But, when you're in your twenties, you're crazy. You'll do anything.

Today I consider myself a lucky man that I didn't lose an arm or a leg. When I go to the V.A. Hospital and I see guys without a limb, some walking around like zombies, I'm just happy I'm able to talk about it all with you today.

Stan was awarded three Purple Hearts for his wounds. He received four Battle Stars, the Combat Infantry Badge, and a Presidential Unit Citation. He returned to Stamford where he operated the Waterside Food O Mat for over twenty five years. He still carries shrapnel in his left leg as a permanent reminder of the war.

"American Parachutists — devils in baggy pants are less than 100 metres from my outpost line. I can't sleep at night; they pop up from nowhere and we never know when or how they will strike next. Seems like the blackhearted devils are everywhere."

- Found in the diary of a German Officer who opposed the 504th at Anzio[2]

The Nisei

After the attack on Pearl Harbor, a wave of fear and hysteria gripped the nation. Anti-German, Japanese, and Italian sentiments were harbored and, in some cases, encouraged. Nowhere was hatred and bigotry more evident, however, than in the treatment of Japanese-Americans, many of whom came from families that had lived in the U.S. for generations.

In this atmosphere of anger and suspicion President Roosevelt signed Executive Order 9066 which empowered the government to evacuate Japanese

Members of the 442nd Regiment Combat Team in France.

Americans from the West Coast. As a result of this order the War Relocation Authority was created and over 120,000 Japanese-Americans were placed in internment camps which were located throughout the United States.[3]

In most cases, families were given 48 hours notice, packed up a few belongings, and were forced to leave behind homes, farms, businesses, and friends. They were then brought to barren and isolated relocation camps in such places as Topaz, Utah, McGehee, Arkansas, and the Heart Mountains in Wyoming.

Although almost all of the Japanese Americans were released by the end of the war, their personal losses were incalculable and in many cases permanent. Family homes were damaged, possessions stolen, businesses lost, and throughout the war not a single Japanese American was ever even brought to trial for espionage.

Despite the shabby treatment from their government, over 9,000 Japanese-Americans served in U.S. armed forces during the war. These soldiers, also referred to as "Nisei" ("first generation") served with great distinction throughout the Second World War. In fact, one of the most distinguished units in the entire war was the 442nd Regimental Combat Team which was made up entirely of Japanese Americans. These soldiers fought proudly and courageously in the Po Valley in Italy, the Vosges Mountains in France, and finally back in the mountains of Italy during the final assault in 1945. The 442nd sustained heavy casualties in these campaigns and in some battles entire companies were decimated.

By the end of the war the approximately 9,000 Japanese soldiers had earned over 3600 Purple Hearts, 47 Distinguished Service Crosses, one Distinguished Service Medal, 354 Silver Stars, and 1 Medal of Honor.[4] At a staggering cost, the Nisei had proven their loyalty to their country.

- SAM ICHIBA -

Sam Ichiba was born in California, the son of Japanese immigrants. Although he was born a citizen of the United States, his parents were prevented by federal law from becoming American citizens. After the attack on Pearl Harbor, Sam and his family were placed in an internment camp. In 1944 he enlisted in the U.S. Army and fought with the 3rd Battalion of the celebrated 442nd Regimental Combat Team. He saw action in France and Italy and was wounded in action.

My father arrived in the U.S. in 1914. A few years later my mother arrived. Their marriage was arranged by their parents because both families came from the same prefecture near Hiroshima.

When the war broke out we lived on a ranch in Woodbridge, California, where my father worked as a gardener. I attended the public schools, played a lot of baseball and had quite a few Caucasian buddies. Then, when the war started, I was isolated, but, two of my best friends stuck by me. In fact, when one of them was killed in the war, another friend wrote me in Italy to tell me about it.

Right after Pearl Harbor rumors flew that we were going to be sent back to Japan, incarcerated, or even shot. In March of 1942 notices appeared that all persons of Japanese extraction were to assemble and prepare to be moved. We were told that we could bring along only one bag each so we had to scramble to get rid of our belongings. My father had just bought a new refrigerator and I remember that he had to sell it for $30.00. He was particularly fearful because when he had returned to Japan years earlier he could see the handwriting on the wall. The country was being controlled by the military and he did not want to be sent back there.

First we were placed in an assembly center in Stockton, California. We lived in barracks there until the permanent camps were set up. That September we were herded into railroad cars to be taken to Arkansas. Of course, the ride was beautiful. We got to see the country. But this was not the best way to do it. Each time we pulled into a town we had to lower the blinds on the train. MPs guarded the train and they were under strict orders not to divulge the identity of the passengers. Once, we stopped right next to a troop train and they kept asking the MPs who we were. They thought we were POWs.

We finally ended up in Rohwer Camp right outside of McGehee, Arkansas. The people there thought we were POWs, too. But when they saw that we spoke English they were surprised. The administrators were Caucasians but other than that, the camp was run mostly by the Japanese within the camp.

We were kept isolated, but once word got out that there were "Japs" in the camp we had a few shotgun blasts shot into the camp. After this the administrators sent work crews out to clear out the woods around the camp. We went out every day and cleared out about 100 yards width around the camp. It was actually a good idea because we used all of the wood for the potbellied stoves that were our only source of heat.

Once our supervisor took a crew out to help with some surveying and one of the natives of a nearby town thought that he was helping some of the prisoners to escape. He ended up shooting one of the boys and taking the rest of them at gunpoint to the local jail. Luckily the boy was not badly wounded. Members of the Justice Department had to come in and bail the prisoners out.

Although the perimeters of the camps were guarded by MPs, it was more for our protection. After all, even if we escaped, where would we go? Other than that, the camp was run like an army camp: rows of barracks, a mess hall, laundry facilities. Each block had a captain. At first cooks were brought in from the outside but later the WRA (War Relocation Authority) hired two cooks right from within the camp. We ate lots of liver, rice, and fish, mostly tuna and sea bass. You worked in the camp and you were paid. I was a dishwasher and made $7.50 a month. Doctors got $28.00 per month. Other professionals made about the same. We also got $3.50 a month for clothing. We all ordered them from the Sears-Roebuck catalog. They made a lot of money on us. The town of McGeehee also made a lot on us. After a while we were allowed to go into town and we spent our money there. In time we even got better treatment from the townspeople.

There was a big division in our camp. There were some people who were militantly pro-Japanese and against us serving in the American military. Others wanted to enlist. I was one of these. I always considered myself an American. My father asked me not to volunteer. But when I told him that I was going to, he said to me, "Now it is your duty to fight for your country. When you go into battle, fight proudly and don't bring shame to your name." I'll never forget that.

When I went for my physical, the doctor told me that I didn't have to go, I had flat feet. I said, "Major, I have to go. My parents are in a camp. I have to prove that I am worthy of being an American." He was puzzled but he said, "OK, son. If that's what you want, then good luck."

Any Japanese American was automatically assigned to the 442nd (Regimental Combat Team) or Military Intelligence Service. By the time I got in, I was one of the replacement troops. When I got overseas I was assigned to K Company of the 3rd Battalion. Just before this, the 442nd had suffered heavy casualties in northern France when they went in to rescue the 141st Battalion (36th Division). Some companies came back with only handfuls of men. I think "I" Company had only six men who weren't killed or wounded. But after this campaign (in the Vosges Mountains) public opinion turned right around on the Japanese American soldier. It did us a world of good. The 36th Division which was from Texas made every member of the 442nd an honorary Texan, and we are still invited to all of their reunions.

Once I got to northern France and assigned to K Company, I said "Where do I go?" and a guy said "Over there." I looked over and saw a few pup tents. That was all that was left of them. They had to be taken off the line until they could be brought up to full strength again. We stayed in the Maritime Alps in Southern France for a while. We were in a holding action and during this time we had contact with the French Resistance.

In March of 1945 we went back to Italy and were assigned to the 92nd Division for the last breakthrough into the Po Valley. Our job was to clear out the last German holdouts in the mountains. They had General Kesselring's machine gun battalions entrenched up there – mostly SS Troops. Now we had to go dig them out. The 100th Battalion had to make a frontal assault on the German positions. They took a beating. We were going to another point higher up.

We were making our way up the mountains in the fog. It seemed like every time we made it up one crest there was another one in front of us. At daybreak we finally rested in a draw in the mountains and that's when the Germans opened up on us. They must have seen us coming because at first they dropped smoke shells in on us. It quickly ran through my mind that in training I had read that the Germans used the smoke shells to adjust their sights on us. We were all out in the open and they were zeroing in on us.

That's when my good friend Fuka (Yamamine) who was the acting Sergeant jumped up and yelled for everyone to take cover. He wasn't even concerned for his own safety. We all took cover and I wanted to yell for him to get down but it was too late. A shell came in and killed him instantly. It bothers me to this day that I couldn't help him. He was like an older brother to me. When I came in as a replacement he took me under his wing. Most guys wouldn't do that with a replacement.

As we were being shelled I saw one of our guys bringing two German prisoners down the mountain. The last time I saw him, he was running to get behind this boulder. I saw a shell come in and hit right next to him. I always wondered what happened to the guy but a few years ago I ran into him at a reunion. He told me that the shell did hit right next to him but he was shielded by the boulder. He got his two prisoners in.

A few days later we were almost out of supplies and we saw an American plane fly over. We assumed that they were air-dropping supplies. So our commander sent three of us out on patrol to see if we could find the supplies. Even if we found them I don't know how we were supposed to get them back. The three of us went out and had a hard time finding the supplies. At one point we were behind German lines. We finally got to the airdrop site and discovered that the plane had dropped a huge spool of wire. It was starting to get dark and as we were making our way back we were fired on. We were on a ledge and bullets started hitting all around us. Dirt was flying up and I could hear bullets going right by my ear. It didn't make a whining sound. It was more like a snapping sound. It turned out that it was our own guys, Charlie Company, that were firing on us. They must have realized it was us because they stopped firing. None of us got hurt but it was awfully close. At one of our reunions I ran into a guy from Charlie Company and he remembered the incident and seemed a little embarrassed by it. I shook his hand and said, "By the way, what's your name" and he ran off and said, "I'll catch you later".

Now it was really getting dark and after a while all of the mountains started to look alike. The oldest of us, Tom, was leading the patrol and I don't know how he finally got us back. The grass was up to our chests in some places.

It was pitch dark when we finally stumbled back to our lines. The Germans were firing at us and we could make out a building which we thought was our command post. We were running toward it when a guy yelled to us, "What's the password?. We didn't know it so one of the guys just yelled out "Buddha heads," and we all dove into the building. When I dove in I fell through a hole in the floor and I almost went all the way through the floor to the basement. The next morning my commander sent me back to the aid station to get my leg wrapped.

Two Italian partisans walked me part of the way there. Then they gave me a walking stick and sent me on my way. That's when I noticed the carnage there, mules, boots, human limbs. You wouldn't believe it. There were bodies all over the place. No trees left standing, only jagged stumps. The wind was blowing smoke all over the place. What a spooky feeling it was to be alone there at that moment. I felt like I was in Dante's Inferno.

When I rejoined my company we had moved even further and had taken a small town named Tendola. It was one of the last German strongholds and it guarded a highway.

We attacked the town right in the open, in broad daylight, at noon. We crept up and caught the Germans by surprise. I guess they were expecting an attack at night. The entire hillside was lined with German machine guns and when I think about it I still get the chills. If they had caught us advancing we would have been wiped out.

When we reached the town, a machine gunner did open up on our left flank. Instinctively, I shoved the sergeant next to me. We both fell and the tree next to us was hit. I was nominated for the Bronze Star. The citation went in, but that was the end of it *(Sam finally did receive a Bronze Star in 1990)*.

When the Germans finally surrendered it was quite a sight. All of these tall SS soldiers coming down the road in perfect formation. They looked beautiful. We lined the road as they were walking down, all spit and polish and here we were a real rag tag outfit. I remember saying I'm glad we didn't have to tangle with these guys.

After the fighting stopped we went into Genoa and were treated as liberators. The Italians treated us great. Some of them looked at us funny and said, "Chinese?" but others were yelling "Bravo Americans" and were offering us vino. It was also about this time that we heard for the first time that FDR had died. It was at dusk and we were in a schoolyard and a pall just settled over the men.

Once the war ended we had to stay in Italy a long time. We were one of the last combat units to return. We didn't get home until 1946. Then we were asked to march in Washington, D.C. We marched right up Constitution Avenue and right to the back of the White House where we were reviewed by President Truman and given a Unit Citation by him. It was one of the proudest moments of my life.

Sam returned to the U.S. and worked several jobs (including a stint as a semi-pro baseball player) until he finished Art School in Chicago on the GI Bill. His father died in 1953 never having the opportunity to become a U.S. citizen. His mother did live to see the laws change and was proudly a U.S. citizen until her death in 1967. Sam became a Photo-Retoucher, raised a son and daughter in Stamford, and is presently retired. He received the Purple Heart with Oak Leaf Cluster, the Combat Infantry Badge, the Presidential Unit Citation, Three Battle Stars, and the Bronze Star.

In 1988, Congress made an official apology to the Japanese Americans who were interned and voted to compensate the victims. In January of 1993 President Bush expanded the payments to include spouses and parents of the victims in the amount of $20,000 each. The President added that , "No monetary payments can ever fully compensate loyal Japanese -Americans for one of the darkest incidents in American constitutional history. We must do everything possible to ensure that such a grave wrong is never repeated."[5]

- AL BENEVELLI -

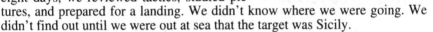

After enlisting in the U.S. Navy, Al Benevelli was assigned to the Fourth Beach Battalion which, at the time, numbered less than 300 men. The job of this "commando" unit was to land on the beach before an amphibious assault to try to clear the way for an invasion. As a member of this unit, Al participated in landings at Sicily, Italy, and Southern France. In 1945, he was sent to the Pacific Theater presumably to prepare for a mainland invasion of Japan.

When we arrived in North Africa, we were assigned to a Combat Engineer Unit where we were trained in Army and Navy tactics. In July of 1943, we left Algiers and traveled in the Mediterranean toward Greece. For seven or eight days, we reviewed tactics, studied pictures, and prepared for a landing. We didn't know where we were going. We didn't find out until we were out at sea that the target was Sicily.

We landed at Gela (Sicily) before dawn. It was pitch black. There were about two hundred of us spread over a ten mile area. We were broken down into groups of thirty and then into groups of four or five. Our area was about one quarter of a mile called "green beach." We had to set up green lights to tell the landing craft where to go. We also had to blow up any obstacles like sandbars or land mines. If we were spotted before the invasion, we were goners. But we were very lucky in Sicily. We hit an area that was not heavily fortified.

After the invasion, our job was to bring supplies up to the beach and evacuate the wounded. We were kind of on our own. Nobody claimed us—not the Army or the Navy. But before an invasion, everybody wanted us. I guess you can say we were the forerunners of these groups like the Seals— except without the equipment. We had a gun, a pack, some TNT and lifebelt. When you dove down with your TNT, you just dove down, no mask or anything. We wore our dungarees.

We stayed on the beach at Sicily for about three weeks. We slept right there—no tent or anything. If it rained, we were out of luck. After this, we went back to North Africa to prepare for another invasion.

In September, we landed at Palermo (Italy), but this time it was a mess. It was a stormy night, and the Germans were waiting for us. In fact, we got screwed up in the storm and landed at the same time the troops did. As we went in with the landing craft, we hit a sandbar, and I was knocked forward. A bullet hit the ensign behind me right in the chest and killed him. If we didn't hit that sandbar, I wouldn't be here today.

The machine guns had us pinned down. We went up the beach on our bellies—bullets going over our heads. We were mixed up with the troops. All the while, our ships were sending shells over our heads. We also had trouble with sand bars there; we had to blow them up.

On the way back to Africa in the fall of 1943, one of our LSTs (Landing Ship Tank) was torpedoed. I wasn't on it, but all of my gear was. In fact, my Stamford

High School ring is still at the bottom of the Mediterranean.

When we went to France in 1944, it was a piece of cake. The Germans concentrated so much on defending Normandy, that we practically walked in. We landed at St. Maxime Sur Mer. After this, we came home for 35 days. We went to California, and I was assigned to the U.S S. Barnwell, an attack transport. We headed back to the Pacific and were practicing for another invasion. But then we dropped the bomb, and the war ended.

After the war ended, we landed in Sasebo, Japan. Looking back on it now, we were very lucky we didn't have to make a wartime landing there. There was very little beach, and the shore was mountainous. It would've been hell. In a lot of places, there wasn't even room for the landing craft. Just getting to shore, we had to weave through these big rock formations that you could practically touch. I can't imagine a landing there.

On one of the trips to Japan, I drew shore patrol and saw Nagasaki. Everything was leveled except for a bank. It was terrible, but I still can't help thinking how bad it would've been if we had to land on those beaches.

Al returned to Stamford in 1946 and went to work at his father's gas station the very next day. He settled down, raised a family here and retired from the Springdale Fire Department in 1987.

STAMFORD SOLDIER
HELPS KING GEORGE

When King George of England began his inspection tour of Allied Forces in North Africa, he developed a severe case of sunburn on his arms. Because he had brought along only a short-sleeved bush jacket, the King seemed destined for misery. That is, until Private Dominick Albonizio of Stamford came to the rescue. While the King rested overnight, Albonizio, a local tailor before the war, stitched new, long sleeves on the King's jacket. The improved jacket passed the careful inspection of the King, and he used it for the duration of his tour.[6]

- LEON DZILINSKI -

Leon Dzilinski was working at Pitney Bowes when he entered the army in 1943. He was trained as a medic and assigned to the 5th Army headed by General Mark Clark. After being stationed in North Africa he participated in the invasions of Sicily and Italy.

At first I wanted to join the Marines so I went into New York with my buddy Matt Guzda to sign up. He got in but they wouldn't take me because I was colorblind. I guess I was the lucky one. He was killed at Guadalcanal.

I was trained as a medic. We were aidmen, litter bearers (stretcher carriers), ambulance drivers, whatever. Each infantry company had 125 men. They had one aidman and one medic. While they were in combat they couldn't take care of all those men so that's when they called us. We were the reinforcements to help them clean up the wounded. We gave them morphine and carried them back to the aid station. From there they'd get to a hospital.

We didn't carry any weapons. We were non-combatants. But the only way to tell was by the cross that we had on our arms.

I landed in Oran (North Africa) in 1943. We stayed there until we made the invasion of Sicily. We landed at Gela and from there we went to Palermo, Messina, and later to Italy.

In Sicily I was attached to the 54th Medical Battalion. I think the whole campaign only took 43 days. We went right in with the infantry at Gela. We had to evacuate the wounded on foot because there were no jeeps on the front line. It was bad there and we had to administer a lot of morphine. Then we'd have to tag the guys so that the doctors wouldn't repeat the dosage. You did whatever you could. You'd take the first guy you came across, pick him up, and get out of there. After a while you got used to it and it became a routine job. *(In Sicily alone the 54th Medical Battilion won 2 Silver Stars, 55 Bronze Stars, and 26 Purple Hearts.)*

It was dark before daybreak when we hit the beaches in Sicily. It was so bad because there was so much confusion there. Our paratroopers were supposed to be dropped in 10 miles behind the German lines and fight back toward the beach. But before this happened some German bombers came over and attacked us. So when our planes with the paratroopers came over later, our own ships fired on them because they thought it was the Germans again. I saw Stan Kasilikowski there. He was wounded but he had already been cleaned and taped up. I had a pair of rosary beads and gave them to him.

When we invaded Italy we went over the Straits of Messina to Napoli. This time it wasn't bad. The Germans had already taken off and we just walked right in. Probably the scariest time I had was when we had to walk right over Mount Etna. It was an old volcano and all I kept saying was, "Don't blow up now! Don't blow up now!"

We went through town after town–Santa Maria, Casserta. We moved so fast

143

I can't remember all of them. At Cassino the Germans had a vantage point that overlooked the entire Po Valley. The British 8th Army finally took it but they were using Polish troops...and over 5,000 of them were slaughtered. We went in later to clean up .

After the Po campaign we went into Rome. This time we were attached to the Special Services because they needed medics. They were good soldiers and nobody wore stripes so you didn't know who the officers were. Once I asked a guy who was in charge and he said, "We're all equal here."

After we took Rome a few of us were awarded the Bronze Star. I don't know why. All I know is that one day in Traversa our commander called us in and told us to put on our dress uniforms. Then General (Geoffrey) Keyes awarded them to us right in the field. *(The Bronze Star was awarded to Dzilinski and two other medics. The citation reads as follows..."For heroic action in combat on June 4, 1944 in the vicinity of Rome, Italy...These enlisted men advanced under enemy fire and our own troops crossfire across 200 yards of open field in front of our advancing tanks and successfully evacuated three machine gun casualties.")*

We were attached to a lot of units in Italy, the Third Army, the Ninth Division, the 85th, 88th, the 96th. I was even with the 34th Division for a while. That's the one Senator Inoye was with when he lost his arm. They were the Japanese-American unit, the 442nd Regiment, 100th Battalion. They were called Nisei. They treated me the best out of any other outfit I was in. One guy always used to say, "Leon, we're not Japanese, we are American." One of the guys was from Stamford. His family owned a restaurant above Frank Martin and Sons. When the war was over I looked him up and they gave me a huge meal, for nothing. They were great fighters and showed that they were just as American as anyone else.

For a while I was even attached to Senator Dole's 10th Mountain Division. They even trained us on how to bring the wounded down the mountain by rope. We never did it that way because it was quicker just to slide the stretcher down the slope.

We saw a lot of young soldiers get killed. When the infantry was losing a lot of men they brought in a lot of replacements. These young kids were called "Repo-Depos." They were green and sometimes didn't even get down when a shell came in. You'd have to yell at them to get down. Compared to them I was a seasoned old vet.

We slept outside a lot of the time. When it was cold you'd do anything to get warm. I even remember once we were near a cemetery and we slept in the mausoleums just to stay warm. I was lucky though. I never got hit. I don't know why. I remember one night we were getting shelled and an infantry man ran up to me and said, "I'm not getting in that hole with you. You don't even have a gun." I thought, "What the hell good is a gun going to do?" So he dove into another hole and was killed. He would've been better off with me.

All of the infantry guys were wonderful men. They'd have head wounds or stomach wounds but they never complained. They were so happy to see us. Sometimes at night it would be so dark you couldn't see a thing in front of you but you would hear moaning all around. I'd get my men together and we'd go out there and find them. Somebody had to get them. You couldn't just leave them there. Sometimes you'd pick up a guy who was over 200 pounds but you had to do it. They never complained. So you'd lug a guy in and you'd be exhausted and the Sergeant would order you back out. My nickname was Diesel and I remember he'd say to me, "Diesel you just have to get those men out of there."

Sometimes we'd follow the infantry right into a town. If somebody got wounded, we'd have to run right out into the street to get them. It wasn't good for other men to see their buddies lying there wounded so we had to get them to the rear as quickly as possible.

One time my brother looked me up and found me in a small town in Italy. He was with the 8th Air Force and he was used to good treatment. The first night he said to me, "Where do we sleep?" And I said, "Right here on the ground. Where do you think?" The next morning we went to the evacuation hospital for breakfast and he said, "Leon, you guys live like bums."

Toward the end of the war I ended up in Cortina, a resort town. We were like prison guards watching over the Nazis. I met a few of the Polish P.O.W.s and they told us that they were forced to fight with the Germans. Later, a few of the guys refused to go back to Poland and went to live in Canada and England.

The Italians were glad to see the Americans. A lot of them couldn't wait to get rid of the Germans. They treated us wonderfully and gave us wine and cheese. We had no trouble with them and were greeted with open arms.

After a while the Germans began to surrender by the thousands. They knew that the war was lost and some simply walked into town and gave up. Once, when I was in a bar in Cortina, a bunch of Germans just walked in and tried to get a drink. Then they surrendered.

When the war in Europe ended we were supposed to go to Japan, but then we dropped the bomb and that was it.

I never met General Clark during the war but a few years ago he came to the Memorial Day Parade in Stamford. I went up to him, shook his hand, and showed him my 5th Army Patch. I said, "Sir, you were a great General." And he smiled, put his arm around me and said, "I'm always so happy to see men who were under my command."

Leon returned to Stamford and to his job at Pitney Bowes. He worked there for over 40 years until his retirement. In addition to his Bronze Star he was awarded a "V" for valor and second Oak Leaf for evacuating patients under fire on the Gothic Line.

- DANNY ROSA -

Danny Rosa graduated from Stamford High School in June of 1942. A little more than a year later he found himself on the beaches of Salerno during the Allied invasion of Italy. As a member of the 45th Infantry, nicknamed the "Thunderbirds," Rosa saw action throughout Italy and spent the remainder of the war there.

When I was at Camp Croft, South Carolina, the Adjutant General called me in. He asked me if I'd like to go to Italy as a spy. He told me that they'd teach me fluent Italian and that I'd be eligible for a lot of promotions. I don't know why he asked me. Maybe it was because of my name. In the army records I was down as Donato Salvatore Rosa. He said, "Don't answer now. Come back in two weeks." He also warned me not to tell anyone or I'd be court martialed. When I got back to camp, my Lieutenant asked me why the Adjutant General called me in. I wouldn't answer and for the next few weeks he was nasty to me.

Well, two weeks later the Adjutant General called me in again. I told him that I wasn't interested. He said "What's the matter son? Don't you want to help your country?" I told him that I did want to help the country and that I'd do my part, but with the infantry. I just was not interested.

I got to Northern Africa at the tail end of the fighting there and we were all over the place, Oran, Tunisia, Arzu, Bazerta, all through there. At Arzu we began to train for the invasion of Italy. They didn't tell us it would be at Salerno. We didn't find out until we were on the way over.

By the time we got to Salerno we had plenty of company – ships, planes, everything. We were frightened. Anyone who tells you that they weren't scared is lying. You just pray that you can do your job and put all of your training to good use.

It was still a little dark when we went in and the Germans were waiting for us. They were up in the mountains and we were down on the beach. It seemed like forever. Our ships kept going around in circles, shelling and shelling, blasting at the Germans in the mountains. There were rocks flying all over the place.

As we went in, the ramp dropped down off the boat and you ran right into the water. You had to hold your gun up high so it didn't get wet. If you were lucky like us, the water wasn't deep, but some guys did drown.

When I got to the beach, I took cover behind the first thing I saw, bushes. I dove into them and the thorns ripped me up. We were pinned down for some time, I can't remember how long. But finally, we fought our way off the beaches and began to go inland. We lost a lot of men there, a lot of my friends. But what choice did we have? There was no other way to get in (to Italy). I was very lucky, but I still try to forget it.

From there on, we went through dozens of small towns. I forget most of their names. In one of these towns, I think it was Benevento, they made liqueurs. The Germans had left a lot of booby traps. They figured that the Americans would try to get their hands on something to drink so we were told to pass the word that no one should touch any bottles. But we had guys who wouldn't listen and some of them were killed.

There was combat in all of the towns we hit, Avalino, Casserta, Florence, and right up to Naples. Sometimes it was house to house and street to street, taking buildings one by one. Usually, a few of us would be sent on patrol to try to see where the Germans were. We were usually on foot, two or three of us with a radio. If it was clear, you'd radio back and the company would advance. We'd go out into the fields, check the trees, check the bushes and the haystacks. You had to be sharp though, because the Germans wanted you to feel safe. They didn't bother you. They wanted you to call the entire company up and then they'd open fire. Once when I was coming back from patrol, my buddy, Goo Goo (Dominick) Tamburri (from Stamford) was on his way out on patrol. We went through basic training and everything together. That was the last time I saw him. He was killed later in the Po Valley Invasion.

We went town to town that way across Italy. In one of these towns we met General Clark. *(General Mark Clark was the commander of the Fifth Army and the entire Italian campaign).* He was very pleasant and he talked to all of us young kids. He asked how old I was and I told him I was nineteen and he said "Soldier, I just ask that you do your best so we can all get out of here quickly."

When we got to Cassino the battle was already on. We helped a Ranger outfit when we got there. We were firing mortar shells constantly but instead of setting them up on a tripod we'd just lean them up against a curb or something. The shells got so hot that we ripped off our shirts and wrapped them around our hands. When it was all over I don't think there was a building left that still had a roof on it. After the war, I went back and took pictures for my brother Charlie to see because he was on Iwo Jima. *(This is an accurate assessment of the damage done at Cassino. One of the casualties of the Allied assault was the Benedictine Monastery that sat atop Monte Cassino. The Abbey, which was over 500 years old, was reduced to rubble by Allied air bombardment.)*

Finally, after Cassino, we went into town and we were being bombarded. I took cover and this was the last thing I remember. The concussion of one of the bombs knocked me clear out of where I was. Later I was told that they had to pull me out of the water. The next thing I knew I was on a hospital ship. I said, "What the hell am I doing here?" A man told me not to move. I could barely move my legs. To this day I don't know exactly what happened. One minute I was on the ground. The next minute I was in a hospital.

They took me back to Northern Africa and after I got well again they sent me back to Italy and I was assigned to a Postal outfit. We worked out of Naples and our job was to gather up all of the packages that were broken or lost and donate the goods to the men that were in hospitals. I stayed with this outfit until the end of the war.

When the war was over, a lot of us young guys had enough points to go home but we let some of the married guys with kids go first. So I stayed over in Italy and while I was there I got the chance to meet some relatives I had there. They treated me well and I had a great time with them. But when I got back to the States, in Newport News, Virginia, I'll never forget what I did. I took dirt and rubbed it on my face. I never thought I'd make it home.

I have no desire to go back to Italy. There are too many bad memories. I lost a lot of friends there.

Today I consider myself very, very lucky. People tell me that I'm always happy and I say, "Of course I'm happy. I'm a lucky guy. God gave me another day."

Rosa received combat ribbons for the African, European, and Mediterranean campaigns and returned to Stamford at the end of 1945. He and his brother Charlie, who had just returned from the Pacific Theater, opened up the Rosa Brothers Gas Station which stood at the corner of Stillwater Avenue and Spruce Street for over thirty years.

- SYDNEY MEYERS ' WALK-

During the battle for Cassino, Corporal Sydney Meyers, a radio chief in the infantry, decided to take a walk while he was off duty. As he was taking his stroll, he heard voices in a ditch and realized that they were German soldiers. Armed only with his carbine, he managed to take all five prisoners

along with their two machine guns. Because he spoke German, he was also able to act as interpreter when the five soldiers were interrogated.

Just a few months later in France, as his battalion was under intense enemy fire, Meyers carried several wounded men to safety and administered first aid to them. For "courage and initiative" Meyers was awarded the Bronze Star. By the end of the war, Meyers had also earned the Purple Heart and four campaign stars for Italy, France, Germany, and Austria.[7]

- TONY PIA -

Tony Pia was scheduled to graduate with the class of 1943 at Stamford High School. In the middle of his Senior year, however, he was drafted and along with several of his classmates, was given his diploma and sent off to join the Army.

In the fall of 1942, I was playing football for Stamford High. We had two games left and I had just turned 18 when I got my draft notice. Back in those days, the big rivalry was with Norwalk High. We used to draw eight to ten thousand for those games. So, when I got my draft notice I went to Paul Kuczo and said, "Coach, I just got drafted." He took me immediately to see Carl Nutter, who was Chairman of the Draft Board. He was also a History teacher at Stamford High School. Mr. Nutter looked at me, patted me on the head and said, "Don't worry laddie, you won't be drafted. You'll have a chance to finish your Senior year."

Well, we played the final game against Norwalk and we won 6-0. I scored the only touchdown and we had a big celebration afterwards. Less than a month later, I got my second draft notice. Coach Kuczo and I went to see Mr. Nutter again, and this time he said the country needed us boys. So right after Christmas I was inducted.

At school they called 19 of us up on stage and in front of the entire student body, wished us well and said goodbye. The following July, my parents received my diploma in the mail. I still think they waited just long enough so that I could play against Norwalk.

I reported to Fort Devins in early 1943 where they processed us, and gave us a bed in a big hangar there. It turned out that the guy in the bunk next to me was Nick Amalfitano. We called him "Tabs." He was a little older than me and he used to manage Abbey's Pharmacy. He was a small guy and we all wondered how he got into the Army.

About 3:00 a.m. on the second night, I heard a little commotion, and when I woke up, Tabs was standing there getting dressed to ship out. As he was leaving, he grabbed my arm and said, "Don't forget kid. Right after the war, drop by and see me at Abbey's". He ran out and I never saw him again, because he was killed in the war *(Amalfitano was killed in Italy in 1944)*. Whenever I visit the cemetery, I still go over to visit Tabs' grave.

Later, we got on a train and they didn't tell us where we were going. One day we were in Pittsburgh, the next day West Virginia. We were zigzagging all over the place and, finally after four days and four nights we woke up in Florida. It was a makeshift camp with tents all over.

We practiced marching in the sand, and it was rough. The hot sun was on our heads and our muscles ached. The two guys in charge of our training were "Gorilla," because he looked like King Kong, and Lt. Pay Day, who we never saw until pay day. Our drinking water came from suspended pipes with water trickling out. We'd rinse out our mess kits in three separate barrels of water. Imagine 1000 guys washing their mess kits in these barrels three times a day. The first week, hundreds of guys were sick.

I ended up with an engineering outfit in Virginia, and we traveled up and down the east coast. Then in April of 1944, we were shipped overseas. The trip took 33 days and we were in a huge convoy of 92 ships. Talk about sick!

At nightfall, about a day or two out of Gibraltar, at twilight, we heard alarms and then little pops coming from the rear of the convoy. One of the ships was hit by a German sub and that night we could see an orange glow in the sky from the burning ship. The next morning when we woke up, everything was quiet and the ship wasn't moving. They wouldn't let us out on deck and we had no idea what was going on. Finally, they let us go up on deck and it turned out that our ship had broken down and we were all alone, except for a PBY flying overhead. Finally, we were towed into Gibraltar and we stayed there for six days.

After this, we went to Oran (Africa) and then Sicily. From there, we were sent to the east coast of Italy with the British Eighth Army. We were assigned to the British because they had been in the war so long that most of their construction equipment was gone. Because we were an engineering outfit, our job was to rebuild roads and bridges. Once we needed a steam shovel badly and didn't have one so a sergeant said, "You speak Italian, don't you? Come with me." We went out and hunted a steam shovel down and I had to negotiate with an old Italian guy and buy it off him. The machine only went about 2 miles an hour, but we used it for a long time while we were there.

Later, we were reassigned to the American Fifth Army again near Rome and we dug up Calicci stone, which was like sandstone, pulverized it, and used it as a base for roads. We also worked at Fifth Army Headquarters where we acted as interpreters for some of the Italian prisoners that were being interrogated.

My parents came from Settefrati, which at one point was only about 10 or 15 miles from where we were working. So, during a lull, I asked my Captain if I could visit the village. "I have to get there," I told him.

Well, a friend and I hopped in a jeep and went as far as we could until we came to a bombed out bridge. I got out, told him to go back, and waded across the river. When I got across the river, I walked and walked and there was not a soul around. Finally, I came across a man sitting on a stone. I asked him where Settefrati was. He pointed to a long road that wound up a mountain and told me that it was near the top. I walked for hours and hours and I met a man on a bicycle, gave him some cigarettes, and asked him to take me the rest of the way there.

Finally, just before dark, I reached the village. I had this strange feeling that I had been there before. It was so quiet there you could hear a pin drop. I heard some wooden shutters open and I yelled out, "My name is Tony Pia. My father, Frank, came from this village." Before you know it, a crowd was there, greeting me. Most of them grew up with my parents. They fed me and treated me like a king.

I stayed there the night and told them that I had to get back to my outfit. One of my cousin's sons showed me a shortcut and escorted me back down the mountain. I walked a few more miles and then I ran into a convoy of American trucks. An officer in a jeep picked me up and brought me back to my outfit.

Once, around Naples, a very odd thing happened. A bunch of us were standing around when in the distance we saw 5 or 6 women coming towards us. They were coming down a mountain and they were in bad shape. They were all dressed in brown and looked like they were starved. It turned out that they were Russian soldiers. They were captured by the Nazis and brought to Italy for slave labor. As the Germans were retreating, they just abandoned them. I'll never forget that one of the women just grabbed a stalk of garlic and ate it raw, with all of the skin on it. We took these women in and got them food, then turned them over to the military police.

I acted as an interpreter for a lot of Italian P.O.W.'s and got to know a lot of them well. They used to cook up these great meals for me. They had no interest in fighting. I became good friends with this barber in Naples and many years later, I looked him up and visited him. You'd think the Pope had just arrived.

I met my future wife, Liliana, while I was in Italy. When we were in Rome in the winter of 1944-1945, I visited a small shop. Half of it was a shoe repair store and the other half sold light garments. One day I went in to see if I could buy some gloves and I saw this lovely woman in there and began talking to her in Italian. She was the owner's sister-in-law. After that, I visited her there every chance I got. One day I went in and her father was there. I thought to myself, "Oh no. He's not going to like this." But we were introduced and he was very nice to me and

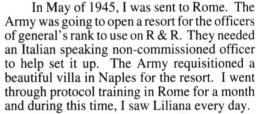

Pia and his wife, Liliana

I wrote them and continued to visit with her until the end of the war.

In May of 1945, I was sent to Rome. The Army was going to open a resort for the officers of general's rank to use on R & R. They needed an Italian speaking non-commissioned officer to help set it up. The Army requisitioned a beautiful villa in Naples for the resort. I went through protocol training in Rome for a month and during this time, I saw Liliana every day.

When I got to Naples, the villa was ready. It had 10 bedrooms, a huge dining room, a bar, and some of the best chefs in Italy. They had chambermaids and a three piece string band for the weekends. Nothing was too good for these officers. Once, I even had to fly to Sicily once to pick up lobsters for two generals who were staying there.

Around August of 1945, Liliana and I were engaged, but we couldn't get married. There was a rule that no American could marry a foreign national until the war was over. When the war did end, I sent in my paperwork, but for some reason it was being stalled. One of the generals at the villa found out about it and cut through all of the red tape and got me the papers within a day. We were married and had our reception right at the villa, and the chefs fed us and made a beautiful cake. Several Generals were at the wedding. After our honeymoon in Capri, we lived right in the villa. I reenlisted and we spent several years in Europe.

When I was with the Fifth Army as an interpreter during the war, I had the opportunity to meet General Mark Clark. I even drove him around from time to time. In 1983, when he came to Stamford for the Memorial Day Parade, I had a chance to see him again. When we met, I saluted him and we put our arms around each other. He was so old and frail, but still very much in command.

"Sarge" Pia stayed with the Army for 23 years, until his retirement as a Master Sergeant in 1967. He and his wife have been married for almost fifty years and have raised two children. Pia went on to work with the Human Rights Commission and has remained one of the town's foremost advocates for veterans.

- THE SERVICE ROLL -

For over three decades, one of the most distinctive structures in downtown Stamford was the World War II Service Roll, located in Central Park across from the Old Town Hall.

The construction of the monument was spearheaded by a large committee, which included Kingsley Gillespie of the Stamford Advocate, First Selectman George Barrett, and Mayor Charles E. Moore. The original structure, which was designed under the supervision of Frank Laney of the State Trade School, was intended to hold approximately 3400 names, but had to be constantly modified to accommodate the ever increasing number of citizens who were entering the armed services.

On Memorial Day, 1943, the unique triangular white structure was dedicated. An estimated crowd of 10,000 turned out to watch the unveiling of the Service Roll, which included the names of 5555 men and women. These names were provided by the Stamford Advocate. Each nameplate was handpainted and a gold star appeared near the names of those who gave their lives in the war effort. Inscribed above these names was, "These be our valiant sons and daughters who have gone in jeopardy of their lives –let none who remain be found wanting".[8]

By the war's end, there would be almost 10,000 names on the Service Roll. For years, the adults and children of the town could visit the monument to find the name of a relative, or friend, and reflect on the town's contribution to the war effort.

In 1972, Central Park, which housed the Service Roll, was removed, the monument was demolished and never again would the names of all those who served their country be preserved in one place. In 1977, however, due in large part to the efforts of Tony "Sarge" Pia, a new "Veteran's Memorial Park" was constructed directly to the rear of where the old Service Roll once stood. Today, four vertical monoliths pay tribute to those who gave their lives in World War II, the Korean War, and the War in Vietnam.

- LOU DEBRISCO -

Lou DeBrisco had finished High School and was working at Plastics Manufacturing Company in Stamford when he was drafted into the Army. After initially being assigned to the Medical Corps he became a translator with the Allied Government in Sicily.

Six of my buddies and I went up to New Haven to enlist. Eight months later I was drafted into the Army and ended up in the Medical Corps. After basic training I went out to Camp McCoy in Wisconsin. While I was there they grabbed me and a few other men and asked us if we could speak and write in Italian. I could, so they shipped us all back east to Camp Shanango in Pennsylvania where I was placed with Italian speaking men from all over the country.

I was 19 years old and they sent me to North Africa, first to Casablanca, then to Tunis. We stayed there until July when the Allies invaded Sicily. We went in several days after the invasion and landed in Palermo. We reported to our headquarters which was called AMGOT (Allied Military Government of the Occupied Territories) and were connected to the Civilian Intelligence Corps.

One of the first things I remember when we got there was that one night we were listening to "Axis Sally" on the radio and she was telling us, "We know you're here. We're going to get you." Later a couple of Nazi planes came in and bombed some ships in the harbor. They hit one of them and I remember seeing the bodies of all these sailors in the water. We helped to pick up some of the dead and wounded. It was horrible.

When we got back to the house we were assigned to, the area was roped off. A bomb hit one of the houses but didn't explode. As the men were trying to defuse the bomb a lady was climbing right over them trying to get her jewelry out of the house before it blew up.

Right after that, I contracted malaria and spent 29 days in the hospital. The Italians were good to me and they kept feeding me lots of garlic. I guess it worked because I regained my strength and I was assigned to the town of Caltinesetta, which was around the center of Sicily, and we set up headquarters there. There were only 11 of us, 2 English Officers, 3 American Officers and 6 GI's. We considered ourselves lucky because it was a nice little town and we lived very well. Our job was to help set up the new government, get the town settled and then move on. We also interviewed a lot of the locals, searched for collaborators, and also tried to help them if they needed food or supplies.

I was the receptionist and handled the people as they first came in. But I had a lot of trouble with the Sicilian dialect, but they managed to get their point across. I had a POW, a Carbonari with me who spoke the dialect perfectly and he would help me interpret. People would come in with different problems. A guy's house would be damaged by a bomb and he'd need some money to rebuild. Another would come in and tell us his son lost a limb and he needed help. Sometimes we'd give them food and supplies. We would either deal with it there or would pass it on to the officers who would ask, "What do these blokes want? Tell them to come back and we'll deal with it tomorrow."

The people in the town treated us like kings. I met a good family there and they used to feed me. I'd get some food, bring it to them and they'd cook it for me – spaghetti, pasta fagioli, meatballs, and everything.

One of the American Officers, a lieutenant, would take us around at night and try to break up the Black Market. He was a mean SOB. He'd beat the civilians with a cane and treat them badly. We'd raid a house, confiscate cases of guns or cigarettes. We worried that one night the people in the town would get even and kill us. But I guess the Italians didn't want any more problems.

The Black Market was a big operation there, especially cigarettes. American cigarettes were going for $20 a case, even back then. Many Americans got rich over there by selling flour, guns, gasoline. Any of that would make money for you. One guy was sending thousands of dollars a month home but finally he was caught and court-martialed.

We did a lot of work with POW's and believe me none of them wanted to escape. They were just waiting for the war to be over. They weren't like the Germans who you had to watch every minute. Most of the Italians didn't want to be in the war in the first place. They hated the Germans.

Once we took 10 POWs out to clean up this Big Estate. They were all Italian Generals and one of the guys, who I became friendly with, was able to get his hands on some food and wine and he said to me, "Don't worry Luigi, we'll take care of this place." And he did.

Once in Caltinesetta, I was ordered to drive two nuns back to their home. Instead, at the last minute I was sent out to pick up some supplies and my two friends took them home. On the way back they were all killed when they collided with a train. When I got back to headquarters the British Officers were having a good time. When I told them about the accident they didn't even seem to care. I was so mad that I wanted to get back at them. So a few days later I went to a pharmacy and asked him to give me something to put in their food. He gave me laxatives. One night I put it in their stew and for the next few days, the British officers lived in the bathroom.

Six months later, we left Caltinesetta and were sent to Naples on a Hospital Ship and evacuated the wounded from Anzio and brought them to Naples. The guys I felt the worst for were the guys who were shell shocked. I felt sorry for them.

One of the best things that happened to me while I was in Italy was that I met my grandmother for the very first time. A few of us had a couple of days off and we were walking around Casserta. I went to a barber shop and asked the barber where the town of Madelone was. He said it was only 5-Kilometers away so we decided to find it. I promised my father that I would visit her if I could. When we got to Madelone I was climbing these high stairs and an elderly woman ran up to me screaming, "He's here. He's here." I asked her how she knew who I was and she said, "You look just like your mother." She told me that every time soldiers came through the town, she would look for me. She had a picture of me when I was five years old and said, "I knew it was you when I saw that curly hair." It was such a wonderful experience, I'll never forget. She cooked for us and I got to spend a few hours with her before I had to get back. When I got back to the States we regularly sent her packages of food or clothing and I corresponded with her for years.

Lou returned to the states, raised his family, and worked for Borden's Dairy for several years. He also worked for the Stamford Public Schools as a custodian for fifteen years until his retirement in 1993.

- JOSEPH FARRELL -

Sergeant Joseph Farrell was a member of a special reconnaissance battalion based in Italy. On the night of March 22, 1944, he and 14 other soldiers were taken by PT Boat to LaSpezia, Italy, where their job was to blow up a strategic tunnel that aerial bombing had failed to destroy.

Once the men went ashore, however, they were never seen again. The PT Boats that brought them there were attacked and had to flee. When they returned the following night to pick up the men, they were unable to locate them. All were listed as MIA until the end of the war.

After VE Day, the fate of the men became known. Their bodies were found in a grave in Genoa. Their hands had been tied behind their backs and it was obvious that they had been executed. The men's bodies were exhumed, brought to an American cemetery, and those responsible were punished. Joseph Farrell was just 21 years old.[9]

[1] Ogden Tanner and Robert Wallace. The Italian Compaign. (Alexandria, VA: Time Life Books, Inc., 1978)

[2] Combat Record of the 504th Parachute Infantry Regiment. April 1943-July 1945.

[3] John Tateishi. And Justice for All: An Oral History of Japanese-American Detention Corps. (New York: Random House, 1984), Introduction.

[4] Ogden Tanner and Robert Wallace. The Italian Campaign. (Alexandria, VA: Time Life Books, Inc., 1978), p.188.

[5] "The Quan". American Defenders of Bataan and Corregidor. Vol. 47, January, 1993.

[6] "Soldier Aids King George". Stamford Advocate, June 21, 1943.

[7] "Corporal Meyers Takes a Walk, Brings Back Five Prisoners". Stamford Advocate, September 6, 1945.

[8] "Memorial Design Given Approval" and "Stamford Honors Living and Dead of US Wars". Stamford Advocate, March 6, 1943, June 1, 1943.

[9] "Stamford Soldier Among 15 Raiders Slain by Germans". Stamford Advocate, September 13, 1945.

CHAPTER TEN

THE AIR WAR

When the U.S. began its first European air attacks on the Axis in 1942, the American command decided on daylight "precision" bombings rather than "area" bombing. During the day, American pilots could see their targets and concentrate on special factories, plants, or transportation centers. At the same time, this would limit the number of civilian casualties.

Initially, however, this strategy proved costly because the daylight also gave the Germans the opportunity to see the approaching planes. Even the heavily armed B-17 Flying Fortresses and B-24 Liberators were no match for German fighter planes. There were a variety of other dangers for the American crews. Whether it was unpredictable weather, mechanical malfunction, or white hot flak that filled the sky, combat airmen faced death each time they took off and, indeed early on, the Americans suffered heavy casualties.

As the war dragged on and the Allies achieved air superiority, the constant bombing wreaked havoc on German cities. Once proud cities like Hamburg and Dresden were reduced to rubble. By war's end the air attacks on Germany had killed thousands, destroyed millions of homes and factories and, most importantly, crushed the Third Reich's capacity to wage war.

- MIKE BOCUZZI -

Mike was one of four brothers to serve in World War II. Assigned to the Army Air Corps, he was a radio operator and gunner for "Rosie's Riveters," a B-17 so named for its pilot, Robert Rosenthal. As part of the Eighth Air Force, Mike flew 25 bombing missions over Germany from October 1943 to March 1944. This was one of the most dangerous times in the war, and at one point, one out of three crewmen did not return from a bombing mission. The B-17, or "Flying Fortress" as it was called, had a ten-member crew, and Mike worked every position except as ball turret gunner.

I was 20 when I went in. I got the nickname "Foxhole" because of my height (5' 3"). One time during the roll call, the Drill Sergeant yells to me, "Hey, Bocuzzi, get out of the foxhole."

"Rosie's Riveters" had great ethnic balance. We had an Italian, a Jew, a German, an Irishman, and a Scotsman. (An article in YANK, a military magazine, once referred to them as a "mongrel crew.")

My first actual bombing missions were October of 1943, the 12th, 13th and 14th I think. We hit Munster, Bremen, and Schweinfurt. Munster and Bremen were marshalling yards.

Schweinfurt was a ball bearing plant. We flew out of Thorpe-Abbotts, England. At that time we didn't have flying escorts. Once you got over the (English) Channel, you were all alone. The only time it was quiet was when you were climbing and forming into a group, and even at that time, you had equipment to check and a lot of heavy flying equipment. We had to wear an electric flying suit because it could get to 60 degrees below zero in the B-17. You had a heated suit that plugged into the airplane. We had no helmets or anything. Parachutes? We didn't know what they were. We'd move them out of the way; push them around the plane. With all the stuff we had on, we couldn't be bothered with a chute.

We went through four different airplanes while I was there. In fact, one time when we came back from a raid on Bremen, our number two engine was shot out, the number four engine was out, and we had a hole eight feet in diameter in our right wing. Later we counted 176 holes in the plane.

There were times that we were coming in and we had to dump all the excess weight off the plane—chutes, bullets, the magazines, everything. One time I even threw my pilot's hat off—imagine that!

On one mission, we came back alone. It was October, 1943, a bombing mission over Munster. One by one the planes went down until it was just us. Our two waist gunners were wounded. *(One later died.)* This was right at the beginning of the war for me. We were broken in right. After the mission, we were all drained. To be honest, when we landed, I couldn't move. I just couldn't move a muscle. But the other guys left me alone. They didn't make a big deal of it. After this, they sent us on R & R. *(This episode is written up in YANK April, 28, 1944.)*

I shot down my first plane that same month—a 190. In fact, I swear to this day that I saw a kid's face as the plane was going down. He was so young. As he came toward us in a swoop, I hit him, and he came in so close that he took the antenna right off our ship. I can visualize that today like it was yesterday.

You always had to stay in formation, no matter what. Once you dropped formation, you were dead. The B-17 could take a lot of punishment. You'd see planes come in with a tail torn up, an engine out, a fuselage ripped open. Sometimes the flak was so close that you could smell it. Of our ten crew members, four were wounded and two didn't come back. I was never wounded. I guess I ran faster than the bullets.

The Hamburg mission was horrendous. The British bombed them by night, and we bombed them by day. What we did there was unbelievable. Fires everywhere—everything destroyed. But you couldn't think about that. You had a job to do. *(Accounts of the Hamburg bombings bear this out. The fires were so severe that fire storms were created by the temperature.)*

Yes, one time I did help the pilot land, but it was no big deal. The co-pilot, "Pappy" Lewis, was wounded. We pulled him out of the seat, and I had to jump in. I only assisted the pilot. The plane was damaged, but we made it back all right.

We also flew one of the longest raids in the war—all the way to Trondheim, Norway (1900 miles). We didn't know too much about this mission except that we had to bomb some plants. I think they may have had something to do with the atomic bomb. *(Accounts of this raid mention only that German naval installations were bombed.)*

We needed every drop of fuel to make it back. The average mission was about 6 hours; Trondheim was 12 hours.

My last mission was March 3, 1944. We were among the first Americans to hit Berlin. But the difference between this and our earlier raids was like night and day. Now we had escorts—Spitfires, P-51 Mustangs, the works. It

Bocuzzi (back row, 2nd from left) and the crew of "Rosie's Riveters"

was like going for a joy ride compared to our first missions.

None of us ever felt like heroes. We just felt like it was something we had to do, not by choice, of course. I always complained and moaned that I wasn't going up anymore, but when they called the next raid, we were always there. They say we were heroes. But we did what we had to do. One time Shaeffer (the waist gunner) got hit and had a hole in his chest. I unplugged my oxygen and went to help him. I found some rags and packed them into his chest. Then I gave him the portable oxygen tank. I didn't make it back to my oxygen and passed out. Then Bill DiBlasio (waist gunner) plugged me in and saved my life.

I was in trouble a lot of times. I was busted to Private a few times. One time two MPs came to get me. They were so much taller than me that everyone would say, "Look at that poor little guy." One time, instead of busting me, they gave me K.P. Imagine—I was a Tech Sergeant and I was on K.P.!

All in all, though, I don't think I would trade my experiences with anyone. Sure it was dangerous, but we did our job, and I made a lot of lifelong friends.

Mike won two Distinguished Flying Crosses and five Air Medals, one of which was presented by Jimmy Doolittle. Many of the exploits of "Rosie's Riveters" were subsequently written up in "Yank," "The Bridgeport Herald," and "The Advocate."

- BOMBING SCHWEINFURT -

Ball bearings were vital to the war efforts of both the U.S. and Germany. Airplanes alone required thousands of these steel balls in order to reduce friction. Norma Hoffman of Stamford was one of the major ball bearing factories in the nation and, as a result, there was considerable local fear that it would be a target for bombing or sabotage

In Germany, one of the major targets of Allied bombing was Schweinfurt, in particular the George Schafer Bearing Company, which produced half of the ball bearings needed to keep the Nazi war machine running. As early as 1943, the Allies began bombing Schweinfurt at a very heavy cost. The city was well defended, and on the first raid alone, the U.S. Eighth Air Force lost over fifteen percent of its bombers. The factory was never completely put out of production.

Ironically, in 1969, the Schafer family, which owned the ball bearing factories bombed at Schweinfurt, came to the U.S. and bought Norma Hoffman which then became Norma F.A.G. Bearings. In 1974, it became F.A.G. Bearing, which still operates in Stamford. Schweinfurt remains a leading city for ball bearing production with F.A.G. as one of its main producers.

- ROGER PREU -

Roger Preu left college in 1942 and enlisted in the Army Air Corps. Between 1944 and 1945, he flew 30 heavy bombing missions into Germany, the last 18 as the group and wing lead bombadier.

I originally started out in pilot training, but I had trouble landing the plane smoothly. My depth perception at 20 feet was off, and I'd always come in a bit too high and bounce the plane. My instructor used to say that if he was twins, I would have killed two of him.

I was unhappy at the time, but in the long run, it worked out well. I trained as a navigator, bombardier, and I loved it. In early September of 1944, I arrived in England and was assigned to the Eighth Air Force. We flew four engine B-24 Liberators, and at this point in the war, we were forced to fly at 20,000 feet because even though the Germans were losing ground, they were assembling more and more antiaircraft as they retreated. A target might have twice the guns in 1945 that it had in 1944.

My first action was as a nose gunner in our B-24 called "Slightly Dangerous." After 12 missions, I was assigned to a lead crew. Shortly after that, another crew flew old "Slightly" and was shot down over Frankfurt.

My first lead mission was as a group lead towards the end of the Battle of the Bulge, in January of 1945, and it was shortly after this that we had a very close call. We were supposed to bomb Berlin but it was clouded in. Our secondary target was an oil refinery at Ruhrland but it was also clouded in. Our third target and nearly our last was Lauta, a big aluminum plant. About five seconds before we dropped our bombs, we received four solid hits by antiaircraft, probably 88's, our most feared enemy weapon. One shell went through the fuselage, just behind the pilot and didn't explode. The second hit the wing, one hit below the right wing and one went right through the center of the aircraft. We managed to drop our bombs, but we dropped them past the target. We were later told that we hit railroad cars. A lot of planes in our squadron were shot up pretty badly.

On the way back, we just couldn't keep up. Two engines were out, and we were leaking fuel badly and had to pull out of formaton with a long ride home. My original crew with whom I had trained, flew right by us and it certainly was lonely as we waved to each other. There was nothing they could do. We were sitting ducks, but lucky for us, the German fighters went after planes that were even worse off than us. I really thought this was it for us. I remember thinking that my folks would need a map to look up where I died. Who ever heard of Lauta?

At one point as we were near the Rhine, we were flying so low that soldiers were shooting at us with rifles. We actually got hit a few more times, but another one of our B-24s slid underneath us, crashed, and blew up. We finally ditched the plane in Saarbrucken (on the Rhine) and were picked up by the infantry.

It took us two weeks to get back to our base in England and during that time, we were listed as M.I.A. When we got back to base, the Colonel called

Washington immediately and made sure that my parents never got an M.I.A. telegram. I was thankful to him for that.

We flew more missions, four to Hamburg alone, hitting oil refineries, V-2 Rocket plants, and the like. On one mission, an Air Force lead to Augsburg, we were the first lead in the bomber train.

I flew until a month before VE Day, and I was on a boat on my way home when the war ended in August of 1945. We never lost a member of our crew but our squadron had many losses.

The nicest thing about being a bombadier was that you were the busiest when things got the worst, and I could see everything. Our radar navigator never saw anything. He said that's just the way he wanted it. Me, I wanted to see everything. I could never do what he did and he could never do what I did.

I was never an athlete in high school, never excelled in any sport. But as lead bombadier in a great crew, in a top outfit, I felt on top of the world. Maybe I was cocky, but I thought I lived up to my grandfather, an infantryman in the Civil War and my father, a sergeant in World War One.

> *Roger won two Distinguished Flying Crosses and five Air Medals. He finished college and came to work for the Stamford Public Schools. He taught for 42 years, including 29 years as the Head of the Art Department at Stamford High School. He retired from the Air Force Reserve as a Lt. Colonel.*

- SHE GAVE HER HAIR FOR HER COUNTRY -

How could a six-year old Stamford girl help her country to win the war? By donating her hair to the government.

Whether it was collecting scrap iron or selling war stamps, young Margaret Nicholson was actively involved in the local Youth Civilian Defense Group. So, when she got the word that her blond hair fit the exact specifications the government had set for use in bombsights, Margaret didn't hesitate. She went to a hairdresser, had her hair cut, placed it in an envelope and mailed it in. As the war progressed, few bomber pilots ever suspected that they owed some of the success of their missions to a six year old girl from Stamford.[1]

- HOWARD JOHNSON -

After graduating from Princeton in 1936, Howard Johnson went to work for American Airlines. After the war broke out, he left behind his new bride to join the Army Air Corps and served with the 467th Bombardment Group, which was part of the Eighth Air Force commanded by General Jimmy Doolittle. Between April and August of 1944, Johnson flew 33 combat missions, most of them in the "Ruth Marie," the B-24 named in honor of his wife. On D-Day he piloted two missions over the beaches of Normandy.

I arrived in England in March of 1944, and there we followed the war by reading the "Stars and Stripes." They covered the war pretty well and really gave us the big picture. We knew that the big invasion of France was going to come soon.

When we had a pre-midnight briefing on June 5, 1944, we knew that this was it, not only because of the timing of the briefing, but also because there was a General in attendance. We rarely had one present at a 467th briefing. General Peck was a real Hollywood type. I remember him saying, "Men, we are going to push the Germans back until their hats float."

This was the mission we all wanted to fly, to be a part of history. But I have to say that neither mission on D-Day was particularly difficult. By the time I got to Europe, the U.S. fighter planes had practically run the German fighters out of the sky. On D-Day in particular, we encountered very few fighters. Part of that was that the Germans did not want to waste their fighters on what they considered was a diversionary tactic at Normandy.

We left at about 3:00 a.m. and were due to be at the beaches at 6:30 a.m. What people didn't realize though, was that the greatest hazard for us was the English weather and the heavy amount of air traffic that day. The amount of planes in the sky over England posed a greater danger to us than flak or German fighter planes.

You have to remember that on D-Day about ten thousand planes filled the sky. In order to get that many planes up and into formation, we had to fly out at an assigned altitude over "Splasher 5," a lighthouse located several miles north of Rackheath, England. That night, in order to find our planned place in formation among thousands of planes, we had to look for certain light signals from the tail of another aircraft. These signals came from an ALDIS lamp which, in actual terms, was a big, powerful flashlight. I think the signal I was looking for was four dots and four dashes. The weather at that altitude was good that night, and somehow we managed to find our group.

There was one way traffic that night. We went north to Scotland, east over the Irish Sea, and then south on a course to Normandy. This indirect route was the only way to get all of those planes in the air.

The weather was very poor over the beaches. This was very good from the standpoint of deception, but very bad for the purposes of bombing. The clouds broke a few times though, and I actually got a view of the whole thing. I could see our ships below. When we got there, we were supposed to meet up with a high-tech plane and follow it to the bomb site. Something went wrong though, and we were never able to find it, so we ended up going along for the ride that night. All we provided was a little more noise for the boys on the ground to hear. When we returned to England a little before noon, we still had our bombs with us. I will always remember that on the way back our radio operator handed me the earphones to hear General Eisenhower announcing the news of the Normandy invasion to the rest of the world.

Johnson and his B-24, "The Ruth Marie"

We were able to get a little sleep and at 4:00 p.m. on that same day we went back for another mission. This time our target was some of the German defenses on the beachhead, and we made sure we dropped our bombs. On the way back, as we were approaching Rackheath, the radio came on and told us "Bandits in the area." This meant that German fighters were around. It was nighttime and according to procedure all aircraft lights and all lights on the ground were turned off.

We were low on gas and tired, but we had to head back out to "Splasher 5" and then out to the North Sea. As we were approaching Rackheath for the second time, my co-pilot announced that he thought he saw the perimeter lights were turned on. As usual, he was right and we finally landed safely, about 24 hours after our initial briefing.

D-Day was one of the very few "tactical" missions we flew. "Tactical" bombing was designed to deal directly with the enemy or his defenses on the ground. The vast majority of our missions were what was called "strategic" bombing. That means hitting things like oil refineries, marshalling yards, trains, or bridges. In other words, "strategic" bombing was aimed at the German infrastructure.

On most of our missions, the flak was far and away more dangerous than the German fighters, but one place you could always count on seeing fighters was Brunswick. If you stayed in formation you were usually safe, but this time a German fighter managed to make it right through our formation. He was so close that I looked through the co-pilot's window and could see his oxygen mask. That was about as close as I ever wanted to get to one.

Probably the most memorable mission I flew was over Hamburg in August of 1944. It was very heavily defended and the flak just covered the sky. It was said that the flak was so thick, you could walk on it. We were shot up pretty badly on this mission, and one engine was shot out. On the way back, the plane was just marginal. I could look out the right and see Sweden. If we landed there, the war would be over for us. Sweden was neutral. They would have interned us until the end of the war. They would have treated us nicely and I have to say, it was a temptation. But I really didn't have any excuses, so we headed home.

When we were coming in for a landing, the hydraulic fluid was leaking, and we didn't think we had any brakes left. So, as was our policy, I had two of the men stationed at the windows with parachutes to slow down the plane. This was the emergency procedure, but luckily we didn't have to use it. When we got on the ground, we had enough fluid left to stop the plane. After we landed, we counted 92 holes in the plane, but no vital parts or nobody on board was hit.

Of all the missions we did, we had to come in alone four times. Oddly enough, two of them were in my last four missions. Each of these times an engine was shot out. When you're on three engines, you have to make a decision. You can either push the engines to keep up with the group, or you conserve your engines by falling out of formation and take the chance of making it on your own. I usually opted to slow down and conserve the engines. One of these times I remember being alone and feeling particularly vulnerable, and just then an American fighter showed up. He radioed, "Big friend, are you all right?" and I answered, "Little friend, I'm a lot better since you arrived." After that, I said that I'd buy a drink for any fighter pilot I met.

Jimmy Stewart was with the Second Air Force. He had a very good reputation and was a Princeton boy like me, but I never had the chance to meet him during the war. Many years later at a reunion, we were told that there was going to be a surprise. The Glenn Miller band played for us and during one of the songs, who stepped out to conduct them, but Jimmy Stewart. *(Stewart played Glenn Miller in the biographical movie.)*

I came home in late 1944 and pulled some strings to get assigned to the Air Transport Command. I flew C-54's to Paris two times a month. And the "Ruth Marie"?. It was taken over by another crew, and later crashed. I think it ran out of gas.

> *Johnson was discharged shortly after V-J Day in 1945. He received the Distinguished Flying Cross and the Air Medal with Three Clusters. He returned to work with American Airlines where he stayed for almost 40 years. Although Johnson was a First Lieutenant during his combat tour, he remained in the Air Force Reserve and retired as a Colonel. He remains an active member of the Power Squadron, the Western Connecticut Retired Officers Association, and teaches meteorology courses in the area.*

[1] "Stamford Girl Gives Hair for Bombsights". Stamford Advocate, December 21, 1943, p.7.

CHAPTER ELEVEN

D-DAY

By 1944, the Allies had pushed the Germans out of North Africa and had launched successful amphibious invasions of both Sicily and Italy. Hitler's forces were being defeated in the Third Reich's underbelly. Meanwhile, on the Eastern Front, Russian casualties were in the millions and growing. To take pressure off the Russians and to begin the push toward German soil, the Allies needed to open up a Second Front. Nothing less than an invasion of France would be needed.

However, the coast of France was well defended. For years Hitler used slave labor to construct the Atlantic Wall, a seemingly impregnable defense stretching almost 2400 miles along the coast of Europe. In particular, the coastline of northern France from Cherbourg to Calais was crowded with logs, steel beams, antitank weapons, mines, and other barriers designed to repel an Allied invasion. To add to allied pessimism, the natural topography of France made an assault difficult. Rugged coastline, cliffs, hedgerow, and the unpredictable waters of the English Channel would certainly impede any invasion.

Nevertheless, Allied leaders were called upon to plan a major invasion of France by 1944. Code named "Operation Overlord" the plan called for a massive assault along 59 miles of Normandy coastline.

In the early hours of June 6th, 1944, with rain falling in "horizontal sheets", the greatest amphibious invasion in history began. Thousands of seacraft, aircraft, and landing craft, along with thousands of paratroopers, infantry, and glider troops made their way toward the coast of Normandy. By dawn, the battle for French coastline was in full swing and although, at first, the invasion looked as though it would end in disaster, by the end of D-Day, the Allies had secured a hold on the beaches. Over the next few days, the Allies continued to pour onto the beaches and by the end of July almost one million troops had arrived.

By August the Allies had won the Battle for Normandy and less than one month later they liberated Paris. For Hitler and the Third Reich, it was the beginning of the end.

Photo courtesy of U.S. Coast Guard

- EDDIE PAGE -

As a member of the 82nd Airborne 507th Parachute Infantry, Eddie Page participated in four major campaigns including Central Europe, the jump across the Rhine, and the Battle of the Bulge. His first combat jump, however, took place in the wee hours of the morning on D-Day. Before the allied invasion at Normandy, the American Airborne divisions were supposed to be dropped inland and secure the port of Cherbourg. But a combination of cloud cover and intense antiaircraft fire created confusion and forced thousands of paratroopers to be dropped miles from their intended drop zone.

I went into the Airborne for the adventure and for the money. We got an extra 50 dollars a month for each month we jumped. In the spring of 1944 we were situated in Nottingham Forest in England training for the invasion. Every jump we made was in full gear and with full ammunition. We never really knew exactly which jump would be for real. Finally about a week before the invasion they told us, "This is it." They put up sand tables and told us that we'd be hitting the northern coast of France around Cherbourg. From this time on, we were confined to a hangar and guarded around the clock. Nobody was allowed in or out.

I don't know why, but the night of the invasion I wasn't frightened. I was concerned, I was intense, but for some strange reason I was not afraid. I remember looking around and seeing a sight that will probably never be seen again. It was like a wall of steel flying through the air — all of these planes. And over and around them were the P51s and P38s protecting us.

We were prepared so perfectly that going across the English Channel I recognized the Jersey Islands exactly as we saw them on the sand tables. Then below us we saw the flotilla that was getting ready to hit the coast of France, and then finally, we hit the coast of France. It was virtually silent but then as we got closer, "pow" the flak started coming up. Other planes were hit, some went down.

I was always the first guy out of the plane. Then I felt our plane get hit. I didn't know where or how bad it was, but it began to shudder and shake and vibrate. I saw other planes go down so I just yelled "let's go" and out I went. When I got out of the plane the worst feeling came over me. It was dark and all I could think of was, "Jesus Christ. Maybe I jumped all by myself. Oh my God." But then I looked around and there I could see "pop, pop" other parachutes opening up, coming out all around me. We were 20 miles off our drop zone and coming down behind enemy lines.

I was coming down all set to hit the ground and roll but the Germans had flooded the area and a lot of us landed in the water. Some of my buddies drowned in six or eight feet of water. With a hundred pounds of gear on they didn't have a chance. One of the guys was badly wounded. I didn't know what to do. I couldn't do anything for him. As part of our equipment we were given a morphine surret (syringe). I just pulled his out, and stuck it in his leg. I didn't know what else to do. Later we had to pull the dog tags off some of them so the Germans couldn't identify them. I landed in only about three feet of water and had to reach down and pull my rifle out of the muck. The first rule of the army was to keep your weapon clean and here mine was, mired at the bottom of the swamp.

On the ground we got a group together – about twelve of us. Some of them, I had never seen before. We went from swamp to some high ground, saw the steeple of a church and headed for that. On the way, we ran into a small house, and about four or five of us surrounded the house, kicked in the door, and charged in with our machine guns pointed. And there were two little old ladies in an old down feather bed so scared they couldn't even talk. We kept pointing to our sleeve saying, "Don't worry, we're American" and finally we just left.

We walked into a village and we grabbed a civilian and showed him a map. I put my flashlight on the map and motioned to him to point to where we were. He took his finger and pointed to a place off the map. We weren't even on the map! So we just folded it back up and put it away.

Within a day about 170 of us got together and organized. We were on the ground, probably six hours before the Allies were even set to hit the beaches, so we were on our own. From our vantage point we were stuck, so we stayed with the village. *(The French village was Graignes, located about ten miles from Carantan.)*

Every day and every night we'd patrol and see if we could find out what the hell was going on. We found out that Carantan was back in American hands and that the Germans were retreating down some of the roads. So we'd go out and do as much damage as we could. We had a few skirmishes with the enemy and even managed to blow a bridge. *(In his book Graignes: The Franco American Memorial, Gary Fox describes the bridge as being at a place called Port Des Planges.)*

The people of the village were so good to us. They helped us, they fed us and even hid us from the Germans. After a while the Germans knew we were there. In fact about a week later they sent in a battalion to get us. We were at Sunday mass and they came in and tore us up. We were running out of ammo and it was every man for himself. One group of Germans came pouring across a big field. We had a machine gunner on a roof and he just ran that gun dry. He was mowing them down but they just kept coming. He ran out of ammo and started to pull slate off the roof and throw it at them.

We all scattered. We had to try to get to Carantan. I was with two buddies hiding just outside the village. We must have been the last three Americans in Graignes because at daybreak I decided to check and see what was going on. I told my buddies to stay where they were. I was going up there to look for food. I was about to walk across a field but decided that I'd better stay close to the hedgerow. When I was near the center of town. I could see two soldiers behind an American machine gun. I thought they were American and was going to walk right up to them. But then a third solder walked out of a building eating what I though was an American K-ration. As he turned around I could see all the black gear on his back. "Germans" I thought, and I ran like a son of a bitch. I thought for sure that they saw me and were going to start shooting. They didn't. I got back to my buddies and yelled, "There is a town full of Germans. Let's get the hell out of here."

After we scattered out of the village we found a civilian who took us to a barn. In the hayloft there were another few paratroopers hiding. They fed us for about four or five days. One day a German came right up to the barn and walked right in. I pulled the pin out of a hand grenade and just clenched it. The guy finally left and my hand was shaking so bad I said, "Hey guys, help me get this pin back in."

A few days later a young French fellow took us to a huge rowboat and up the river toward Carantan. Carantan kept changing hands between the Americans and Germans so he just let us off a few miles away. We got challenged on the outskirts of town but finally found our way back.

A few years ago we went to Europe. I told my wife, "I don't care where we go but I have to go to Graignes." I wrote ahead of time and when I got there a woman came up and hugged me and started crying. She was one of the young girls who helped hide us from the Germans. She was only sixteen or seventeen the last time I saw her. We both cried. Later she took me to a boatyard and said "Does that look familiar to you?" And there it was, a huge black rowboat, the one that took us to Carantan. I could still see exactly where I was sitting in that boat. The people were great to us and we still write to them. *(The woman's name is Odette Lalavachef.)*

After we escaped from Graignes the Germans came in and destroyed the place. They took two priests, slit their throats, and killed our wounded paratroopers and over 30 civilians. Just murdered them. Not war. Murder.

They also took a century old church and just blew the hell out of it. Four of my buddies were killed there. There's still part of it left and inside there's a memorial for the civilians and paratroopers that were killed. *(The Germans punished Graignes severely for assisting the Americans. Over the next three weeks they murdered 24 wounded paratroopers, 32 civilians, and jailed 44 citizens. In addition to this 66 homes were destroyed and 159 damaged. Only 2 houses in the village remained intact. On July 18, 1944, Graignes was finally liberated by the Allies.)*[1]

When we got to Carantan I thought they'd say, "Oh These guys are heroes" and send us home. Instead, they fed us, gave us clean clothes, new weapons and off we went to St. Lo. We just kept on going. Outside of St. Lo there were some Germans trapped in a valley and we were hitting them from the air. One day this big guy with a shellacked helmet comes walking up with a bunch of officers. It was Patton. We had been fighting our hump off and he says, "You guys take that valley and then I'll take over." "He'll take over?" I said. Son of a gun. He did just what he said he'd do. By the time we got back to England he was almost to Paris.

While I was at Normandy I met an officer from Stamford named Ken Ballard. He was a big athlete in town. One night he went out on patrol and was shot in the stomach. I saw him on a stretcher. He was pea green. I was sure he'd never make it. When I got back to Stamford after the war I went up to Boucher's restaurant and who was behind the bar? Ken Ballard. Two weeks later, he was killed in a car crash.

Before I jumped on D-Day I met another guy from Stamford. One day a Platoon Sergeant came up to me and introduced himself. His name was Harry LaChance. He had al-

Page and Odette Lalavachef reunited in 1991

ready jumped in Sicily and Italy, and said he wanted to give me a little advice. "Don't try to be a hero. Do your job and watch out for your own ass." I spent the rest of the day with him, we talked and off we both went. After Normandy, when we went back to England I went over to C-Company and asked if Harry LaChance was around. They told me he had been killed. When I went back to France in 1991 I visited Carantan and St. Mere Eglese. My brother-in-law and I walked down to the cemetery. All we could see was rows and rows of stones. Something drew me over to one and I looked at it. It said Sgt. Harry LaChance, 82nd Airborne, Connecticut. That was the only stone I read in the whole cemetery. (*From England, Eddie was then sent back to Belgium during the Battle of the Bulge.*)

We left on Christmas Eve, 1944. They flew us outside of Bastogne to relieve the 101st that was trapped there. That was great, the guys were in bad shape. Surrounded, cold, dysentery, trench feet. It was just great to make contact. We fought our way through the Ardennes and down to Luxembourg. That winter was the coldest in 20 years. Some mornings you'd get out of your foxhole and your joints were frozen. You could hardly move. We had to fight the Germans the whole way and you hardly ever slept. They gave us benzedrene tablets to keep us awake but you didn't need them. Most of the time you couldn't sleep. The fear takes over. I just cut two holes in my sleeping bag for my feet and pulled it up around me. I wore it like that all day. (*In March of 1945 Page took part in the jump across the Rhine. Known as Operation Varsity, this was the largest single airdrop in history.*)

The 507th was supposed to spearhead the drive across the Rhine. It was a morning jump, just before noon. As we got close to the Rhine, you could hear the artillery and anti-aircraft going off. On D-Day, you had night cover but this time you could see what was going on. It was just like the movies. You could see everything happening at once.

We actually made our jump at only 300 feet. This was the lowest I ever jumped. If you didn't do everything just right you were dead. Again I yelled, "Let's go" and out we went. I cringed as I was going down. I was waiting to get hit by something. But this time we landed safely at the far end of the drop zone.

We were warned that the civilians would fight us to the death but one of the first things we did was take a castle in Munster where the Germans had retreated. We took hundreds of prisoners including women and children but we had no problems with any of them. We went through Munster and Essen, and then they pulled us back into France. While I was there a buddy talked me into signing up for six more months of duty in Berlin. The war had ended and he told me to bring a lot of watches. When I got to Berlin, the city was leveled. The Russians had annihilated everything. The Russians were paid and had nothing to do with their money, so I sold my first watch to one of them for $1500 invasion currency.

While I was in Berlin I used to go to a German dentist. The last time I went to him I told him that I would be going back home. I'll never forget what he said to me. He said, "You wait. You'll be back here again. Next time to fight the Russians." He was right, in a way.

Page was wounded three times in action, surviving a concussion, shrapnel, and a bullet wound in the chest. We was awarded the Purple Heart and the Bronze Star for "meritorious service in the European Theater of Action." His unit, the 507th, won a Presidential Unit Citation, the French Croix de Guerre, and the Belgian Croix de Guerre. In 1992 he was named the "507th Paratrooper of the Year" and is only the third recipient of this award.

- JOHN JAY GINTER, Jr. -

John Ginter was one of four brothers to serve his country during the Second World War. As a member of the 92nd Troop Carrier Squadron, he flew over 200 missions transporting paratroopers, towing gliders and supplies throughout Europe. He participated in seven major campaigns including the Invasions of Southern France, Holland, and the Ardennes.

On D-Day, John was an Aerial Engineer on a C-47 which was part of the airborne assault that brought paratroopers into France five hours before the invasion of Normandy.

When the war broke out, I was working at Luder's Shipbuilders in Stamford seven days a week. I had a deferment because I was working in a "vital industry" but I decided to enlist anyway. I ended up as part of the 92nd Troop Carrier Squadron. We got to England in March of 1944 and trained constantly in simulated paradrops and glider towing. We were up all hours of the day and night. All we did was TRAIN, TRAIN, TRAIN.

We used a C-47 which General Arnold called the "aerial mule." The C-47 was a vulnerable aircraft. It had no armor and no self sealing gas tanks. So, if we were hit by anything that caused a spark, we'd just explode. Later we found out that the projected casualty rate for this plane was about 70%, but they never told us that. We had regular airfields in Chateaudun, Cherbourg, and Verdun. Most of the time we landed in wide open fields. All we asked of the people on the ground was to run heavy equipment across the field to make sure it didn't sink. Then, in we'd go. it was a rare occasion when we'd go up to 10,000 feet. Most of our paratroop drops were between 500-700 feet and in addition to the paratroops we'd often carry 6 bundles on the pararacks which were underneath the plane. These bundles contained supplies, rations, ammunition, antitank mines, and grenades. In Giessen, Germany we carried 115 5-gallon cans of gasoline to General Patton. This was in addition to 800 gallons of gasoline that we had in our own tanks. Later we were told that when Patton saw us he said "Look at those sons of bitches. I could kiss every one of their asses. They have my gas."

On June 4, 1944, we went into a briefing. That's when they told us that we'd be going into Normandy. Then they put us into a high security compound with armed guards. Now we finally knew where we were going. At the briefing, we were issued an escape pouch that contained French money, area maps made of silk and a photograph. The photo was taken five days earlier. The French underground would issue false identification in the event that we were shot down. We were briefed in escape tactics with a code enclosed.

The June 4th invasion was postponed 24 hours due to bad weather, but once we had the D-Day secret, we were put in a heavily armed, guarded compound. On the night of June 5th, we got the go-ahead. We were hauled out in 6x6 trucks. We got to the airfield (*in Upottery, England*) and picked up a "stick" of paratroopers

(*18 troopers*). We were all nervous. The paratroops were nervously milling around, constantly urinating under the wing, chain smoking, checking each others chutes and gear, short-tempered, and worried if the "GREASE GUN" would perform. (*This grease gun was the newest issue of a machine gun with a folding handle replacing the Thompson*). I sensed their behavior when I checked out the pararack triggers for the proper sequence of release. We loaded and locked the pararacks, preflighted the engines. Finally, we took off at 2325 hours.

Normally, in a sealed cabin you would hear loud talking. But that night SILENCE – just the engines' roar. I surmised that each of us was communing with himself, reliving the past and thinking of loved ones we had left back in the States, . . like a Communion with death. Normally with a gang like that you'd hear a lot of noise in the cabin. But that night, nothing. Just the roar of the engines.

I was an aerial engineer. When it was time to drop the paratroopers I'd be near the cargo door and my job was to see that every one of them made it out. If someone froze, I was supposed to kick them out...or shoot them.

We were each issued a .45 shoulder holster pistol. Because I was wearing a chute, I would strap the gun onto my leg. We also had a sub-machine gun in the plane and I set it up so that if I had to bail out I would be able to take it with me. I'd keep six clips of cartridges strapped to my legs.

On the way to France we had a series of checkpoints. The first few ADA and ELKO were land radio signals. Then to Portland Bell, a lighthouse, the Gallup, a Navy ship sending out a beacon. At Hoboken, we turned and I checked the time. We picked up speed due to a tail wind. I removed the jump door. That's when we saw the first flak from the Alderny Islands and it was pretty heavy. At first I thought we weren't going to get it because they didn't have our range yet. Then as we got to the Guernsey and Jersey Islands, we saw even more. It was really heavy there, then it settled down like nothing happened. We entered France at St. George de le Riviere and for the first 8 miles it was quiet. Two groups went in before us and the German air defenses didn't pick them up. They were unscathed.

Then when we got there it really opened up and all hell broke loose. Our drop zone was near Blosville and as we approached it was like the Fourth of July tenfold. All you saw was red, green, yellow, and blue tracers – like fireworks. The Germans had timers in their shells and they would explode at certain altitudes. They called it flak because that's exactly the sound it made...flak...flak. Finally they zeroed in on us and that's when they started to knock some of our planes down.

Two hours before we went in, groups of Pathfinders (troopers) were supposed to set markers out in the fields for us. These markers would show us where to drop. But when we got to our drop zone there were no markers so we had to find it by following radio signals sent out by the Pathfinders. "Rebecca" was one signal and "Gee" was another. The Germans had jammed the "Gee", so we tried to stay between both signals to make the drop. I am not sure why "Gee" was jammed. It was jammed for 30 miles and cleared up. Also, as a guide to the DZ (dropzone) we used landmarks as per the mockup at the briefing. Our DZ was west of Blosville, some of the sticks landed near Sainte Mere du Mont.

At precisely 1:15 a.m. I jumped the troopers between Hiesville and Blosville. Then I saw a big orange fireball coming straight at us. I was sure that we were going to get hit. It was about 2 or 3 feet in diameter and I just looked at it, mesmerized, praying, scared. Miraculously, it missed us. Then it hit the plane right behind us – a direct hit. It lit up the sky and disintegrated. The pilot's name

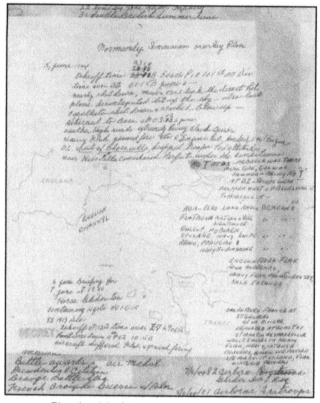

Ginter's original invasion map for June 6, 1944

was Muir. Then Capelluto's plane on the other side got hit, crashed and blew up. The flak seemed to be concentrated in one area. After that, we got hit in the right engine. I'm not sure if it was flak or small arms fire.

We departed Normandy and headed for our checkpoints. On the way out we caught more flak from Marcouf Island. The right engine began to overheat. We were all crowded up in the front of the plane like small children trying to console each other. No words were spoken. We were all frightened but we still had to do our jobs. The oil pressure was dropping slowly and the engine was about to seize up. So I cut the right engine power, we saw land and slowly limped in with the left engine doing the work (this same engine was hit and knocked out on another mission), however, we landed in friendly territory. We were hit in the oil cooler and landing gear strut.

We were all shook up when we landed. They took us into interrogation and forced us to swallow a half a tin of alcohol. It was a hot room and pretty soon you settled right down. They interrogated us at about 3:30 a.m. and then I went right to sleep.

We thought we wouldn't be flying again, but the next day we went right back out. This time we were towing English Horsa gliders into Normandy. Each of the gliders was carrying 30 or so troopers. We released the gliders in about the same place that we dropped the troopers. We went right over Utah Beach and this time it was quite a chaotic scene. There were so many ships below, it was unbelievable. Barage Balloons were everywhere and the troops were running around like ants. We had no idea that what we were witnessing was historic. We were just doing our jobs. There was no real flak this time, just small arms fire. The biggest danger was that one of the navy ships would shoot us down like what happened at Gela (Sicily). We were ordered to paint black & white 18 inches wide stripes on the rear fuselage as a precaution against friendly forces shooting us down.

After D- Day we flew primarily supply missions. On July 23 we flew into Sainte Mere-Eglise with ammunition. As we were loading the wounded soldiers into our plane for the return trip, this big tall Frenchman walked up to us. The officers that were with him started to ask us questions but we just wanted them out of the way because we had critically wounded guys to deal with. The big tall Frenchman turned out to be Charles DeGaulle.

The drop in LeMuy, France, was a champagne run compared to Normandy. We did get some flak and when we landed in Italy I saw that the propeller had been hit. There were no other propellers available so I spent hours filing the propellers until the blades were perfectly balanced. That's what we call American ingenuity.

(*For the next few months Ginter flew many missions into France and Italy transporting medical supplies, plasma, rations, artillery shells, and wounded soldiers. In August of 1944, he participated in the invasion of Southern France and later Holland and the Ardennes*)

On December 23, 1944, just as the Battle of the Bulge was starting we were supposed to pick up the 17th Airborne in England and fly them to Prum (on the border of Germany and Belgium). We loaded them up on Christmas Eve but the weather got bad and ice began to form on the wings. So we landed at Chateaudun (FR) and decided to do what we could to entertain the guys. We picked up some Vin Mousse and Cognac and they had a great time — our Christmas present to them. On Christmas Day we landed them in a cow pasture in Germany.

The last bad mission we flew was during the invasion of Holland. This was our longest flight over enemy territory. It was a beautiful fall day and we were flying so low that people were waving to us. We were carrying the Parachute Infantry of the 82nd airborne. We got hit with some flak on the way over but we dropped our "stick" of troopers exactly on the drop zone.

I came back to the states in 1945 and my wife and I had a son. One day my friend Major General Charlie Imschweiler came to visit me. He was the pilot of our plane and we flew every single mission together. He was having trouble finding work in Pennsylvania and was begging me to re-enlist with him. He said, "Gint, we'll have our own plane. Nobody will be shooting at us. It will be like a vacation." I took him into my son's room and we both looked at my son. I said, "Charlie, this son of mine is going to be famous someday and I'm going to dedicate myself to him."

> *By the time the war ended, John had participated in eight campaigns and received one Silver Service Star, two Bronze Service Stars, the Air Medal with two Oak Leaf Clusters, and two Croix de Guerre with Palm Leaf for "Valor Above and Beyond the Call of Duty." When he returned he joined The Electric Service Company and later opened "Jay's TV Service," which he operated for over thirty years until his retirement.*

- THE "WILLING SLAVE" -

Ginter had sketched out the name "Willing Slave" and logo onto the side of his C-47 but never had the time to formally paint the name onto the side of the plane. After over 125 missions with the same plane Ginter's crew was given a new plane, a C-47B and later a new C-46.

After the War, the original plane changed hands several times ending up with Scandanavian Airlines, Piedmont Airline, the Spanish Air Corps, and finally with the French Navy. The plane was used as a navigational Trainer until it was finally retired in 1983. That same year, a Frenchman, Yves Tariel, who was 10 years old at the time of the Normandy Invasion, decided that he wanted to do something to commemorate the great event. When he built an Airborne Museum in Sainte Mere Eglise, the French Ministry donated Ginter's C-47. Today it stands in a separate building in the museum, restored to the way it looked in 1944. The name Ginter is visible on the nose of the plane and although a sign on one of the engines identifies it as "Willing Slave" that name has not yet made its way onto the side of the plane.

- WALTER WESTCOTT -

Walter Westcott enlisted in the U.S. Navy in November of 1942 and was assigned to the Naval Amphibious Force. As a Motor Machinist Mate aboard an LST (Landing Ship Tank), he was involved in the initial landings at Utah Beach on D-Day and made several other landings at the Normandy beaches.

I went overseas in 1943 and was stationed in Wales, Plymouth, England, and finally at Southhampton, which became our base. I was assigned to LST 294 and that was my duty until the end of the war. Our job was to transfer men and supplies to the beaches. Later we took German prisoners back to England. Our ship was about 300 feet long, and we had a crew of about 115 and could carry around 400 infantry troops.

All the while we were in England, we knew we were going to be involved in something big, but we had absolutely no idea where it was going to be. In fact, even when we were on our way, we didn't know where we were going—at least the enlisted guys didn't know. We had done so many drills in the channel and hit so many beaches, it was tough to know when the real thing was coming. But when we saw all the soldiers come aboard with live ammunition, we pretty well knew that this was it—we were scared silly.

We actually landed on the seventh of June. It was dark and stormy. We hit Utah Beach with men and supplies. We didn't have the terror or the danger that the infantry had, but we could have been hit at any time. Going in, we did lose one of our smaller boats, a LCVP (Landing Craft Vehicle Personnel) with 25 men on it.

I don't remember all of the details of that day. There are a lot of things I've tried hard not to think about. A lot of the time we were busy just trying to keep the engines running. I also had to operate the ramp crank and at times assist some of the soldiers off the craft.

When I was off duty – I think the schedule was two hours on, two off–I went up top. There was a lot of confusion. Some of the boats stopped too short. There is no way to describe what it looked like; no picture, not even a panorama, can capture it. Dogfights, planes, balloons, bombs dropping, things going in all directions. I'll never forget, one of our planes was hit and crashed right into an ammunition dump on the beach. There was a huge explosion and a lot of people were killed in accidents like that. You couldn't possibly see everything that was going on. You'd be looking in one direction, and there would be a hundred things happening in another direction. We actually thought we'd get hit by one of the planes that was shot down. One landed right next to us. But we were lucky. We made a lot of runs, maybe a dozen, maybe twenty, and we weren't hit.

Later on, around the fourteenth or fifteenth of June, we had to take a shipload of German prisoners with us—about three or four hundred. Like anything else, there were a few troublemakers. We had an officer who tried to instigate a riot.

We used to have to lock him in the head to isolate him. He was kind of arrogant. Occasionally he'd yell something at us in German, but other than that, he did not speak a word to us. When we got back to England, I was the one who had to take him ashore. When I finally handed him over, he turned to me and said in perfect English, "Thank you, young man, for your kind and considerate treatment." For the most part though, the Germans were kids just like us and scared the same way I would have been if I was captured.

Once when we were on the beach with the ramp down, I heard a noise like I never heard before—loud and scary. My first response was to run as far as I could. It turned out to be a buzz bomb. It sounded almost like a motorcycle. We saw more of them, and they always scared the hell out of me.

For the next few weeks, we shuttled back and forth. We hit about every beach except the British beaches. Later we spent time in the harbor at Le Havre. You could actually look down and see all of the mines in the harbor. What a sight!

Later, in May of 1945, we went to Hamburg to pick up some American and British officers to help liberate Norway. We were told that when the Germans were defeated, they would not surrender to soldiers of lesser rank. Evidently the Norwegians did not have a fleet of officers and soldiers to formally accept the surrender. It was a little scary because the Germans were still armed.

That summer, I came back to the states, and on August 8, 1945, I was married.

Mr. Westcott married his sweetheart, Mabel Burnes, of Stamford whom he had met in 1943 while on leave with his friend. He has lived here since the war and was employed as a carpenter before going to work for Pitney Bowes.

- MICKEY DONOHUE -

Mickey Donohue was one of the most promising boxers to come out of Stamford. As a welterweight he had fought all over New England and won the Westchester Diamond Gloves Championship. When he entered the Army, he had already been boxing professionally and later became a member of the Army Boxing Team. At the same time, his brother Tommy, another local fighter, was the Pacific Fleet Heavyweight Champion.

On June 6, 1944, Mickey was seriously wounded during the invasion of Normandy. His dreams of a boxing career were ended when he suffered spinal injuries and was confined to a wheelchair for the rest of his life.

- HARRY VANECH -

Harry Vanech graduated from Stamford High School in 1938 and went to work at the Stamford Rolling Mill. In early 1941 he enlisted in the Army Air Corps and became a pilot with the 98th Troop Carrier Squadron. On D-Day he was among the first of the airplanes to cross the Cherbourg Peninsula. Before the war was over he would fly scores of other missions including the Holland and Rhine jumps.

I was originally trained as a fighter pilot in the single engine planes. But about that same time in 1943 they formed the Troop Carrier Squadrons. So they took our entire class, transferred us to that, and trained us to fly C-47's.

We spent several weeks at Fort Bragg training with the Airborne Divisions and then in January of 1944 we were sent to England. We practiced our formations and drops for months. After a while we knew we would be dropping paratroopers over France but of course we didn't have any idea of exactly when we'd be doing it. We also knew it was going to be a big drop because we were put into a large command of about 1000 planes.

We were told what our mission was two days before the drop and everyone was confined to the base. We had a full briefing the day before and we left about midnight on the morning of June 6, 1944. There were so many planes that it took us a long time to get all of them in the air and into formation. When we flew across the English Channel we had boats that flashed signals to us from below.

I think that the most frightening thing about the invasion was the weather. We had to make the drop about 1:30 AM and the weather was terrible. We had to fly in real tight formation and we had to fly low at about 500 feet. The bad part of it was that there was a solid overcast below and no lights below. We had no references whatsoever. You were always afraid that you were going to fly into someone and all you had to go by were the blue lights on each wing. If the plane in front of you dropped its speed, you had to adjust accordingly. But in the bad weather you couldn't tell exactly how far away you were. At some points you were only 15 or 20 feet away. We had to fly in such tight formation because we had to drop the paratroopers as close together as possible.

When we left England we were told to maintain a speed of 145 miles per hour and then once we reached the continent, we were supposed to drop down to 110 mph. because you couldn't drop the paratroopers at high speed. But when the planes up front dropped speed what happened was that everybody else began to gang up. So we had to chop our power and for a while some of us were flying just a few miles per hour above stall speed.

All the way over we were supposed to maintain radio silence but at one point one of the guys in the plane came over the radio and yelled that he was stalling out. He told us to increase our speed. You just couldn't cruise at that low speed and I was fighting a stall myself so what I had to do was drop my landing gear and dump both of my flaps. Then I could increase the engine power. This gave me a little more lift but still, a few times I had to pull out, increase my speed, and then fly back in again. This was the only way you could avoid overrunning the plane in front of you.

Even before we hit the mainland you could see the tracers being fired up. I don't think there was a plane that night that didn't come back with at least one hole in it. Every time you saw a tracer come up you knew there was at least 4 or 5 other bullets with it. The danger here was that one of the tracers would hit the fuel tank. The planes were supposed to have self sealing tanks but they didn't. They weren't installed until after the war.

We finally got over the drop zone and at the signal we dropped our paratroopers over Tarantan, which was right near the Ste Mere Eglise. At the time we dropped them we were only flying about 75 miles per hour. We were very vulnerable at this point because you were close to a stall and you were an easy target. I never knew what happened to the guys we dropped that night. I took it upon myself to try and find out about them but I couldn't. Later we got reports that a lot of the men were dropped into the water because the Germans had flooded the area. To this day I wish I knew what happened to them.

We flew another mission on D-Day but this one was in broad daylight at about 7:30 A.M. This second run was to resupply the men and this time the Germans knew we were coming. We were so low that we could actually see the guys below shooting at us. But as soon as we dropped our load we got the plane up to 200 miles an hour and got out of there. Then once we were over water again we'd get back into formation.

I couldn't tell you exactly how many total missions I flew, but we dropped paratroopers, supplies, and even towed gliders. For a while we were flying gasoline to General Patton. We'd carry over a hundred "Jerry cans", which were 5 gallon cans of gasoline in our tanks; all you needed was one well placed hit and it was all over. We did this almost every day for a while and during this time it was absolutely impossible to get an accurate weather forecast. In Europe, from one hour to the next the weather could change. But we had to get him the gas at all costs and about 95% of the time we were successful at it.

One of the missions I most remember was at Mortain (France). There was a Battalion that was surrounded by Germans. The Americans were up on a hill right near a church. They were outnumbered and needed supplies badly and our squadron was picked for this mission. We were able to get them the food, ammunition and medical supplies they needed and they were able to hold off the Germans. *(This mission took place in August of 1944 and although there was dense flak and German small arms fire all 12 planes returned safely).*

The Rhine and Holland jumps were, in their own way, just as hairy as D-Day. In Holland we had to fly over 400 miles over enemy territory. We lost one plane there and one during the Rhine crossing, but fortunately we got both crews back.

In Holland we also towed gliders. On the glider missions your formation was much more spread out. We towed the gliders on a rope about 200 feet long and you had two formations, ours and the gliders. The most difficult part about these was finding the right field. In Holland they all looked alike. Someone on the ground was supposed to fire a smoke signal to indicate the correct field. Then, the glider pilots could determine the best landing direction by watching which way the smoke blew. These guys were a courageous bunch. Once they were cut loose they were probably flying only 50 to 80 miles an hour — just hovering there, so easy to pick off. While they were being towed they were also sitting ducks because if an enemy plane approached you couldn't take an evasive action.

I flew the same plane on every mission. The C-47 was a remarkable plane. It could take a lot of punishment. If it was damaged they'd just patch it up. Once, over the Rhine we were hit by a 20 mm shell. This was the closest we came to being destroyed. It blew a big hole in the plane but a few feet either way and it would have hit our gas tanks.

When the end of the war came most of my friends decided to stay in the Air-Corps. I decided against it. I was anxious to get home back to my wife and to my little daughter who was born just before I went overseas.

Harry Vanech logged over 1500 hours in the C-47 and received the Air Medal with Oak Leaf Cluster. He worked at Pitney Bowes for several years until his retirement in 1983. One of his passionate hobbies is rebuilding and refurbishing World War II planes. At present he owns two, one of them a BT-13 that he still regularly flies.

- EUGENE GODLIN -

Eugene Godlin graduated from Stamford High School in 1941 and joined the Navy the following year. He became a Signalman 2nd Class in the Amphibious Forces and as a crew member on LST 359 he participated in the landings at Tunisia, Sicily, Salerno, Anzio, and finally Omaha Beach on D-Day.

I was sent to Arzew in North Africa in 1943 and our first landing was in Tunisia between Bizerte and Tunis. In Arzew, some of the bombing raids were frightening. The bombs sounded like sirens as they came down and one night when I was in sick bay with a fever, the bombs were hitting all around. I remember the sweat dripping off me and the bombs sounding like they were getting closer and closer. A few days later when I was better, I went outside and there were these big holes in the ground all around the sick bay. As we went in I remember a lot of ships, mostly German, that were sunk in the Bay. It was just about impossible for a ship with a keel to get to the beaches. German bombers were overhead and all you could do was take in the action, like watching a show. The American searchlights were zeroing in on the bombers and knocking them out of the sky.

Our next operation was Sicily. This was really our first major invasion and there were hundreds of ships as far as the eye could see. We made our initial landing at Licata after a stormy trip, and as the troops moved up the coast, we'd make our landings further and further up the coast. Our Captain, Jimmy Ferreola, volunteered us for two landings behind enemy lines at a town called Milazzo in Northern Sicily. On the second landing, our troops were among the first to enter Messina. Ferreola was a fiery guy, very excitable, and very impatient. Before the landings, he told us that he'd volunteered us for these missions and said, "If anybody doesn't want to go, I'll put you ashore now." Well, nobody wanted to back out, not so much out of patriotism, but more because no one dared to ask to be put ashore. I wouldn't have put it past him to dump us off in the middle of nowhere or maybe even an island occupied by the enemy.

The Salerno invasion was particularly difficult because the German planes kept diving at us. Then, at one point after we landed, we were told that the Germans were counterattacking and were pushing the Americans back to the beach. So we actually spent a few days on the beach and were told not to unload until we got further instructions. We were carrying airborne troops and I remember them saying, "If we get hit, we're going to need these parachutes" because we were carrying lots of ammunition and high octane gasoline. We were desperate to get the high octane gas and ammunition off the ship. We were not high and dry, so we finally formed a human chain and in the middle of the night, in water up to our waists, we passed the gasoline drums and ammunition along until it got ashore. Almost everyone got in on it. Even some officers, who didn't have to, stripped to the waist to unload the ship. It was quite a sight I'll never forget.

The Germans really surprised us here because normally, before they came in, we'd be warned over the radio. But here we never got any advance notice. They just surprised us. The sun was at our backs and when we were on the beach the planes just came at us right out of the sun and dove on us. One time I was on the bridge when a bomb hit right near the tail end of the ship in about five feet of water. Ferreola and I were next to each other and we both hit the deck and were covered with sand. We pinched ourselves to see if we were all right, and then he looked at me and said, "I saw St. Peter that time." Then he got up, went into the wheel room and grabbed a gun. Then he went around to each gun crew and said that if he caught anyone of them not looking into the sun, he was going to shoot them.

When we made a landing, we'd usually go in and help pick up the wounded. Before this, I could never stand the sight of blood, but after a while you got used to seeing everything. We were told never to stay too close to another LST, because you were too easy a target, and while we were at Salerno an LST right next to us took a direct hit from an incendiary bomb. We took in the wounded and it was just terrible. The stench of burned human flesh was very bad and never quite left the compartments where the men stayed before we got them to a hospital.

On the second trip, we went back to Oran and loaded up the First Armored Division. I never made it a habit of listening to the radio, but one day "Axis Sally" came on and said that she knew the First Armored Division was on its way to Italy and that they were all going to be killed. At sundown, we joined a convoy and were attacked by torpedo planes and subs. The planes were circling around the convoy making it difficult to fire on them without hitting another one of our own ships. That night, our commander told us that if we were sunk, we would be responsible for our Signal Books. If we couldn't save them, we were to keep them from the Germans by putting them in a sea bag, tying it with lead line, and throwing it overboard. So many ships were getting hit that we had the books all ready to go, but luckily we were not hit. To me, Salerno was the worst because just when you thought it was getting quiet, the action would pick up.

After Salerno, when we made our practice invasion for Anzio, which was staged at night, some of the men were dropped in water that was too deep. I knew this because the signal for this was three red lights, one over the other. That night the water was filled with red lights. We heard men yelling for help all night. We were able to pick up a few of them, but from what we heard later, a lot of men were lost that night.

Altogether we made 23 trips into Anzio. There was only a small port there and when we made our initial landing, it seemed like it was going to be easy. But after a while, the Germans began shelling us and we pulled up a lot of shrapnel. Fortunately, we never had a direct hit. The port at Anzio would only accommodate one LST and one or two smaller landing craft at a time. We got shelled every time we went in. The Germans had a railroad track in the middle of a mountain and they'd wheel out a big gun. Then it would go back into the mountain when our aircraft went over and bombed them. Our modus operandi was to come back with the wounded and German prisoners.

After Anzio, we went to England. I can't remember when we were told we were going to make a landing, but for a long time we made a lot of practice runs. Any one of them could have been the real thing, but we didn't know until we were well underway. One day, before Normandy, the Captain said to me, "Godlin, we're going to Omaha." I said, "Oh boy, we're going home?", and he said, "No, we're going to Omaha Beach." Going into Omaha Beach, it was clearly the biggest invasion force of them all. We were getting fire from the beaches, and it was landing close to us but it was almost like God had ordained that they would come close without hitting us.

We went in one time on the first day and altogether over the next month we made nine landings at Normandy. But at about 10:45 on July 12, we were hit by a magnetic mine. I was scheduled to go on watch and was down below brushing my teeth. I was talking to one of my shipmates and he was telling me how one of our sister ships was hit and the crew got shore leave. I joked that it would be nice if we took a little hit and got a little time off. I just finished saying that and BOOM! I don't remember what happened next, but I slammed into the sink. The lights and mirrors exploded. Then, I was lifted up and must have hit the ceiling because I was knocked unconscious. When I came to, everything was pitch black and I was laying in a few inches of water. Two guys ran right over me. I managed to get up and get on deck and they put me on a stretcher. The ship was taking in a lot of water, but they pumped it out and got it back to England. I was put up in a British hospital and then later in an American hospital. (*Godlin remained in the hospital for 5 weeks for injuries to his head, neck and stomach. Twenty eight others were injured when LST 359 hit a German mine.*)

When I got out of the hospital, I rejoined the crew in Scotland and from there we were going to be towed back to the states to do a War Bond tour. On December 20, 1944, while we were underway, we were hit again. This time by a submarine. I had just finished an 8 hour shift on watch and was in my bunk when we were torpedoed. The concussion threw me out of the bunk and into a locker. We were hit in mid-ship. I ran like hell to get on the bridge and then I remembered the signal books. They were supposed to be on the bridge, but someone had taken them down to the officer's quarters. So I ran down below and grabbed them. It was dark and eery down there and the ship was making screeching noises and tipping back and forth, so I grabbed them, put them in a bag, and threw them over to the tug.

On the bridge, a few of us saw a periscope sticking up on our starboard quarter. It was incredibly close and some of our men shot at it, but even though it was close we couldn't hit it. Our main blinking signal lights were inoperable, so I immediately ran up a flag hoist saying, "Periscope on our starboard quarter." Then I found a smaller signal light that we used on invasions and used it to send signals to the U.S.S. Fogg, a destroyer that was nearby. They were reading me with the signal light and were heading for the periscope when they were also hit by a torpedo. They weren't sunk, but I later found out that they lost 22 men. Anyway, the Fogg and another destroyer in the convoy dropped depth charges and thought they sunk the sub.

The water was rough and we had to hop over to the seagoing tug one by one, and the tug took us over to a cargo ship, the U.S.S. Mattole. But some guys were still trapped in the engine room on board, so the Captain ordered a welder to go and cut them out. Once they cut through the deck, they were able to save a few men who were hanging onto the pipes. Two men were still trapped down below and died. One of them had just turned 18 and just joined the crew. As we sailed away on the reserve ship, our ship was a sorrowful sight. The colors were at half mast – I had lowered them. The ship lumbered, split in half, and was sinking. Tears were running down my face and I was embarrassed, but when I turned around everyone else was crying as the ship went down. In addition to losing the men, there was something about losing an inanimate object that was almost like losing a friend, especially one that got us through so much.

Gene attended college on the G.I. Bill and majored in accounting. After graduating from the University of Bridgeport, he went to work for the Internal Revenue Service for almost 40 years until his retirement. Godlin received the Purple Heart, 5 Battle Stars, the Presidential Unit Citation, and the Navy Commendation Medal.

- A TIMELY REUNION -

Godlin later related another story about the Anzio landing.

"*Just before going into Anzio, I opened a hatch and a paratrooper was coming down the ladder. We got to talking and he said he was from Stamford. I said, 'I can't believe it. I'm from Stamford, too.' I wished him well and when I got home after the war I meant to look him up and find out how he made out, but I couldn't remember the name.*"

In May of 1994, fifty years later at a Veteran's gathering at Darien High School, Godlin told this story in front of the audience. From the back

of the audience, a voice said loudly, "That was me." It was John Kaslikowski, a member of the 82nd Airborne, who was in atten- dance with his brother Stan. As the two embraced after, Godlin said, "Glad you made it through."

Kaslikowski and Godlin in 1994

- CLEMENT TURPIN -

Clem Turpin enlisted in the Army in January of 1941, before the United States entered the war and was assigned to the 2nd Division, 23rd Infantry Regiment. Between June 1944 and May of 1945, the 2nd Division spent 337 days in combat and traveled 1750 miles across Europe. Turpin landed at Omaha Beach on June 7, 1944, subsequently participated in five campaigns, and was wounded twice.

When I enlisted, I requested the Coast Artillery, but after basic training in Fort Mead, Maryland, the men were separated and went where the Army needed them. I had seen a Sergeant wearing an Indian Head insignia patch and I thought, "That's the outfit for me!" Sure enough, that's where they sent me – the 2nd Infantry Division. I was sent to Fort Sam Houston, Texas, and then on to Dodd Field, an old Air Force base where they trained flyers in WWI. Here we trained for five weeks in mud that stuck like glue. In the summer, we ran maneuvers to Louisiana, training in swamps. We received Ranger training which gave us excellent preparation for combat. We learned Judo, Karate, map reading, climbing, how to disarm mines, bayonet, airborne training, how to use all kinds of weapons, cross rivers, make rafts and all phases of infantry training. Upon completion, we received a skull on a black insignia patch for this ranger training. Afterward, we were sent to Camp McCoy in Wisconsin, where we were trained to ski and operate in the snow.

In early October of 1943, we were shipped overseas in a large convoy. Years later I read that ten ships in this convoy were sunk on the way to Europe. We stopped at Glasgow, Scotland, where some troops were taken off and the rest of us were taken to Belfast, Northern Ireland, where we stayed for eight months in a British army camp. In May of 1944, we were sent to Swansea, Wales, to another camp right by the docks where every day we practiced getting on and off the ship. Then, one night they told us that we were going to see what it was like sleeping on the ship. Well, in the night we felt the ship moving and we woke up wondering what was going on. Everyone was excited as we were issued invasion currency, on the night of June 5th, when they told us we were headed for the invasion of France.

We were only one of thousands of ships going in on the morning of the invasion. On my troop transport, I had a ringside seat for the invasion, watching planes going in overhead, big bombers, small fighter planes, watching dogfights in the sky, ships going in and wondering when it was going to be our turn. I watched the battleship "Texas," nearby, firing all day long, blasting the shore and targets further inland. Every once in a while, the Germans fired back and huge geysers of water would shoot up in the air.

About 200 of our engineers went in that morning. I don't know if we were supposed to go in the first day or not, but finally at 3:00 a.m. the next morning, they got us all together and we climbed down a cargo net to a Landing Craft

Infantry. It went in as far as it could, then shot out its ramp. With full gear, we jumped into chest high waters and headed toward the shore as it started to turn daylight. Occasionally a man would step into a shell hole and disappear beneath the waves. There was sporadic fire. Here and there were underwater obstacles. We could see bodies floating around, but we just kept on going. I was lugging a 21-pound Browning Automatic rifle with a clip of 20 rounds that would be gone in one or two blasts. We passed trucks and tanks stalled in the water. We were like mechanical men as we headed in, 300 feet to shore. I don't know if it was a stroke of luck or a diversionary movement, but the Germans weren't heavily engaged in defending the point where we landed on Omaha Beach. Our job was to expand the beachhead and we had a clear corridor to go through troops that were stalled on shore. There were obstacles all around, angle irons and damaged equipment. We heard the firing, but it was like Moses parting the Red Sea. We got in a line and went right in up the beach to a big field just over the top of a bluff where a whole battalion stopped there to reorganize their units. We immediately dug slit trenches for protection out in the open, when I saw a soldier running, yelling, "Gas! Gas!" We had gas masks, but he was out of his mind. There was no gas.

We spent the night here, dug in at the edge of a forest, and during the night, the enemy flew over and dropped bombs all around us that shook the earth. The next morning we proceeded forward into the hedgerows, which were terrible. These were small farming lots of an acre or so, surrounded by stone walls, held thick with overgrown vegetation. All the Germans had to do was poke their weapons through and let you have it, but you couldn't see them behind these walls. We took a lot of casualties here and our tanks couldn't plow through. They were gunning us down. If you were exposed, bang, you got hit. (*The hedgerows in France threatened to stall the Allied advance until an Army Engineer, using some of the German obstacles placed in the water, rigged makeshift plows which allowed the tanks to bore through the vegetation.*)

We used the phones on the back of the tanks to tell the crew inside where to fire. We'd take one field, then move to the next, and went all through Normandy like that. It was like taking one fort at a time. At one point they sent me and a young kid to act as an outpost in front of the rest of the company and if it was clear, we'd signal for the company to move up. At night we dug in near a wall, exhausted from going through bush all day long. The next thing I knew, it was dawn and the Germans were right there. At this moment, one of them hung over our hole and fired about 50 rounds with his machine gun straight down at us. Dust flew up all around and we jumped out and ran towards our line. As I was running for a break in the hedgerow, their tank fired low and made a ridge as it skidded across the ground before it exploded into a tree. As I lifted my leg to jump the barbed wire I could feel the projectile swoosh right between my legs. How lucky can you get?

Inside of three days, we had gone inland about 15 miles, field to field. We kept progressing, but we took heavy casualties. We stopped at Hill #192, the highest point in Normandy. This high ground was heavily defended and the Germans employed all weapons against us, and from this vantage point they could see all movement in the harbor taking place and direct their fire. We attacked this hill many times, but were driven back. Finally our artillery came in to support us with a rolling barrage and we followed it right up the hill. Lieutenant General Leslie McNair, head of the ground forces, was observing the infantry/air corps coordination when a wave of U.S. bombers dropped their bombs too short into our lines and he was killed. I was only about 100 yards away from him when it happened. Half-way up, a machine-gun fired at us from a few feet away. I hit the ground and could feel the bullets going between me and the ground and shattering my cartridge belt. We got up and charged the hill again. I looked around and saw an enemy antitank gun and a hole near by. I fired into it and heard screams. The crew, three German paratroopers, crawled out and surrendered. I captured their anti-tank gun and took them prisoner. Walking them down the hill, I told one of my men (by this time I was squad leader) to take them the rest of the way to Battalion stockade. He was gone only about five minutes when he returned. I knew it was much further than that. Who knows what he did with those prisoners. They had been trying to break our communication wire stretched along the ground with their feet. I had fired at their boots to make them stop when I had them, so who knows what happened after he took them. After capturing the anti-tank gun, I turned it around and fired it five times into the German lines. We got to the top of #192 and our Captain told me, "Turp, take your squad to the next hill, keep in contact by radio, I'll watch you through binoculars." It was exhausting encouraging the men to move through positions, advancing through the enemy fire and in three months time, our company suffered 750 casualties. One time in the woods, I spotted a German scout. He was so close, I could have touched him, but I told my men to stay quiet. Sure enough, he returned to his squad, but we had set up two BARs and wiped them out when they came back. The 2nd Division was in skirmish after skirmish and that's how we made our way across France.

We reached Brest, France, an important submarine port for the Germans. One night we set up a position and were camouflaged behind some trees and brush when SS troops came running through the woods screaming and shouting like a huge wave of fanatical wolves. They stormed through the forest and we didn't budge an inch or even breathe as they ran right past us. We waited and later they came back through, but they didn't detect us and we certainly conserved our ammunition on them. Our orders were to capture the city and I was wounded here for the first time. We were on a hill firing into the enemy position. Our new Lieutenant stepped on a mine and the explosion took his leg off. He had only been in combat for 15 minutes. We advanced to a wall and the Germans were on the other side of it. I was told to take my squad 100 yards out to meet another squad. We came upon another enemy position and I yelled out in German, "Come out with your hands in the air" and 30 Germans surrendered. As we went further down, Germans fired on us and I was hit by a wood-tipped bullet which grazed my face and the splinters entered my temple. I didn't know it until one of the men said, "Hey Turp, you're hit."

By October we were taken in box cars out to the Seigfried Line. The 2nd Division normally covered a front of five miles. Here we were thinly spread out covering a 25 mile front. I remember looking through my binoculars and seeing the bodies of the 28th Division ahead of us where they got slaughtered, and were piled up like logs. It was such a sad sight. We were spread so thin that the German patrols would go right through us and capture men behind us at times. There was a lot of artillery/mortar action back and forth and in early December they took us out of the line and replaced us with three new divisions, green troops, that had just come from the States. The Germans knew they were green and hit them hard during Hitler's big drive through the Ardennes (The Battle of the Bulge).

We were in a drive going through the Seigfried Line headed for the Roer River Dam. At the same time (December 16), the Germans attacked the positions we had formerly occupied. We were called by radio and had to stop, turn around, come back and make a line in front of the German's armored division. The German attack in Belgium failed because of the 2nd Division. Years later, the German general Manteuffel said that one of the reasons the German attack in the Ardennes failed was that they, "Ran their heads against a stone wall in the Monschau forest" (*against the 2nd Division*) We did our job well. We moved a lot through Belgium, plugging holes where the Germans were breaking through. We were constantly moving, shifting, wherever they needed us. On January 16, 1945, our regiment was to make an attack in the Ondenval-Inveldingen Pass and secure a valley for the whole corps to pass through. On the day of the attack, they put my company in a wheatfield unprotected. At daylight, the Germans saw us there and started dropping mortar. We were pinned down by artillery and a machine gun set up in a farmhouse window started mowing us down. It was bitter cold and we were laying in snow about a foot and a half deep, trying to dig holes to get into for cover. A mortar shell hit near one of our guys and he just shook the dirt off. Then a second one came in right in the same place and took his leg off. I remember his screams – we couldn't do a thing. We had a lot of other casualties. Finally, tanks with plows came in to clear the road ahead so our tanks could come in and support us. A medic

Photo taken from a captured Nazi soldier

came up there and asked the sergeant, "Where are your casualties?" The Platoon Sergeant, my best friend, was bending on one knee to point when he was shot through the forehead and fell dead in the snow. I was the Platoon guide and next in line for the job, so I took over. When our tanks started firing, the Germans moved back. By nightfall we came to the edge of a forest and it began to snow heavily. We went up the side of a hill along the trees' edgeline. We found prepared positions and one huge hole that an entire platoon could use to take cover. We occupied that position that night and we were freezing. We were trained not to make fires, not even for warmth, which would give away your position. We had no food, no extra ammunition, no radio for communication, nothing! We were on top of this hill by ourselves.

The next morning, we discovered that our man on outpost had been killed by a treeburst. So the Lieutenant and I went on a short reconnaissance and had gotten a few hundred feet when I saw three soldiers in white camouflage. I said, "Lieutenant, the Germans..." He looked and said, "That's F-Company." I said, "We don't wear those black belts." So I took aim, shot one down, and a firefight started. There were no more than 30 of us with no replacements and we were freezing to the point where we didn't care if we lived or died.

It was hard to see where the Germans were, so I kept yelling to the men, "Fire low! Fire low! Fire at the base of the trees where you think they're hiding!" Then we heard this roar getting louder and louder and it was what a foot soldier fears the most, a tank. As it got closer and closer, we realized that it was a Tiger Tank. The tall pine trees began to bend and break under its weight and I could see its muzzle coming right at us. It looked like a monster coming through the woods, crushing the pines in its way. Then the turret turned and aimed in our direction and BOOM! it fired at us. Some of our men got up and ran. I hollered, "Stay here and fight!" I picked up rocks and threw them at the foxholes to rally the men to fire their weapons. Our gunner had run away, so one of my squad leaders and I jumped into a hole where the machine gun was. He fired away at the tank, but it did nothing. The tank kept firing and it dawned on us that we were all going to be killed if somebody didn't do something! I crawled through the woods to get our bazooka. I had been trained on the bazooka, but had never fired it with live ammunition. I looked out of the hole after he fired to see where his gun was aiming. After it fired, I got out of the hole on one knee and from behind a knocked-down limb, fired at the tank. It hit and just bounced off. I jumped back in the hole and it fired again – I got out and fired another round. I must have hit it about ten times, but I couldn't do any damage. Then out of the corner of my eye I caught movement to the side. I was on my knee ready to shoot at the tank when I whirled around with my bazooka and saw three Germans about 50 feet away. I took aim at a tree next to them and fired. The round blew the tree apart and killed them. If I had missed, they would have killed me. Finally, the tank backed off and retreated with its troops. When things quieted down, we got out of our holes and started counting bodies. We had lost three men, the Germans 37. *(For this action, Turpin was awarded the Silver Star by General Courtney Hodges. The citation reads as follows: "When an enemy tank began firing pointblank into the foxholes, Sergeant Turpin secured a rocket launcher and while subjected to intense small arms fire, crawled through the dense woods to within 50 yds. of his target, firing his weapon until the tank was forced to withdraw. This action allowed the men to concentrate their fire upon the enemy infantry to their front. Then, Sergeant Turpin, at a range of 20 yards, killed three enemy infantrymen with the rocket launcher. This bold initiative and gallant actions were an important factor in repelling the enemy drive.")* So we stopped the tank, we stopped their attack, and we held our position. We carried our dead down to the road so their bodies would be found.

In March, we came upon the Ludendorf Bridge. We crossed the Rhine here by barge. We continued into Germany and fought through different towns. The last one I was in was Gottingen. We were riding on tanks in pursuit of the retreating German Army. We came upon a bridge here that wasn't defended by the enemy. I felt it was safe, so I proceeded across the bridge and could hear talking half-way across. I was by myself when I leaned over the side and spotted three Germans getting ready to blow up the bridge. They were about to set off an aerial bomb electronically with a generator. I hollered at them to surrender, they came out and I took them prisoner. I jumped back on the tank and we now proceeded across the bridge. On the other side was an airfield with 15 fighter planes just sitting there. I asked one of the Germans there, "Was ist los mit der Deutschen Luftwaffe?" (What's the matter with the German Airforce?) He replied, "Nichts benzene" (no fuel). As we continued through Gottingen, we heard there were over 7,000 wounded enemy within the city. We passed a building with a high barbed-wire fence around it. Outside was an armed member of the Volksturm (local guard). I told him to get out of my way and when we went inside, there were 150-200 women and children slave laborers. They told me they were starving. I remembered seeing sacks of potatoes by the town university. I went back there and grabbed two bags and flung them over the fence so the liberated prisoners would have something to eat. We proceeded further when that night I was told I would be going back to the States on a rest and rehabilitation furlough. The next day I was taken by truck to France and from there to England and then back to the States. Before my furlough was through, the war in Europe had ended and I was discharged June 28, 1945.

By the end of the war, I was the only man on the front lines from our original company of 186 men to finish the war without being killed or seriously wounded. I was always on the front lines with my men and I was the luckiest man in the US Army. What kept me going was constant prayer. I carried one very sacred prayer with me at all times throughout the war. If I were asked to pass one thought on to future generations concerning this war, what comes to my mind the most are the words I heard once to a song..."The greatest thing you'll every learn is to love and be loved in return..."

Turpin served on the Stamford Fire Department for almost 25 years and presently makes his home in Florida. In addition to the Silver Star, he received the Bronze Star, a Purple Heart with Oak Leaf Cluster, and five battle stars for Normandy, Northern France, the Rhineland, Ardennes, and Central Europe.

-THE TIGER TANK-

Turpin faced the most formidable tank in the entire war, the German Tiger. Not only did the Tiger have greater firepower than any other tank, but its six inch frontal armor, which was slanted to deflect enemy fire could not be damaged, even by a direct hit from an American tank. In fact, more than one Sherman Tank commander reported multiple hits on a Tiger without consequence. On the other hand, the Tiger's 22 pound shell could knock out a Sherman from more than a half mile away.[3]

The original Tiger inflicted heavy damage on allied tanks at Normandy and the newer and improved Royal Tiger used in the Ardennes was even more destructive. Although the Germans were ultimately defeated in the Battle of the Bulge, the Royal Tiger emerged as one of the most feared and most respected weapons of the Third Reich.

---

[1] Gary Fox. <u>Graignes: The Franco American Memorial</u>.

[2] "Donahue Enters Hospital in West Virginia". <u>Stamford Advocate,</u> September 9, 1944.

[3] William Goolrick, <u>The Battle of the Bulge</u>. (Alexandria, VA: Time Life Books, Inc., 1979), pp. 54-55.

CHAPTER TWELVE

THE DRIVE TOWARD GERMANY

Now that the invasion of Normandy was successful and the allies had opened up the second front, the stage was set for the drive eastward toward the German homeland. In July, 1944, General George Patton spearheaded the drive across France and on August 25th Paris was liberated. Within weeks, the Germans were driven completely out of France and most of Belgium was also in Allied hands. On September 25, 1944, the US First Army entered Germany. During the Allied offensive, the Germans lost hundreds of thousands of men and the ultimate outcome of the war was no longer in doubt.

Photo courtesy of U.S. Army

- EDWARD KOVACS -

Ed Kovacs enlisted in the U.S. Army in 1942 after his Sophomore year at Yale University. He served in the 100th Infantry Division and saw four different European countries— France, Belgium, Austria, and Germany. At one point, his division saw action for seven consecutive months, from the fall of 1944 through the spring of 1945.

I was 18 when I went in. I was part of the Yale contingent who joined the infantry. We were supposed to be a "show division." They'd march us around in parades and things like that. We never thought we'd ever see action, but we ended up in Marseilles after D-Day, 1944. No sooner did we get there than we were visited by a plane every night. We called it "Bedcheck Charlie." The Germans knew we were there, and they knew exactly who we were and what our capabilities were. They knew that we were commanded by General Withers Burgess. They used to broadcast this on the radio. They also dropped a lot of propaganda leaflets on us, mostly telling us that our girlfriends back home were with other men.

In the fall of 1944, we were on our way up the Rhone Segonne Highway, up toward Strasbourg. All along the road there were cars, tanks, and jeeps piled up, shot up and crushed. We were supposed to be relieving the 442nd Regiment, a Japanese/American Combat Team. It was one of the most decorated units in the entire war. (*Indeed it was, with some 3,600 Purple Hearts and 354 Silver Stars.*)[1]

Some of the first planes we saw were Thunderbolts captured by Nazis. They inserted them into their air force. One day I was coming out of the Battalion Aid Station, I had chilblaines (blisters). All of a sudden, this T-bolt comes flying overhead, and I was strafed. The guy must've been a rotten shot. I finally dove into a house and hid behind a door. But I got my revenge. A few days later, I shot down one of those sons of bitches with a .50 caliber machine gun.

The worst action I saw was in the Vosges Forrest. It was there that we encountered our first tree bursts. Incoming artillery would hit the trees above our heads and the impact would send tree fragments flying all over. If you didn't get hit, you were lucky; some were killed. It was scary. During this engagement, three of us were separated from our unit and marooned for three days. We were between lines. We were so hungry we ate snow; we ate the grass underneath the snow; we even ate dirt to fill our bellies. We didn't know where the hell we were. One guy had a switchboard so my job was to keep him awake so we could keep communications alive. They thought we were captured, but finally they sent a jeep for us. We were so glad to see that jeep.

On Thanksgiving of 1944, we were finally able to get a hot meal. That night I awakened from a terrible nightmare. I was yelling. I dreamed I was looking at my brother's tomb. I should have known something was wrong. Three weeks later I got a letter from Lucy (*Lucy Lannie, later to become Mrs. Kovacs*). She told me my brother had been killed. George died the exact day that I had that nightmare. He died in a town called St. Avaol, Belgium. The crazy thing is that he didn't even have to be in the war. He had a bad heart, but they took him anyway.

During the Battle of the Bulge, the Germans tried to disorient us any way they could. They changed road signs; they even had soldiers who spoke perfect English infiltrating our ranks, and even directing us right into German lines. Because I spoke German, I had to drive around and look for anyone believed to be a GI that was really a German.

All through France we had to slug it out all the time. It seemed like we barely moved. After the Bulge we really moved, sometimes 40-50 miles a day, through South France, across the Maginot Line, and into Germany.

In March of 1945, they finally put us in reserve because we were in combat so long. On VE Day, I was in Bavaria. What a beautiful feeling—nobody's out to kill you!

After VE Day, I was placed with a Military Government Unit because I could speak German. I was in evaluation. After the war, every German who wanted to work had to fill out a questionnaire. I had to evaluate the applications to determine if the people had Nazi backgrounds. If not, they could work. The funny thing is that a lot of the Germans turned the Nazis in. They would do anything if they thought they'd get a little extra butter or food. We actually captured Ribbentrop's secretary that way. *(Joachim von Ribbentrop was Hitler's Foreign Minister, most famous for the Molotov-Ribbentrop Pact or Non-Agression Pact with the USSR in 1939).* I spent a year with the Military Government Unit and was back in the states on Easter Sunday, 1946.

Mr. Kovacs was awarded the Bronze Star in 1946 but is most proud of his Combat Infantry Badge. After the war, he finished college at Yale and taught in the Stamford Schools for over 30 years. He was Chairman of Social Studies at Stamford High School until his retirement in 1986.

- PRIVATE BENJAMIN PRAEGER -

By the time Benjamin Praeger and his wife arrived in Stamford in 1940, they had already fought their own private war against the Nazis. The Praegers were living in Vienna, Austria at the time of the Anschluss with Germany in 1938. They were arrested by the Gestapo and placed in Buchenwald, one of the infamous Nazi death camps.

The Praegers were released in 1939 and went to England before settling in Stamford. Praeger was inducted into the service in 1944, and served as an infantry-man with the First Army in France and Belgium. On November 3, 1944, Praeger, who had just received the Combat Infantry Badge, was killed in Europe. He died just one day before his daughter, Shirley Esther's, first birthday.[2]

- SAM ROUMELES -

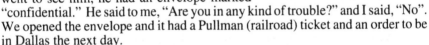

Prior to entering the Army, Sam Roumeles was an accountant for Schick, he was almost immediately recruited to become a Special Agent with the Counter Intelligence Corps (C.I.C.). Four days after the invasion of Normandy, Roumeles and eleven other agents went ashore attached to XIX Corps. As the Allied troops swept through France, Belgium, Holland, and Germany, their job was to apprehend enemy spies and others who collaborated with the Nazis. They were also to arrest high ranking members of the Nazi party.

After I entered the Army, I took a battery of tests at Fort Bliss in Texas. Then one day I was told that I was wanted by my C.O. When I went to see him, he had an envelope marked "confidential." He said to me, "Are you in any kind of trouble?" and I said, "No". We opened the envelope and it had a Pullman (railroad) ticket and an order to be in Dallas the next day.

There I was interviewed and told that I had the qualifications to become a Special Agent in counterintelligence and counterespionage. You had to be over the age of 25, which I was, and they were looking for lawyers, auditors, F.B.I., and Secret Service men who spoke foreign languages. I also spoke a little French and fluent Greek. I was also told that I could be sent anywhere in the world. Well, at this time in my life, it sounded like the most exciting thing in the world to me. So, I took some more exams and a few days later, a Special Agent handed me a check for two hundred dollars, which was a lot of money at the time. He told me to go out and buy a completely new wardrobe from socks to boxer shorts to suits.

After this, I was placed in school and attended classes from 8:00 a.m. to 10:00 p.m. for eight weeks and then we followed with field training. In the fall of 1943, I was sent for advanced training in Chicago and then operated as an agent in Chicago. We investigated and interviewed suspects who were thought to be saboteurs or enemy agents. I also worked in Washington, D.C., and New York City. At that time there was a lot of fear of Abwehr, the German Intelligence organization. It was, without question, one of the best intelligence organizations in the world.

The entire time I operated in the U.S., my wife was the only person who had my non-military address. My parents' mail was given to her for forwarding.

While I was in New York City, I was told that I was going to be sent to Alexandria, Egypt, and there I was to wait for the invasion of Crete and Greece. But when it was decided that no American troops would be used in this operation, I was reassigned to London. Then I was sent to Matlock, England, where we trained with the British Military Intelligence. In March and April of 1944, we brushed up on our French and were assigned to XIX Corps which was scheduled to take part in the invasion of France. There were eleven Special Agents, and we worked out of XIX Corps Headquarters.

On the morning of June 9, 1944, we boarded an LST and joined the Allied convoy in the English Channel. On D-Day, plus four, we landed at Omaha Beach Red. We were expecting some small arms fire, but we were very lucky because the battle was now further inland. When we arrived on the beach, it looked like a tornado had just struck. As we made our way past hundreds of German prisoners, we knew that our safety was bought by the blood of the men who preceded us.

In France we worked in groups of two. My partner was Larry Myers, who was head of the Foreign Language Department in the Fullerton, California, school system. He was fluent in French, Spanish, and German. We were sent to the town of Isigny, where the people were very hospitable and helped us with our investigations. We worked extensively with the French Forces of the Interior (French Underground) and from the day we opened our office in Isigny until the end of the war, our living quarters were almost always provided by residents who were active in the underground forces.

Our primary objective was the apprehension of enemy agents and we usually were able to get reliable information from the underground, local politicians, priests, or others. Everywhere we went we were treated as liberators. People would cheer us, give us fruits and vegetables, and some restaurants and stores would invite us in for food and drink. At Isigny, we stayed with an electrical engineer and his wife who was a school teacher.

From Isigny, we traveled through north central France and by September of 1944, we were in Belgium. There, we were again greeted enthusiastically by the Arme Blanche, or White Army. They were comparable to the F.F.I. and gave us good solid information. Like the French I stayed with, I formed some lasting friendships with these people and still correspond with some of them. From Belgium we went to Holland, but then in December, the Germans broke through at the Bulge and we were delayed there for the winter.

After the Battle of the Bulge, the next target was the industrial Ruhr section of Germany. We arrived in Munchen-Gladbach on March 1, 1945. This was one of the largest industrial cities in the Ruhr and because of its importance, we arrived there immediately after the troops. The Nazis had been very active in the city for years, but we found many sources who could be trusted to give us reliable information. Right after we arrived, we received a tip that there were two young women in town who were radio operators for the Lufwaffe. We found one of them and she admitted that she had worked for the Nazis and that she was currently a "Stay Behind Agent" who was ordered to report the movements of British and American troops to the German Centrale. After hours of questioning, she admitted that another young woman was involved and we quickly apprehended her.

As the interrogation progressed, we were given three other names and they too were quickly arrested. All five girls, whom we nicknamed "the Rhine Maidens," were between 18 and 25 years of age and were trained agents who were skilled at sending and receiving radio messages. Originally, they had been drafted and recruited by Hauptman Cloeren of TRUP 122. They told us they agreed to work for the Germans because they received extra ration cards, 250-300 marks per month, and exemption from further military service.

Since two of the girls still had their radios, we decided to take advantage of the opportunity and have the girls work for us. From that point on, we gave the girls the cover names of "Blaze" and "Lazy," and they transmitted only the information that we wanted the Germans to receive. When the British 21st Army

Group was to cross the Rhine at Wesel in March of 1945, "Blaze" reported three American and British Infantry divisions moving toward another area. This little deception kept the Germans in their positions south of where the crossings were to take place. "Lazy" also transmitted information of little or no value to the Germans and both were awarded the Iron Cross II Class by the Germans.

Roumeles taking VonEpp into custody.

In April, we crossed the Elbe River and began to make plans to enter Berlin. But a few days later, we got the disappointing news that we had to stay where we were and await further orders. On May 5, 1945, just before the Armistice, we were told to go to Bad Nauheim, a resort spa, which was about 20 miles from Frankfurt. It was untouched by the war because most of the fine hotels were converted to German Military Hospitals. We moved into a comfortable villa and began to look for some of the important Nazi personalities that were still unaccounted for. We visited the German hospitals then and one day a reliable informant at one of the local hospitals informed me that Franz Ritter VonEpp was on the fourth floor (*Franz VonEpp was a veteran of the Boxer Rebellion, World War I, and a Lieutenant General in the regular German Army. He was one of Hitler's earliest military backers and was made Governor of Bavaria when Hitler came to power. He was later made an "Obergruppenfuher" [4 Star General] in the Storm Troopers*).

When I went up to the fourth floor and confronted him, he denied who he was. But after questioning him further, I told him to save us both a lot of trouble. I knew who he was. I had a dossier on him with his picture. He finally admitted who he was.

After checking with my superiors, it was determined that he was wanted, possibly for trial. VonEpp complained that he couldn't be transported because of ill health, but we gave him a physical and he was found to be suffering from severe depression. As soon as he was fit for travel, a guard, another agent, and I drove him to Mondorf Les Baines, Luxembourg.

The ride to Luxembourg took a long time and we talked for many hours. He told me that he was friends with Hitler and also of the many conversations he had with him. They were both fanatically anti-Communist and he considered himself an authority on Communism. And then he told me something I will never forget. He said that for the past four years we had been aiding our real enemy, the Russians. Then he said, "Although the U.S. has won the war, it has not yet defeated its greatest enemy."

We delivered VonEpp to Luxembourg, but he never made it to trial. He died on February 8, 1947.

Roumeles returned to Stamford and his job at Schick in 1945. Later, he went to work for Sun Chemical Corporation where he worked for 32 years until his retirement as Vice President in 1982. Much of the story he related here was not declassified until 1991.

- TED REWAK -

Ted Rewak was one of the five "Fighting Rewaks" who served the country during World War II. In addition to brothers William, Peter, Stephan and Walter, the oldest brother Carl was a veteran of World War I. Leaving a wife and seven month old daughter behind, Rewak went overseas with the 557th Field Artillery Battalion. Between August 1944 and May of 1945, he spent 239 consecutive days in combat and saw action in France, Belgium, Holland, and Germany.

The 557th was a so-called "bastard outfit." Nobody wanted us. We were different from the regular artillery because our 155mm gun was mounted right on a Sherman 32 ton tank. We had an advantage over the tractor drawn or 6 x 6 artillery, because we could fire in six minutes flat while they took about sixteen minutes to start firing. We'd just back onto our spade, get laid in, and start firing. We'd never been tried in combat before and nobody was sure how well it would work. We were great.

My particular gun section had twelve men, six ammunition carriers and six to fire the gun. Of these twelve guys we had seven different nationalities and we all got along beautifully. The shell itself was 94 pounds and it took two men to load it, but we could blow a hole about 25 feet wide.

While I was in England training, we were moving in an ammunition carrier and suddenly one of the tank carriers caught fire. It was loaded with live ammunition. I jumped on top of the tank, unloaded the ammunition, and quickly handed the shells and powder to my buddy on the gun crew. I was burned badly and they wanted to give me a Purple Heart but I refused. I hadn't been injured in action.

By the end of the war, we fought with Patton's Third Army, the Eighth Corps, Tenth Corps, and I think altogether about twenty-two different units.

Just before we went into France, I found out that my brother was nearby in Birmingham, England. I was in Staffordshire and I went to see the First Sergeant to see if I could get a pass. Colonel Whiting (Commander of the 557th) came out to me and said, "Rewak, we ship out in two days. I'll give you twenty-four hours and if you're not back, I'll throw the book at you." I knew I might not ever see my brother again so I said, "Fair enough," and I was back in twenty-four hours.

When we got to France we had no radio communication between each tank. There was just a small strip of red lighting mounted on the rear of each tank and you were just supposed to follow the tank in front of you. Ours was the last tank off the LST and we lost the tank in front. We were about six miles into enemy territory before we realized something was wrong. We turned right around and using a small flashlight we had to follow our tracks all the way back to the beach where we started.

We got our baptism of fire in Brest, France, which was defended by an estimated 35,000 German troops most of whom were in heavily fortified bunkers and pillboxes. I honestly felt that the way the Germans were dug in they could have lasted for six months but we took them in six weeks. We were trained to hit targets from six to eight miles but here we were only four hundred yards or so away and from that range we were deadly.

Brest was a city under ground. Some of the Germans were six stories below ground level. We were under constant fire and every one of us was scared. I was the gunny then and the gunner's sight was located right next to the barrel. The noise was unbelievable but you couldn't wear ear plugs because you had to be able to hear firing commands. When the city fell we took thousands of P.O.W.s, many of them were just young kids, fourteen and fifteen years old.

After Brest all of the outfits wanted us because we could fire so quickly. This was our only mission in France and after this we went through Belgium, then Holland, then Germany. We were in combat for so long, that I have only a few specific memories of the times and the places we were in. However, I remember Christmas Eve very vividly. We were in Belgium during the Battle of the Bulge. We were in the middle of firing when suddenly there was a lull. It grew quiet and we began to sing Christmas carols. Even the Germans were singing.

We only spent a day or two in Holland. We were in a town called Maastricht which had the largest outdoor pool in the world at that time. We had an extra few hours so we decided to take a swim.

But other than that we were almost always in action, day and night, with cold food most of the time. We were under orders not to steal anyone else's food but then we found out that the P.O.W.s were getting K-Rations and we were getting C-Rations. Finally we hijacked a train and took enough food to feed a hundred guys for almost a week. We got a reprimand for that.

We lived outside through all four seasons. Our tank had a spade on it so when we set up, it would start a big hole for us. Sometimes we would be able to use an old German trench but most of the time we would dig a hole big enough to accommodate six people. This was against regulations but we did it anyway. Then, if we could, we'd put a few doors or railroad ties on top to cover us from the rain and snow. We never had regular living quarters until the very end of the war.

It is absolutely remarkable what the human body will take. Sometimes it was 25 or 30 below zero. They used to call me the "Crazy Russian" because no matter how cold it was I would wash myself outside every day. We'd sleep in our clothes in a sleeping bag with our boots on. One night my friend took his boots off. I told him not to take them off but he did anyway. The next morning they were frozen solid and he couldn't put them back on.

One of my best friends overseas was Dutch Schulman from Texas. He couldn't read or write in English because he'd only been taught German back home, so I used to write all of his letters for him. He started off as a cook for the officers but ended up with our battery and we became fast friends. Because Dutch was a cook, every once in a while he'd give us a good meal. We had orders not to touch any of the animals over there but one time I caught a wild turkey and Dutch cooked it. I was worried that we'd get in trouble but Dutch said, "Let me take care of this." So he ripped a drumstick off, gave it to Colonel Whiting, saluted him and just kept on walking. The Colonel didn't say a word. Another time, toward the end of the war, we were occupying an estate belonging to one of the Nazi High Command. It was about 1600 acres and had about a thousand prize chickens on it. We were ordered not to touch them but by the time we left there wasn't one left.

By the time we entered Germany a lot of the country was destroyed. We fought at a place called Krefield for about three days and while we were there I picked up a little puppy that was only a few weeks old. This was "verboten," of course, but I kept her anyway. She traveled with us all through combat and we named her Daisy May. At night she would run from trench to trench trying to find a warm place. The funny thing is that whenever that dog started barking we knew that planes were coming. After the war, when we got back to England, the dog got distemper. We couldn't do a thing for her, so we had to just let her die.

Our battery usually fired faster than anybody else. When I was a gunner, I used to have guys put out stakes at even numbers so that I could adjust my sight without adding or subtracting. One time we got three Tiger Royals before anyone else even got a shot off. They were no more than 1500 yards away. That was one of the few times I actually saw a target that I hit.

Another time I got the order to fire on a German F.O.P. (Forward Observation Point). It happened to be a Catholic Church. I was a Catholic and it broke my heart to do it. It took me three shots to lay in and twenty-five to destroy the church.

After over two hundred days of firing without a break, I had a stretch where I fired from 6:00 p.m. to 6:00 a.m. All of a sudden I couldn't gun anymore. I developed so-called "combat fatigue." I just forgot how to do my job. They wanted to send me back to the base hospital but I begged them not to. We'd been together as a team all of this time and I wanted to finish with them. Fortunately, they allowed me to stay and twenty-four hours later I was fine.

In April of 1945 we knew the war was coming to an end. We were in a place called Leasche which was less than fifty miles from Berlin and we were among the first Americans to make a juncture with the Russians. My father and mother were born in a Russian speaking village that was part of the Austria-Hungary Empire and I spoke a fair amount of Russian. So one of the Lieutenants invited me along. About nine of us crossed the Elbe River in little rubber boats. It was close to Easter so when we got there I began to sing "Hristoss Wosscress" a Russian song that means "Christ Has Risen." When the Russians heard this they dropped everything and hugged me. Then they began to sing. We were there for a little over three days. We drank a lot of beer and vodka and talked. We got along famously. I became friendly with a Russian Sergeant and he kept telling me that he did not want to go back home. He wanted to come to the U.S.

While we were there I asked the Lieutenant if I could stay a little longer and he told me that it wouldn't be a problem. I was the last guy to return and they were getting ready to court martial me. I said, "Look, I volunteered for this mission. You guys weren't doing anything back here anyway." They decided not to punish me.

We all know that we could have gotten to Berlin long before the Russians got there but instead we sat on our fannies and allowed them to get there first. This was a big mistake. There is no question whatsoever that we would have been there first. (*This controversial Allied decision to allow the Russians to occupy Berlin would shape Cold War History for more than forty years after the war.*)

Later, when we got to Wolfsberg, Germany, the Russians tried to get us to move out of the city. Colonel Whiting said, "Rewak, tell them that if they want us out they'll have to put us out." We were facing an entire Russian regiment but fortunately they backed off and left us alone.

When the war in Europe ended, Colonel Whiting offered me a permanent ranking of Sergeant Major if I stayed on. I asked for twenty-four hours to think it over but finally I turned it down. I missed my family too much. My daughter was already three years old.

Rewak was discharged in November of 1945, as a First Sergeant. In addition to four Battle Stars, he was awarded a Bronze Star for "meritorious service against the enemy in France and Germany." Now that he had returned home safely to his young family, he went to work for Remington Rand and stayed with them for almost thirty years. He was one of the founders and first Post Commander of VFW Post 9617 in Springdale and served as its Quartermaster for twenty-three years. In addition to this Rewak was honored as the Grand Marshal of the Memorial Day Parade in 1984.

- LT. MICHAEL D'AGOSTINO -

On September 20, 1944, Lt. Michael D'Agostino, a popular local man, was killed in Germany. Prior to his death, the people of Stamford followed his progress in Europe and rapid rise through the ranks. D'Agostino travelled across Africa and Europe with the Fourth Division and held the Purple Heart, Bronze Star, Combat Infantry Badge, and Distinguished Unit Badge. Three months after his death, he was awarded the Silver Star for leading his platoon against a heavily armed German position. This citation further states that in the face of artillery and machine gun fire:

"Lt. D'Agostino made three trips across the 300 yard space in order to evacuate the casualties of his platoon. By his actions, he saved the lives of several seriously wounded men. Lt. D'Agostino's consideration, military courage, and tenacity are in keeping with the highest traditions of the military service."

Michael D'Agostino receiving the Bronze Star in France, 1944

- LENNY PAGLIANO-

Lenny Pagliano joined the US Army in 1943 and became a wireman in a Sound Observation Unit attached to the 8th Corps of the United States Army. He arrived in Europe in the summer of 1944 and before the war was over participated in five major campaigns, Normandy, Northern France, the Rhineland, the Ardennes, and Central Europe.

Not too many people have ever heard of a Sound Observation Unit. We usually worked with an artillery or tank outfit. Our job was to lay out microphones and wires. We would start at the Post Command and we would run our lines from there out to where we placed the microphones, then from the microphones to an Observation Post or Lookout Tower.

The observer in the tower would have binoculars on and would wait for the German artillery to fire. When he saw the gun fire he would press a button that would activate the microphones that we put out. The mikes would pick up the sound of the shell as it came over and send a signal back to the Post Command. The mikes were so sensitive that they could tell exactly where the German artillery was. Then the machine would be able to give exact coordinates to our own artillery or tanks. We would be able to use these coordinates to knock out the German guns.

Most of the time we would be a half mile or so behind the infantry. It depended on where there was high ground for the observation tower. We moved around a lot and were attached to a lot of different units like the First Army, the Third Army and the Ninth Armored Division.

We left England and arrived at the Utah Beachhead (France) in August of 1944 but we didn't see our first action until we got to Brest (France) a few weeks later. There was a German submarine base there and they were dug in pretty good. But we had them cornered. We laid out our lines the whole time and had a few narrow escapes but we were lucky. I never saw so many airplanes in all my life and they just kept bombing and bombing the Germans. I remember thinking, "Thank God they're ours." We were there until September and finally the Germans gave up.

There were bodies everywhere and we were given orders not to take souvenirs. They told us not to pick anything up because the Germans booby trapped bodies and things. Well, this friend of mine went up and picked up a German helmet and there was still part of a skull in it. He was so shaken up that he had to be treated for battle fatigue.

After Brest, we had to move right out. We went to Paris, then Luxembourg, then Belgium. That winter (1944) we went to Binsfield and St. Vith (Belgium) with the First Army and that is when all hell broke loose. It was right before Christmas and one night three or four of us went out on patrol. We knew the Germans were around but we didn't know they were that close. All of a sudden we started getting shelled. This was the beginning of the Battle of the Bulge.

Our front lines were so weak that the Germans had us. We had to retreat over thirty miles, with Germans right on our tails. It was freezing and we were praying that they didn't catch us. We left behind equipment and everything. We drove day and night in the snow.

Once we regrouped, we joined up with the Third Army in Luxembourg right after Christmas. From there we went to Bastogne to help relieve the 101st Airborne. We got there on December 28th. *(During the Battle of the Bulge, the 101st was trapped by the Germans in the Belgian town of Bastogne. Although they were cold, tired, hungry, and on the verge of collapse, they courageously refused to surrender. When the Germans issued an ultimatum to their commander General Anthony McAuliffe, his famous reply was, "Nuts.")*

Bastogne was three quarters surrounded and when we went in the Germans were shelling the city. Even the cemetery was destroyed. Some of the shells were "high bursts" that would explode in the air and send shrapnel flying everywhere. Some of the shells were called "screaming mimis." They didn't do a lot of damage, but they were morale busters because the sound was so loud.

While the shelling was going on we continued to lay our lines. You got used to diving under anything when the shells came in. One night, my buddy and I were working and just as we finished a shell came in and hit a pole that we had just finished working on. There was a blizzard and it was cold, but we kept laying out the wires day and night. We would have three pairs of socks and two pairs of pants on and a few of the nights we slept in the crawlspaces of some of the homes because the ground was too hard to dig a foxhole.

One night one of the officers of the 101st wanted us to take some microphones and bring them out in front of the infantry. It was snowing that night and a Captain came up and told us not to do it. He said we would be sitting ducks out there. We were very lucky. We were at Bastogne for about a week and we survived.

After the Battle of the Bulge we went back to St. Vith and the town was destroyed. But we knew the Germans were in trouble because they were using horses to pull some of the equipment. They were also using bullets with wooden tips on them because they were running out of metal.

In February of 1945, we crossed the Rhine and went into Germany. We stayed there until the Spring and at the very end of the war we were sent to Pilsen which was in Czechoslovakia. We met the Russians there and right from the start we hated them.

After VE Day we were being trained to go over to the Pacific to fight the Japanese. But then the Atomic Bomb was dropped and I stayed in Europe until the end of 1945.

Lenny was discharged as a Corporal in December of 1945 and was awarded the Silver Service Star for participating in five major campaigns. He returned to Stamford where he worked as a roofer and a painter until his retirement. He was active in the National Guard and the Springdale VFW where he presently serves as its Junior Vice Commander.

- ARTHUR CONTI -

Arthur Conti was drafted into the Navy in 1943. He was trained as a gunner and served on five cargo ships during the war. As a Seaman First Class, he sailed the North Atlantic and the Mediterranean before making the famous "Murmansk Run" to supply our allies in Russia.

I was assigned to the S.S. James Gunn in 1944 and our first run was from Baltimore to Casablanca. It took us about sixteen days to get there. We were carrying planes, trucks, and a lot of other stuff like sugar. When we unloaded, you could see that the trucks and planes were pretty battered from the rough water on the way.

We came back to the states again, got another load, and headed out for the Mediterra-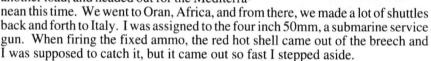nean this time. We went to Oran, Africa, and from there, we made a lot of shuttles back and forth to Italy. I was assigned to the four inch 50mm, a submarine service gun. When firing the fixed ammo, the red hot shell came out of the breech and I was supposed to catch it, but it came out so fast I stepped aside.

We picked up a lot of stuff in Oran, mostly ammunition, and then anchored in Augusta, Sicily. From there we were supposed to bring it to Naples. While we were in Naples, we were attacked by German planes. A troop ship had come in right along side of us and I guess they were after it. That night another cargo ship and a tugboat were hit and sunk. There wasn't much we could do but watch. It was like a firework show with our shore batteries firing at the planes and the planes flying around overhead. The sky was filled with light. But all I could think of was us, with all that ammo, and what would happen if we got hit.

On March 18, 1944, we left Naples, passed Gilbraltar leaving the Mediterranean and headed for the United States. On April 14th, we pulled into New York Harbor and anchored. It was good to see home again! I was assigned to several other ships making uneventful runs.

In October of 1944 we went back to the U.S. and I was assigned to another ship, the S.S. Thomas Scott. We went up to Bangor, Maine, for about a week, picked up some bombs and ammunition, and brought them back to England. Then we went up to Manchester and loaded up with food, some farm equipment, and an L.S.T. Then we headed for Russia.

We were told that this was a dangerous route, that German planes would swoop down on us and we'd be easy to hit. But on the way over I didn't even see a single plane and we landed safely in Murmansk. It was freezing cold up there and there was ice all over the ship. A Russian pilot guided us through a river and ended up grounding the ship. There was no serious damage, though, and we were able to unload all of the food and equipment.

We stayed in Murmansk for about five days while we had some repairs done. Then we anchored at the mouth of the river and waited for orders. We were there for another two days waiting to make convoy. In the meantime we picked up some refugees from Finland and were supposed to bring them to England. There were probably thirty of them, men, women, and infants. I told my friends, "This is bad luck." I thought it was a bad omen that we had women and children on board.

Finally, we made convoy and left for England. Then, about twelve noon it happened. We were on the outside of the convoy. This was known as the "coffin corner" because you were really exposed to subs. I just came off watch and went to get something to eat. Then I heard this bang! It came from the other side of the ship. I ran over to the other side to see if my friends were all right. One of the guys was playing his guitar and was knocked on the floor. Then we found out that we were hit in the boiler room. I don't know if it was a mine or a submarine but the next thing we heard were orders to report to the boat deck to abandon ship.

The refugees were let off first and then the crew, maybe sixty men in all. Everyone was told to stay calm and not to panic as the lifeboats were being lowered. It was important to stay calm because the water was so cold that if someone fell off or a boat tipped they'd only survive a few minutes in the water.

We were the only ship in the convoy to get hit. I got off with nothing but the clothes I had on and my foul weather gear. There were about twenty five of us in the lifeboat and we were picked up by an English destroyer escort. Our ship was still floating pretty much intact and we were watching it when someone yelled that there was still one of the refugees left on the ship. I think he was deaf. Volunteers rescued the lone refugee that had been left behind.

We were picked up by the Russians and brought to an old World War I destroyer. Then they tried to salvage the ship. A Russian torpedo boat pulled along side the English destroyer and took about twenty of us aboard and transferred us to an old U.S. WW I destroyer. Then, the Russian destroyer tried to salvage our ship! First a few of the Russians boarded the ship. I don't know if they ransacked it or not but

The SS James Gunn, headed for the Mediterranean

then they tied a cable to it and were trying to tow it. But the ship was taking too much water and after about two hours they cut it loose. The ship started to lift and then split in half and went down. The last thing you could see was the propeller sticking up in the air. You could hear the suction as it disappeared.

We went back to Murmansk and had to stay there for another three weeks. While I was there waiting to be taken back to England I met a guy from Stamford from the Daly family–the ones that owned Laddin's Terrace. His convoy left before mine and I never saw him after that.

From Russia, the crew was split up and put on various ships bound for England. Once in England, the crew was reunited, and then split up again, and assigned to different ships bound for the U.S. I was on my way back from a Cuban run when I heard that Japan had surrendered and the war was over.

Arthur Conti was discharged on March 8, 1946. He returned to town, married, and raised his family in Stamford. He was employed by the Stamford Public schools and worked as a custodian and in the maintenance department for over thirty years until his retirement.

- PHILLIP LODATO -

Phil Lodato entered the U.S. Army in 1942. As a Staff Sergeant he taught light and heavy weaponry at Fort Bragg, North Carolina. In 1944 he was sent overseas with the 100th Division, 399 Combat Infantry Company, and was taken prisoner by the Germans in December of 1944.

We landed in France in a driving rain and bivouacked right on the ground. We had no tents or shelter and between the rain and the German air raids, it was a frightening experience. Within a few days, we were up at the front lines in action.

I was in a weapons platoon, in a machine gun section. We were advancing pretty fast through a lot of small towns and were meeting

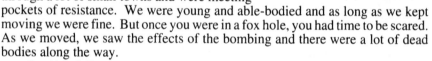

pockets of resistance. We were young and able-bodied and as long as we kept moving we were fine. But once you were in a fox hole, you had time to be scared. As we moved, we saw the effects of the bombing and there were a lot of dead bodies along the way.

By late fall we went through the Vosges Mountains, and as we were advancing through the snow, we were meeting more and more resistance. The Germans were just ahead of us. As we advanced across a field, they opened up on us. One of my guys, a full-blooded American Indian, was our first gunner. He was a big, strong guy, cunning too, a real good soldier. He was one of the guys that made our unit tick. He was shot in the leg and I never saw him again.

Early one morning our company started out over the snowy mountain terrain. We were meeting some resistance, but we kept moving further and further into the mountains. We were cold and exhausted traveling over 40 kilometers. Finally, we came to an area to rest. Our location was in Limburg, near Bitchy, France. It was a very short distance to the stronghold, the Maginot Line.

Just before dark, we heard some rumblings, possibly tanks in the area. We were told to dig in and wait until morning. I placed my two machine gunners in different directions – one towards the road and the other towards the flank. I told my crew that they must dig deep fox holes. Since we didn't know what to expect, we prepared for the worst in the morning. We dug all night. Some men from other units dug shallow fox holes, which was unfortunate because they were not well protected. Our location was a wooded area full of tall trees. At dawn, all hell broke loose when the Germans started shooting machine guns at close range. They were, also using half tracks equipment firing 20 millimeter shells directly into the trees. The shrapnel came down on the men in the fox holes. The men were screaming and yelling. There was much confusion everywhere. One of my machine guns was firing constantly until the Germans overran our position carrying burp guns and potato mashers (grenades). We lost about 60 men. The rest of us were captured, about 22 of us altogether including eight or nine men from the weapons platoon. We were captured by SS Troops. The first thing they did was line us up against a wall. I said to myself, "Oh no. Here it comes," but they searched us, took our weapons, and moved us by truck about five or ten miles. Looking at it now, I'm sure that they didn't have any idea what to do with us. They didn't want to have to feed us. We were captured December 9, 1944, a day I will never forget.

That evening they put us in a barn and all hell broke loose again. There was an Allied air attack and shells were hitting all over the place. The horses in the barn were going wild. After that, we were moved around to different camps, constantly under the threat of bombing. We were taken to a railroad yard and we were bombed once again. We weren't marked or anything so no one knew we were Prisoners of War. The entire time that were prisoners, the biggest threat was air attacks from Allied Forces.

I ended up in three or four different camps. In Limburg, Stalag XII A, we slept on the floor and it was bitterly cold. You usually got together with a few buddies to keep warm. The biggest problem was that we weren't moving around to keep warm. The food that we were fed wasn't nourishing. They would feed us "grass soup." It would go right through us, eventually causing much weight loss. Once in a while we'd get a potato or a little bread, but the amount and type of food depended upon which camp we were in. We did what we had to do to survive.

One of the most dreadful things that happened one night was when they brought us to the railroad yard. We were put into boxcars, which were small, wooden cars that were about 20 feet long. We were packed together. It was so crowded that a person couldn't even lie down. We were in those boxcars for nine days, packed like sardines. If we had to go to the bathroom, we had to use our helmet and dump the contents out of a small hole on the top wall of the car. We received a meager supply of rations, which was to last for the entire trip. We had to guard these rations or someone might steal them. At times, we were like animals stealing from our best friends due to the hunger which plagued us. The train always moved at nightfall. One night we were strafed by Allied planes causing extensive damage to the train.

Everyone needed a buddy to depend on. My best buddy was a guy named Boscoe. He was an Atheist, while I was a Catholic, yet we got along great because we helped each other survive as POW's.

Once we were in a POW camp, life was bearable, but the food was inedible. In between camps while we were traveling, we did what we had to do to survive. Once while we were walking, I saw a huge sugar beet along the side of the road. I grabbed it and the guard next to me slammed me in the shoulder with his rifle.

In the Neubrandenburg camp, Stalag II A, we had Italian, Russian, British, and Canadian Prisoners of War. Towards the end of the War, we got packages from the Red Cross, which included items such as canned food, cigarettes and the like. For some reason, the Russians got nothing. The Russian Prisoners of War were dying like flies everyday from the lack of nourishment. Some of the Russians were so thin, their skin was like cellophane; we could practically see right through it.

I was very fortunate to survive the hardships of War as a POW. I was only twenty-two and in good shape at the time. There were times when we could not give-in to being cold and hungry. We needed a strong will to stay alive. We knew we couldn't give up because only the strong survived.

One of the things I remember most was being transferred to a barn operated by a Polish man and wife. I tried to persuade them to give us some food, but they were afraid of us. The entire time we were there, I was searching around the barn for food. That night it was pitch black, and while I was crawling around the barn looking for anything edible, I discovered some sacks that felt like they had a grain of some sort in them. I used my trusty pocket knife that my parent's gave me that I had hidden in my shoe. I slit the sack open, and sampled some of the contents. It was wheat for sure. I took off both of my long socks and loaded them with this wheat, then I tied them around my waist. This supply lasted for about a month and helped to keep me strong. When we got to camp, I shared it with my buddy, Boscoe. We would take a rock and pound the wheat kernels into a powder, which we diluted with water and cooked in a small can. It was similar to the wheat my mother would cook each year on the feast of St. Lucy. Once I got back home to the States, I told my mother this story and she both laughed and cried upon hearing it.

On December 28, 1944, Allied planes accidentally bombed one of the prison camps that I was in. One of the bombs made a direct hit on an officer's barracks killing about 52 of the Allied Officers. A day later, the Germans asked for volunteers to go to the officer's grave site to represent our government. My friend and I decided to go. Some other nationalities also volunteered to be there.

We walked for about four miles to an open gravesite filled with bodies. Then we realized that the Germans brought us there for propaganda purposes using radio speakers and cameras broadcasting that the Allies were bombing their own men. Unfortunately, we were there to witness this miserable sight.

In late April, we could hear bombings in the distance. The word was out that the Russians were close by. By then, I had been a POW for 6 months. One morning, the Russian tanks came in and surrounded the camp. They had taken the town of Neubrandenburg destroying it. The Russian prisoners were wild running out, jumping on the tanks and hugging everyone in sight. I stayed with the Russians for about ten days, when, finally, we joined up with the Americans. We were brought to a hospital in Belgium for checkups, but what we needed most was nutrition. When I went into the Army, I weighed about 130 pounds, but, now, I was down to about 100. Many of us were shaky, and very sensitive to loud noises. I think for many years, I'd flinch every time I heard a car backfire or a firecracker explode. Finally, the Army brought us home to Lake Placid, New York, where a team of Army doctors treated us until we were OK. After that, I returned home. I had been MIA for six months. My wife, Helen, didn't even know I was alive until the war in Europe ended.

Looking back upon my wartime experiences, I have to say that with all the hard times that I went through, I don't regret any of it. It forced me to have a strong will and a resolute mind. It taught me how to survive against all odds.

Phil Lodato returned home to his wife, Helen, in Stamford, Connecticut and became one of the founders of United House Wrecking Corporation, a salvage business selling artifacts and antiques from old houses. Operating for nearly 40 years, it was one of the main attractions in Connecticut .

- A PRISONER'S DIARY -

In the six months that he was a prisoner of the Germans, Lodato secretly kept a diary which his captors thought was a prayer book. The following are some excerpts from April and May of 1945 which were recorded just before the war in Europe ended.

April 14 - There are rumors that the war is about to end.

April 15 - Today a message was read to us that President Roosevelt was dead.

April 16 - Bought some semolina (wheat) from the Italian prisoners only to find out that it was not semolina. It tasted like rubber, so I went and got my cigarettes back from the Italians.

April 18 - No Roll Call today. Now I know the war is ending. Planes overhead all day. Good news that the Russians are fighting in the streets of Berlin.

April 24 - We are told that our camp will evacuate soon. Maybe tomorrow.

April 27 - Russians are 30 kilometers from here. Evacuation called off because we refused to move.

April 28 - No sleep tonight. Bombs dropped all around the camp. Midnight. Russian tanks blasting everything in sight. No one hurt our camp. Thank God for that.

April 29 - 4:30 Russians blasting the hell out of Neubrandenburg.

May 4 - Captain just announced that war is over. Northern part of Germany has given up.

May 7 - War is officially over at 2:00 AM reported by Dutch radio.

- RICHARD FOLEY -

When Richard Foley was inducted at age 19, he had a baseball contract with the Brooklyn Dodgers and had already played some professional ball in the organization. No doubt he could have served his country by travelling and playing in exhibition games. Nonetheless, he joined the  *paratroopers and made the jump into Holland wearing his catcher's mitt on his belt. He was wounded by sniper fire during the jump but returned to action and a little over a week later, was critically wounded when he was hit by shrapnel from a German mortar.*

Foley suffered severe spinal injuries and never regained the use of his legs. After the war, he moved to Massachusetts to be close to the Veterans Hospital in Framingham where doctors told him that he would probably not live much beyond the age of thirty. Soon he met Sheila Foley (no relation) whom he later married. Branch Rickey, owner of the Dodgers, paid for his honeymoon in Florida and had him trained to be a scout for the Dodgers. Foley scouted for the Dodgers, Mets, and Pirates organizations before going to work for the Major League Scouting Bureau Southern New England.

Although he struggled with medical problems related to his war injuries, Foley maintained an active life working two and sometimes three jobs at a time. He was also one of the original seven men who were instrumental in starting wheelchair basketball. Although there was talk of books and screenplays on his life, Foley was never interested. Life with Sheila and their two boys was fulfilling enough.

He remained involved with professional baseball and his job at the Needham Fire Department. On Memorial Day, 1989, Foley died at the age of 64, outliving the doctors' prognosis by some 30 years.

[1] Ogden Tanner and Robert Wallace. The Italian Campaign. (Alexandria, VA: Time Life Books, Inc., 1978), p.188.

[2] "Pvt. Praeger, Former Prisoner of Germans K.I.A.". Stamford Advocate, November 18, 1944.

[3] "Silver Star for Stamford Officer K.I.A.". Stamford Advocate, December 26, 1944.

CHAPTER THIRTEEN

THE BATTLE OF THE BULGE

As Christmas of 1944 approached, the Allies had every reason to be optimistic. Allied troops had rumbled across France and Belgium and were headed right for the heart of Germany. The German situation was dire. On the eastern front the Russians were decimating the armies of the Third Reich and were now in Poland on their way to Germany. In addition to this the Germans had been at war for over five years and had lost almost three and a half million men.

It was in this atmosphere of German despair and Allied overconfidence that Hitler planned one last desperate gamble. He would launch a massive counter-offensive against the overextended Allied troops. The attack would take place in the Ardennes region of Belgium and would come to be known as the Battle of the Bulge.

On December 16, 1944, in the snow and bitter cold of winter, the attack began. Over 250,000 Germans attacked the Allies along an 85 mile front in hopes of smashing the line. For several days with the American armies surprised and in a state of confusion it looked as though they would do just that. Fighting was both fierce and terrifying. Thousands of Americans were lost, separated, captured or executed. In the cold and dark of the Ardennes forest German artillery fired into the trees transforming them into deadly projectiles.

The darkest moment for the Americans came on December 19th when the Germans surrounded the 101st Airborne in the town of Bastogne. When the Germans called for an American surrender General McAuliffe's reply consisted of a single word—"NUTS." Although the men were trapped, dangerously low on supplies, and wracked with illness, the Americans fought bravely and were able to hang on until the day after Christmas when relief arrived.

When the American forces did not quickly collapse, the German offensive began to sputter and by late January, 1945, the Battle of the Bulge was over. Although it lasted little over a month the Germans suffered over 100,000 casualties. American casualties were only slightly lower. But more important, Hitler's daring gamble had failed and with this the defeat of the third Reich was inevitable.

- FRED GENOVESE -

Fred Genovese was one of five brothers to serve in the armed forces during the war. Prior to this time he was attempting to make his mark as a professional boxer in the welterweight division. As a member of the 82nd Airborne, Fred made combat jumps throughout Europe including the invasions of Sicily, Italy, Normandy, Holland, and Central Germany and was with the American forces when they made the link up with Soviet Forces on the Elbe River.

We landed in Africa in 1943. By the time we got there we were just doing some mop up against the Germans. Then we prepared to go into Sicily. We did a lot of running with 50 and 60 pounds on our back. And it was always so hot, sometimes 130 degrees. You were always thirsty and we didn't have much water. During the day you had to keep all of your clothes on or you'd get sunburned. Then at night, you'd freeze.

The Sicilians hated the British, but they liked the Americans. So, when we landed in Sicily they'd surrender to us. They'd yell, "Paisan" and come to us. The Italians were a little different, though. They didn't like the Americans. They used to sing a song about how the Americans bombed their churches and killed a lot of people.

In Italy I met General Gavin (Commander of the 82nd). He thought my name was Genova. He was a good general and a good man. He'd come up to the front lines and look after us. We were in our foxholes and he asked us if we were warm enough and told us to get some leaves and branches and cover up good.

Once, we were in a place called St. Michelangelo on the side of a mountain. The Germans were at the bottom and we could hear them talking. Sometimes they would yell out in English, "OK., move forward." But we knew better. Every night the hills would be full of sheep and you could see them moving around all night. After a while we got orders to shoot anything that moved because one night we caught a few Germans coming up the hill hiding between the sheep.

Another night I took my gun apart and was cleaning it. What a mistake. All of a sudden I saw something move. It looked like a log or something. I thought I was dreaming. I grabbed a grenade and saw it move again. I thought maybe I was seeing things, so I opened my canteen and poured water on my face. And there it was again – moving – moving. I waited until it got closer and finally when it was about 20 feet away, I threw my grenade at it. It was a German. He had camouflaged himself.

The Germans wanted this high ground and they kept attacking, and we kept repulsing them. We lost a lot of men, but we held the ground. Later our Company Commander won the Silver Star for this.

We were in another town in Italy called "Femina Morta" and we were getting the hell kicked out of us. It seemed like German artillery was hitting us wherever we were. Finally, we figured out that one of the Italians, a well dressed man with a briefcase, was radioing our position to the Germans. He was shot on the spot.

On D-Day, we got charcoal and blackened all our faces. At 5:00 in the morning, we landed near Ste. Mere Eglise. Our job was to cut a path back to the beach. Once we got toward the beach it was like the end of the world. Things blowing up, people screaming. You couldn't believe it. Our commander was an old guy, Colonel Lewis, and he just kept yelling at us to move forward.

Later, when we were moving through France, there was heavy resistance. We were going like hell and for a while, we were hooked up with Patton. When we were moving with the tanks, sometimes a guy would get hit and fall and the tank would run right over him. Sometimes a guy would get wounded, and you could push him out of the way, but others got crushed. You just had to keep moving. One night I was in a foxhole with a buddy and we were getting shelled. It was quiet for a while so I left for no longer than a minute. While I was gone my buddy was killed. I felt so guilty – like I left him flat, like I should have done something.

After a while you got so disgusted, you didn't care. In France, we were so hungry that one time we ate grass. We drank water right out of a horses trough. We didn't care. I would have given $100 for a loaf of bread. You'd be tired, hungry, cold, and you smelled, but you had to do anything to stay alive. We didn't know when the war was going to end. It could have lasted five more years for all we knew. You just had to make the best of it. But sometimes you'd get to the point where you just didn't give a god-damn.

(*In September of 1944, the 82nd and 101st Airborne Division jumped into Holland to clear the way for the final assault on Germany.*)

We jumped into Holland and later ended up in a big Catholic cemetery. Our job was to push the Germans out. They had a lot of artillery and were shelling the hell out of us. We had to creep and crawl inch by inch just worming our way up. All of a sudden I felt something burning in my pants. They were fireproof, but smoke was coming out. A piece of shrapnel went right through my pocket and hit an extra grenade that I had. It sliced the grenade like an apple. It didn't explode, it just sliced in half. In a way it was a good thing because that grenade saved my leg. But if it exploded, I would have been gone. I was bleeding like hell, but I felt real lucky. I carried a piece of that grenade with me for a long time as a reminder. But I finally got rid of it.

We had this guy named Clarence with us, a rebel from Oklahoma. He was a real comedian. While we were in the cemetery, we were crawling near a gravestone with Jesus on it and as we were getting shelled, he turns to me and says in this drawl, "Hey Fred, there's Jesus. Let's liberate him." He was so god damned funny.

(*During Christmas of 1944, the Germans launched a huge counter offensive known as the Battle of the Bulge.*) By the end of 1944, we were all ready to go home. We did our job and a lot of us spent Christmas over there and were ready to leave. We were supposed to go back to the states. We even had our clothes and our guns cleaned. Then about 3:00 in the morning, the Sergeant yelled, "All right men, everybody up." I said what the hell are you doing? He said, "The Germans have broken through. We know you don't want to leave without finishing the job." We all thought he was kidding. We were half asleep and had to get ready to go. Before we knew it, we were on trucks headed toward Bastogne. It was so cold and the snow was up to our knees.

Toward the end of the war we went into one of the death camps. I think it was near Ledwigschluss. The stench was unbelievable. Inside the bodies were stacked up like firewood. You couldn't tell who was dead and who was alive. I couldn't believe it. Some were moaning for help but we were told not to feed them a lot or they'd die. Their eyes were hollow and some of their stomachs were swollen.

The civilians in the town said they didn't know anything about it. So General Gavin gathered up all the people in the town and made them review the bodies. Then, he made them take the bodies to a park and bury them.

After that we crossed the Rhine and I finally got hit. To be honest, I really don't remember what happened. I was knocked out cold. I was hit in the leg and was taken back to France to a hospital. The French took good care of the Americans and after a few weeks I was right back on the line again.

We were in one town in Germany mopping up. By this time the Germans were in bad shape. I remember we were going house to house when my friend Homer threw an apple core through an open window. All of a sudden, two Germans came out with their hands up shouting, "Comrade."

The concentration camp at Ledwigschluss

When we got to the Elbe River we met up with the Russians; they were worse than the Germans. They were burning houses and putting the people out on the streets and pushing them into this big open field. It was cold outside and babies were crying and people were being pushed around. A lot of the Russians were drunk and were grabbing the women and knocking them down. I remember a few of them going over to a stable, letting the horses out, and then throwing rocks at them.

I never thought I'd make it back home, but when my mother got sick while I was there I said, "I'm going to go home. No son of a bitch is going to kill me." But, the longer you stayed there, the more chance you had of getting hit. Your chances of making it were getting slim. Every time we went up in a plane, somebody had to die. The plane could crash or you could get shot out of the air or you could get killed on one of the traps that the Germans had waiting for us. But finally, in March of 1945, I had enough points to come home.

I was lucky to come back. I had a lot of close calls while I was over there. I was shot in the leg, hit in the helmet, hit in the canteen.

I don't talk about the war a lot. If somebody asks me a question I'll answer it, but that's it. Once my brother and I went to a war movie at the Stamford Theater and I got the chills and just walked out. It brought back memories. Then sometimes I'd have bad dreams. But after a while I got used to it.

A lot of times I'll sit here and think, "Why did I come out alive?" Maybe somebody upstairs was looking out for me.

Fred returned to the states with his "G.I. Bride" from England. He settled in Stamford and served on the Stamford Police Department for over 40 years before retiring in 1992. He was awarded the Purple Heart and a Presidential Unit Citation.

- PETER LACERENZA -

Peter Lacerenza entered the military some ten months before the attack on Pearl Harbor. He was initially scheduled to serve one year but once the U.S. entered the war he served for the duration. After spending almost 6 months with the 8th Coast Artillery and 3 years with the 240 Coast Artillery Band he was reassigned to the 78th Division, 310 Infantry. He arrived in Europe in late 1944 and was stationed in England, Central Europe, the Rhineland, and the Ardennes before being captured during the Battle of the Bulge.

When I was transferred to the 78th I was trained as a heavy machine gunner. After D-Day we were sent to England, France, then Belgium. This was about the time when the Americans were reaching the Siegfried Line. We went to the Ardennes, then through the line. Our object was to capture a dam on the other side of Kesternick, Germany. (*The dam referred to here is the Schwammenauel Dam*) They were afraid that the Germans were going to blow it up. From December 13th to the 15th we advanced a few towns and got to Kesternick. On December 15th, I was on the outskirts of town manning my machine gun but I had to go back to the first medical station because of some frostbite on my legs and feet. While I was there, one of my squad was killed. We didn't know it at the time but this was the start of a big German push.

After they treated me at the medical station, I had to find my way back to my squad. Going back through Kesternick it seemed like I was detoured a hundred different times. Once, when I helped a wounded soldier, then when I was caught in sniper fire. But then just before I located my squad, I saw a rifleman and he was pacing back and forth. Behind him was a little gully and in it were six or seven American soldiers, all dead. They looked so peaceful–like they were sleeping. The soldier told me that they were hit by an 88mm shell. Then another guy came along and was very upset. He knew all of the guys and started referring to them by name.

I finally got back to my squad later on and all hell broke loose. We had no idea what was happening. We thought Kesternick was secure and that the war was almost over. Now shells were coming right over our heads and hitting the town. This was during the night.

The night of December 15th was bitter cold and snow was on the ground. Our Lieutenant took off and said, "Stay here until you hear from me." We were supposed to protect his flank. There were only five of us left there. We were on a hill overlooking a valley. We dug in for the night, which was a problem as we had to dig through tree roots and we could hear the artillery all around us. There were three of us in one shallow hole and behind us were two sergeants in another hole.

Early the next morning it was foggy and we couldn't see too well. We heard some noise and then a shot. The sergeant peered up and told us that there were a few Germans coming along near a fence that was behind us. I had a pistol and a grenade and, not expecting them to come from the rear, the machine gun was still facing toward the valley, there was no way we could reach out to turn it around. I don't remember what the other two had, probably carbines. One of the sergeants fired his rifle from his hole and I threw a grenade near the fence. Then machine gun fire came in right over our heads from the other direction. McKinney, the fellow next to me, started bleeding from the head. We thought he was shot but it turned out he had a gash from a rock that shot up and hit him. We were surrounded and the Germans started yelling in English, "Hands up, hands up." I yelled to the sergeant, "What do you want to do? We're pinned down." And he said, "We're going to have to give up."

So, for some reason I asked him if he wanted me to get up first. I put my hand up first expecting it to get shot off but when it wasn't, I stood up. Then I saw a machine gun about 20 feet away, and a bunch of riflemen. We were completely outnumbered. One started yelling for me to get my hands over my head and another started yelling for the other guys to come out. As I was walking forward, I could see that a couple of the Germans were wounded. An officer was wounded in the leg and he looked mad as hell. He had an automatic weapon in his hands. We called it a "burp gun" because of the sound. He was aiming it right at me. I was sure he was going to shoot so I did the first thing that came to me. I saluted him. Don't ask me why, it was just automatic. Thinking back, I think it was from our training. If ever in enemy hands, Officers should have the same respect as our own.

He didn't shoot. They captured us and made us carry the two wounded Germans back to their first aid station. As we were being brought to their rear, we noticed that practically the only thing that the Germans had left were tanks. Once you got beyond the tanks there were no trucks or anything. All they had were horses and carts carrying their supplies.

We were lucky that we didn't panic and run because we probably would have been killed. I also think that if we waited any longer someone might have thrown a grenade in at us. (During the Battle of the Bulge many Americans who had surrendered were gunned down. The most brutal incident of this sort became known as the Malmedy Massacre where over 100 Americans were executed after they surrendered.)

As they were bringing us in, we got no more than 25 feet when an American artillery shell came in. We all hit the ground and a few more Germans were wounded. None of us were hit. When we finally got to the rear, which was no more than a quarter mile from where we were captured, we were put in a barn, then trucked to a town called Flemershine where we stayed in the town jail house. We worked there for a day and on December 18th they marched us to Bonn. I think we were moved around a lot because some of the P.O.W. camps were over-crowded. Before it was all over, I spent time in seven camps. The only reason I remember this is that I had a pencil with me and each time we entered a camp, I wrote down the name of it in a little mass book that I kept.

The treatment was different from camp to camp. It depended on who you were dealing with. In some of the camps, if you didn't move fast enough they'd kick you or hit you with a rifle butt. Sometimes they'd poke you with a bayonet, not stab you, poke you. Usually when they marched us, we weren't treated badly because they used the older soldiers, the Home Guard, to watch us. These guys were 50 or 55 years old and they had their own problems marching.

As far as food was concerned–they didn't have much. They'd give us thin soup or this black bread that must have had wood in it. Once in a while you'd get a potato but you'd have to split it with another guy. And you made sure that you cut it exactly in half. The water was bad and I got sick a few times with a fever or diarrhea. Once they took some of us to a hospital where we inhaled steam for a temperature.

You couldn't bathe. You couldn't shave. I think I shaved once in the time I was there and I don't even remember how I did it. You worried about lice. In one camp we had to take off our clothes and they sprayed us and our clothing with a chemical. Then we had to walk outside to get our clothes. This was in the middle of the winter. The cold was always a problem. It seemed that you could never get warm enough. Some camps had bunks and in others we slept right on the floor.

The worst thing, though, was when they transported us in the boxcars. They were so crowded. They'd cram as many guys in as they could and you could hardly move. You could only sit, you couldn't lie down. Sometimes we were in them for days because rails would be destroyed and we'd have to just sit on the track in the boxcar until they were fixed.

Sometimes we marched for days at a time; once, for seven straight days. One time, we were marching and we saw the Germans marching a column of prisoners in the opposite direction. We were told that they were political prisoners but the word was that they were going to be killed. They looked like they were in bad shape. One of our guys tried to pass something to one of them and a German guard hit him.

A strange thing is that while I was in one of the camps I was dishing out soup and I ran into Frank Martinelli. He lived in the same house where I lived, on the second floor. We were in the same camps together but in different groups until we were liberated. When I got back home before he did, the first thing I did was tell his mother that he was all right.

We never talked or associated much with the German guards but one of them who spoke English was telling me that he heard that German P.O.W.'s were treated very well. I agreed and he told me that the first chance he got, he was going to surrender to the Americans. He was a young fellow, maybe 17 years old.

Right before Christmas, when we were in Stalag 12-B, some British Lancaster bombers came in and accidentally hit the barracks right next to ours. A lot of G.I.'s and officers were killed. They must have been way off target.

Toward the end of the war, I ended up near the Polish border. We kept getting information that the war was almost over. I don't know how we got this information but there was an underground. This is how we found out that F.D.R. died.

In late April, we knew something was up because the German officers started panicking. On April 26th, we could hear gunfire in the distance and assumed it was our guys. When we woke up the next morning the Germans were gone. The highest ranking officer in the camp took charge and immediately set up a system of guarding ourselves, so that none of us could get out. He told us that we were safer inside the camp than out.

On the morning of April 28, 1945, we were liberated by the British Welsh Guard. We weren't hollering or yelling or anything but we were elated. The first thing that came into the camp was the chow wagon but they wouldn't let us eat a lot because they were afraid we'd get sick. It was foggy so they didn't fly us out for three days. When it cleared up we were flown into Brussels and from there we were finally turned over into American hands by the British. We were on our way to France by rail when we heard that the war was over.

I was taken to a hospital and treated for malnutrition. Then they put us on a ship and sent us home. Later, I was sent to a camp in Lake Placid and while I was there I met Bill Samela from Stamford. That's where we became good friends.

When I got home I found out that even though I was captured on December 16th, 1944, I wasn't reported M.I.A. until January 2, 1945. Then, my mother didn't find out that I was alive and in a prison camp until May 2, 1945.

Right before I left Stamford for the service, I went down and bought a pair of shoes at Lou Konspore's on Atlantic Street. He told me that I could pay him when I got home from the service. Then, when I was reported M.I.A. he told my sister to forget about the money. Well, when I finally got home, I went right down to the store to pay. When Lou saw me he turned white as a ghost and said, "My God. I thought you were dead." He never took my money.

Lacerenza raised his family in Stamford and worked in the antique restoration business with Williams' Antique Shop, until his retirement. He was awarded the Combat Infantry Badge, the Bronze Star, the P.O.W. Medal, and three Battle Stars

- GENE OFIERO -

Gene Ofiero entered the Army in 1943, and was one of five brothers overseas during the war. He saw action in Belgium and Germany with the 2nd Infantry Division and was seriously wounded just one month before the war in Europe ended.

In 1943, my father got three draft notices on the same day, one for me, my brother Tony, and my brother Joe. We already had three brothers overseas. My father was a widower and had to raise 12 kids, and he said, "Jesus, don't these guys have a heart?" So, my brother Tony had to go down to the Draft Board to try to straighten it out. My brother Joe was a very sick man. He had a rheumatic heart so they couldn't take him. They told me that I could stay home if I worked in a defense factory, Air Radio. I worked there for a while, but I told my father I couldn't take it any more, so I went into the Army.

They shipped me down to Fort McClellan in Alabama, and when I was there I called my sister and she was crying. She told me that Joe was getting worse and was in Intensive Care at Stamford Hospital. She said that my father was going downhill and that he had practically lost the trucking business with us all gone.

So, I went to see my Captain and told him that I had to get home. My brother was dying and I had to see him. The Captain knew that I had done some boxing before the war and he said, "I'll tell you what. If you box this weekend, you'll get a three day pass." I jumped at it, so he took me down to a theater on the base and there was a big line of guys waiting to box. When the promoter, a guy named Shapiro, got to me, he asked me if I was a professional. I lied. I told him I was and that I fought Willy Pep once. I was a featherweight, only 96 pounds, and he wanted me to fight this guy who was undefeated. I would have fought anybody for that weekend pass. I just hoped I could make it the three rounds. Well, I did, but I got beat up pretty bad. I took the train home and got to see my brother Joe. It was the last time I saw him *(Joe died in 1945)*. Three weeks later I was on the front lines.

I got to Europe as a replacement at the end of the French campaign and the first major action I saw was in Belgium. It snowed every day and at one point, the snow was way over my head. So I used to follow this tall guy, Sergeant Butler, and hold on to him while I was carrying the radio. During the Battle of the Bulge, you wouldn't believe the confusion. Sometimes you didn't even know the guys you were fighting with. Your mind just goes. You're practically berserk. It's hard to explain, but guys wanted to die. You couldn't sleep at night with the German shells coming in –ßthe screaming mimis. At times, we were down to only 30 guys, and were waiting for replacements.

We were stuck up in the mountains most of the time. I forget the name of the town. A lot of the time we took cover in these tunnels that the Belgians had. The people there were living on beets they had stored. The entire time we were there, we were down to one ration a day. At one point, we found some chickens and guys were grabbing them two at a time to cook them. We were outdoors most of the time and we slept outside every night. We weren't even allowed to keep a fire at night. The British were and they used to laugh at us. I remember one of the guys saying to me, "You might as well die warm."

We'd go out on patrol with four or five guys and you always had an officer with you, usually a 2nd Lieutenant. A lot of these guys were green and it seemed like they were dying like flies. We'd go out in the snow. You never knew where the Germans were. One time I tripped a flare and it lit up the sky and we were standing out there like silhouettes. The Germans were pretty close and could have killed us, but we ran one way and they ran the other.

You were supposed to go on patrol about once every 8-10 days, but for a while I was getting it almost every night – and at one time, five nights in a row. We'd usually go out and if we saw a building, we'd go into the cellar and radio back anything we saw. One time, two of us went into a damn cellar and we heard footsteps up above. It was German soldiers. We left one at a time, and got out of there in a hurry.

Sometimes you couldn't see through the snow. When you got shelled, the snow would fly around and blind you. You'd just try to find a hole or something for cover. Once when we were getting hit, I jumped into a hole and there was a dead soldier in it. He must have been there for days because the snow was piled up on his helmet. I jumped right back out of that hole.

Finally, in January, we got a nice sunny day. A jeep with a half track, we called it a weasel, dropped off a new supply of C-Rations. Then we saw American planes overhead. It was just like Christmas. There were so many planes in the sky that the snow was moving. Then they let their bombs go and the ground shook. We felt like nothing could live through that kind of bombing.

In April, after we crossed the Rhine, we were in Germany, not too far from Belgium. We were all happy because we thought we'd be going home soon. At this time, Patton was moving fast and we couldn't keep up. One day, five of us were riding on a tank and we got to a German village. We were the

Gene and his brother Lou outside the hospital in France

first tank in and the others were following. As we went around a bend, there was a German tank waiting for us. The muzzle of the gun was aiming right at us and I was looking at it point blank. As the German tank fired, we all screamed. I tried to jump off and get the radio off my back. That's the last thing I remember. I woke up in a field tent and the next thing I remember was being on an airplane with a lot of other stretchers. I never saw my outfit again. I don't know what happened to the tank or the other guys. I don't think they could have possibly survived. I was blown off our tank by the concussion. That's probably what saved me.

For the next few weeks I was out of it. Then I finally realized what happened. My hair was burned off and I guess I had swallowed some of the flame because my mouth and throat were burned. I couldn't see for a while and I couldn't move my left arm and my legs. It was maybe three or four months before I could get around. They gave me a lot of electrical shocks for my muscles and Dr. Ginsberg, who was treating me used to say, "Don't worry, we'll have you walking again." I can never thank him enough. Little by little, the feeling in my arm and fingers returned, and I was sent to Belgium for rehab.

When I was in the 21st General Hospital in France, my brother Lou came to visit me. He saw my name in "Stars and Stripes" and came from Austria. He told me that my brother Nick was wounded on the exact same day as me, April 7, 1945. I had seen Nick while I was in Belgium. He was with the 78th and I knew he was in the area, but one day I was in a 6x6 and he rode by in another 6x6. I screamed as loud as I could, "Nick! Nick!", but he never saw me. He was wounded when a bullet went through his helmet and deflected into his forehead and nose.

I was supposed to go for more treatments, but I was dying to come home, so I signed a waiver to get out. Coming into New York on a boat, there's one thing I'll never forget. I saw the Statue of Liberty for the first time in my life. I ended up on the 92nd Street Pier and when they played the Star Spangled Banner, there wasn't a dry eye on the ship.

Ofiero was back in May of 1946. He operated several gas stations in Stamford and Darien until 1973, when he went to work for the Darien Board of Education. He has been awarded the Purple Heart, the Combat Infantry Badge, and the Croix de Guerre.

- THE BOND DRIVES -

In less than four years, Stamford conducted eight war loan drives. Each drive exceeded its goal and by war's end, the town purchased $69,483,732.00 worth of war loan and victory bonds. With the population estimated at 63,000 people, the town purchased an average of more than $1,100 for every man, woman, and child in town.

In addition to this, the town donated 3,642 pints of blood to the Red Cross for the war effort, and another 300 pints immediately after the war ended.[1]

- GEORGE ZURMAN -

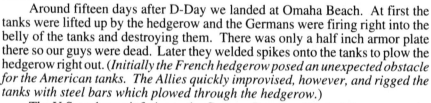

George Zurman graduated from Stamford High School in 1934 and enlisted in the U.S. Army in 1941. When the war broke out he was already married with a young daughter. Just after D-Day he was sent to France with the Fourth Armored Division to take part in General Patton's famous "breakout" from the beaches of Normandy. As a Captain in the 737th Tank Battalion, nicknamed "Patton's Spearheaders" he participated in the five campaigns including Normandy, Northern France, Ardennes, the Rhine, and Central Germany.

I went overseas in February of 1944 and was stationed in Wales. We were supposed to go in two days after D-Day, but they couldn't get the tanks ashore fast enough. They were sinking. So we had to wait until the Americans took the beaches so that we could land in shallower water.

Around fifteen days after D-Day we landed at Omaha Beach. At first the tanks were lifted up by the hedgerow and the Germans were firing right into the belly of the tanks and destroying them. There was only a half inch armor plate there so our guys were dead. Later they welded spikes onto the tanks to plow the hedgerow right out. (*Initially the French hedgerow posed an unexpected obstacle for the American tanks. The Allies quickly improvised, however, and rigged the tanks with steel bars which plowed through the hedgerow.*)

The U.S. tank was inferior to the German Panzers. We had the worst tanks in the war. We didn't have the firepower that they had. The Germans' normal anti-tank shell traveled 3400 feet per second. Ours only went about 2200 feet per second. We couldn't make a hole in their tanks but their shells would go right through ours and out the other end. If they hit you – you were dead. We lost a lot more tanks than they did. In my company alone we lost 44 tanks in less than a year.

When we attacked at Company strength that meant 3 platoons. Each platoon had 5 tanks. Then there were 2 extra tanks and then I was in another. In all, I was in charge of 18 tanks and 90 crew.

There were 5 guys in a tank. Three in the turret, one driver, and one assistant driver. A tank carried 3 machine guns, and one .75 mm gun. The only way we could knock a Panzer out was by hitting the side of it. We could maneuver better than they did but you could never take one head on. Our strength was in our numbers. We had a hell of a lot more tanks than they did. If the Germans had as many tanks as we did, you'd probably be speaking German right now.

It wasn't like you see in the movies where tanks blow up all the time. Tanks were flammable because they carried ammunition. But they rarely blew up. A lot of our tanks burned on the inside like a blow torch but they didn't blow apart. When a tank was hit, a lot of the time you didn't know it until you saw the hole. Sometimes they looked fine on the outside. Only once did I see the turret blow off a tank.

Three tanks that I was in were hit. But I was lucky each time. Twice the hits were low around the tracks. Our company had plenty of casualties though, because most of the time a tank got hit, you lost 2-3 men. While hot chunks of metal would come in and ricochet around.

Another thing that was different from the movies was that you didn't button down. In other words you never pulled your hatch down. You had to stick your head out to see. In training you were told to pull the hatch down but then you were looking through a periscope and you could only see what was right in front of you. That was it. If everything was peaceful and you were traveling up a road, you could close the hatch. But in combat you can't see. You can't tell who's shooting at you. That's why you never saw a veteran tank commander in combat with the hatch closed. Maybe a replacement, but not a veteran. After you were in combat for a while you knew that if you wanted to live you had to see what was going on. Another thing, the hatch was heavy. If you got wounded badly, you'd be trapped in there. You wouldn't be able to get the hatch up and get out. If the tank got hit and flared up you had to get out quickly. Usually a driver or assistant driver couldn't get out in time because their hatches had to stay closed. They were right beneath the guns and if they left the hatch open you wouldn't be able to traverse the guns.

It took a lot to supply a tank. It was built to carry 85 rounds but we always carried 100. We also carried 6,000 rounds for the machine gun. It had a 450 horse power engine and it would use about 180 gallons of gasoline a day. And that was later with the improved engine. At first we were using an aircraft engine but every time you started it, a blue cloud of smoke went up. That was the last thing you wanted, a cloud of smoke to make you a perfect target.

Before you fired your gun you would fire your machine gun with tracers on it to show you where they hit. From 800 feet in, that would tell you exactly where your shell would hit. The Germans had boiler plate steel and sometimes you'd hit them and it was just like a mosquito bounced off them. You had to pray that you hit them just right because if you didn't, you'd watch their big gun turn right your way. Your best bet was backing out and trying to maneuver to the side of them, hit their tracks, and disable them.

After we landed at Omaha Beach, we joined up with Patton when he formed the Third Army. The Allies were about 3 miles inland when we got ashore. Then we got to St. Lo. This was definitely the worst action our company saw. We'd gain 500 yards during the day and they'd take it back at night. We'd attack at 6:00 A.M. and they'd attack at 12:00 midnight. As a matter of fact, I slept in the same foxhole, on and off, for around 3 weeks. This was one of the toughest battles we faced. When they picked up the dead there, they had to pack them up in carts and stack them like cordwood. That's what I saw. The dead stacked 8 high in rows. Every once in a while a truce would be declared to pick up the dead and wounded. We had to do this because at night you'd hear men yelling for water or for help in the fields between the hedgerows.

The danger of war really hit close to me when I was in the Gremecey Forest in France. I was in a jeep talking to a major in the 35th Infantry from Texas. He was telling me how when the war was over he was never going to get angry again. He was going to go back to Texas, get married, and raise a family on a farm, and never let anything bother him again. Then we heard a noise and I barely had enough time to yell for him to get down. A shell came in and caused a tree burst. And the next instant he was dead. There I was, talking to him one second, and the next second he was killed. It could have been me, I was only a few feet away. But all I could think about was how a minute earlier this guy was talking just like a happy kid. He had no idea that he only had a few seconds to live.

Mortagne in France was another bad fight. We had a lot of fights, but none like this one. We pretty near got wiped out this time. We attacked the 2nd S.S. Panzer Division. We attacked at 3:00 A.M. and didn't get back until 5:00 A.M. the next day. For a while they had us completely surrounded and fired everything they had at us. We never really took the town. We just put enough pressure on them so that they had to withdraw. When it was over, we came back with only 5 tanks. They knocked out 12 of our tanks and another crew was missing in action.

Later on, the Army gave us "jumbo tanks." They just put 10 more tons of armor on the Sherman Tank. They gave us 5 and we were the first company to get them. The first time we used them we were going up a hill in Germany and their anti-tank guns knocked out all five right from the front. We didn't get any more after that.

We saw Patton quite a bit. If you acted like you were afraid, he had no use for you. But he'd talk to the GI's just like he was another GI. He didn't care if you saluted or not. He'd joke around and yell to us, "How the hell are you? Did you shoot anyone today?"

When we got to the Rhine, we were supposed to wait there for two weeks while a bridge was built. But Patton got there and said, "What the hell are we waiting for?" So, we ended up going across in barges, and once we got across we knew the war was over.

Toward the end we took a lot of prisoners. Once I was leading a company into a town. I was in a jeep and I stopped to talk to the driver. I felt a tap on my shoulder and when I turned around it was a German soldier surrendering. They had just had it. They were out of food and out of ammunition. In one of the towns we took over 700 prisoners.

At the end of the war we were in Frankfurt, then the Ruhr, and then we made a beeline to Czechoslovakia. The Germans wanted to surrender to us but we weren't allowed to take them. We had to send them to the Russians. (*Before the end of the war the U.S., England, and Soviet Union set up occupation zones. In many instances Germans who were captured in certain areas were not allowed to surrender to U.S. troops.*) One night we could hear the pop of German guns. Some were shooting themselves rather than turning themselves over to the Russians.

We occupied Czechoslovakia and then went to Bavaria looking for high ranking German officers. Then we went back to England. In all we were in combat for 299 days. By the time the war was over there were only 15 men from my original company that weren't killed or wounded. My first Sergeant was killed and I lost 5 Lieutenants.

I don't know why I was so lucky. I didn't have a scratch.

Zurman returned to his wife and daughter in 1946. He established Fairfield Auto Top, which he operated in Stamford for over 35 years. In addition to 5 Battle Stars, he received a Presidential Unit Citation and the French Croix de Guerre.

- CAPTAIN ZURMAN'S SILVER STAR -

While in France's Gremecey Forest, George Zurman was awarded the Silver Star. Facing stubborn enemy defences and "severe enemy artillery, mortar, and antitank fire," Zurman led his company through the enemy defenses and captured the town of Morhange. Zurman is credited with planning, coordinating, and personally supervising all tank action and moving freely among his troops "with utter disregard for his personal safety."[2]

- JIMMY STOLFI -

When the war broke out Jimmy Stolfi was working in the Civilian Conservation Corps making $30.00 a week. At age 19 he was drafted into the U.S. Army and assigned to the Fourth Armored Division. As a member of the Mechanized Reconnaissance Troop A, 25th Cavalry he saw action in France, the Rhineland, the Ardennes, Bastogne, and Belgium.

My outfit was supposed to go into Europe right after D-Day, but I had my appendix out in England and was in the hospital for thirty days. While I was in the hospital they were bringing in a lot of guys who were wounded on D-Day. One day a guy came in and he was passing out Purple Hearts. He came up to me and asked, "Where were you wounded son?" I said, "I wasn't, I had my appendix out."

After that I had to join up with my unit again somewhere in France. What town? I don't know. There were so many names to remember. Some of the towns were so small they they weren't even on the map. A lot of them were little farm villages and we weren't in them too long. The war was on. You'd take a town and move on.

When I joined up with my unit my job was Cavalry Reconnaissance. We were the ones who were always sent ahead on patrol to look for Germans. I drove the lead jeep in my platoon. I had a Scout Sergeant and a machine gunner with me. Altogether my platoon had 6 jeeps and 3 armored cars. Each jeep had 3 guys and each armored car had 4 guys so there was never more than 30 of us. It was tough because we were usually out in the open and you couldn't see the Germans unless they started shooting at you. They were usually dug in and you were going into their territory. In some places they were there for years.

If we spotted anything we would radio back to the command post and they'd bring up the infantry, tanks or artillery. Sometimes, if we were really outnumbered, we'd just have to make a run for it. With the small vehicles, we could usually get out of an area in a hurry. The thing you had to watch for the most was getting boxed in and getting caught in a crossfire.

When you went into a town you had to be careful of booby traps that the Germans left behind. Stairways, beds, doors, anything would be booby trapped. That's why I never slept in a house during the war. I slept on the ground. I slept in barns but never in a house because you never knew. I figured the Germans would never booby trap a haystack.

When you went into a town you didn't take too many chances. You didn't know who the real civilians were or if they were snipers. Some of the soldiers would dress up in civilian clothes. So any young guy we saw, we took in and sent him to be interrogated. We figured that these guys had to be in the army because near the end of the war the Germans were using everybody. We captured guys 60 years old with new uniforms and brand new rifles. That's how old the Germans were taking them. But most of the civilians were friendly. We got along with them. In most cases we were liberating the town. In Germany they figured, we took the town. They weren't going to give us any backtalk. In Frankfurt the civilians were so hungry that they were digging in our garbage cans to get the food that we threw out. We'd clean off our new mess kits and they'd go after that food.

Once in a while we'd get a hot meal. We always had a blow torch with us and sometimes we'd use it to heat up our C-rations or our coffee. It was faster than building a fire. Sometimes we'd find food in a village — bread, a slab of bacon and sometimes we'd come across eggs on some of the farms. The only time we got a hot meal from the company chow wagon was if we were in an area for a couple of days. You'd also go months without a shower. You'd have to wash out of your helmet.

During the Battle of the Bulge, we traveled two days and two nights to relieve the 101st at Bastogne. Most of it was through the woods. It was cold, too, about a foot and a half of snow. The Germans were shelling the hell out of us. They were sending 88 mm shells in. They were wicked. I lost my Company Commander right outside of Bastogne. We were in an open field across from some woods. We couldn't figure out where the hell the shells were coming from. That's when our Company Commander got it. He went out on patrol in a jeep with two other guys. The other two guys came back but he didn't. They just had his helmet. *(The history of the Fourth Armored Division records that Captain Charlie Trover was killed by a sniper on Dec. 24, 1944).*

Finally, one of our guys spotted a German with a white suit and a radio on his back. He was radioing our position back to the Germans and they were firing on us. It was the worst battle we were in but we survived it.

Later, toward the end of the war, our whole Division was going onto Frankfurt. There was a whole column of Germans walking down the main street with their hands up, ready to surrender. There wasn't even a G.I. guarding them. They were just marching, three abreast, about 200 of them. They wanted to know where to go. We couldn't stop to guard them so we just motioned for them to keep on going.

Right after Frankfurt and about a month and a half before the end of the war, I got wounded. It was March 25, 1945, and we were headed for a small town outside of Frankfurt. They sent us on patrol where no one else had been. We were going down a road and we got ambushed. I was in the jeep and they opened up on us. My machine gunner was shot right in the head. As I was getting out of the jeep I got hit in the arm. It felt like a hard slap. I grabbed my M-1 and tried to take cover behind the jeep and I got knocked on my butt by a bazooka blast. I was dazed for a few seconds but my Sergeant turned the jeep around. As he did this I was running to call the other guys from the Platoon up to help us and bullets were flying all over hitting the ground, whizzing by my ears.

Finally, an ambulance came up and took me and my machine gunner away. I heard them say that he was already dead. I was in a daze, a little in shock, and I couldn't feel my arm. So the first thought I had was that I had lost my arm. When we got back to the rear, the medics took the bullet out of my arm. Later they gave it to me. Today I have it framed. I didn't know at the time but I also got hit in the leg with shrapnel. I was on a stretcher for five days before they could get me back to a field hospital.

I ended up in a hospital in Paris for nine weeks. By the time I got out and rejoined my unit, they were in Czechoslovakia and the war was over. We spent the next six months there and in Germany as part of the occupational force. We'd go out on patrol and look for stragglers. There were still some German soldiers that didn't know the war was over.

I don't talk about the war a lot today. It was a long time ago and I try to forget it. I'm just proud that I did my job. I didn't run from it and I got home in one piece.

Jimmy Stolfi was awarded the Purple Heart, four Battle Stars, the EAME Medal, and the Presidential Unit Citation for relieving the 101 at Bastogne. He also earned a Bronze Star for helping some of his comrades who were pinned down by enemy fire. At present, he is retired and working part time as a manager at the Darien VFW and was recently honored as the Grand Marshal of the 1993 Memorial Day Parade.

- ALPHONSE RICH AND THE BATTLE OF THE BULGE -

During the Battle of the Bulge, Al Rich was assigned to the 101st Airborne Division in the vicinity of Bastogne. On January 13, 1945, carrying a light machine gun and ammunition, he charged a well entrenched German position. Running through deep snow, "Rich routed three enemy positions, killed several and captured 12 of the enemy."[3]

For his actions, Rich was awarded the Croix de Guerre with Palms by the Belgian government. In addition to this, Rich earned a Bronze Star, Presidential Unit Citation, and four Battle Stars.

[1]Stamford Advocate, August 15, 1945

[2] "Stamford Officer's Gallantry in Battle Brings Silver Star". Stamford Advocate, February 7, 1945.

[3]"Belgians Honor Stamford Man for Gallant Capture of Twelve Nazis". Stamford Advocate, September 5, 1945.

CHAPTER FOURTEEN

VICTORY

With the Battle of the Bulge ending in defeat for the Germans, the Third Reich was quickly crumbling and the Allied war machine was rolling through Germany. By April of 1945, Hitler was holed up in his bunker waiting for a miracle. In the next few weeks, however, it was obvious that none would occur. Mussolini had already been killed and American and Soviet forces were closing in on Berlin.

On April 30, 1945, Hitler took his own life and one week later, Colonel General Alfred Jodl unconditionally surrendered the remaining German forces. At long last, the Third Reich was defeated.

With the war in Europe over, the United States could now concentrate all of its resources on the Empire of Japan. President Truman was advised, however, that an invasion of the mainland would result in over a million casualties.

On July 7, 1945, a team of scientists tested the first Atomic Bomb and reported its awesome destructive power to the President. Soon after, Truman issued the Potsdam Proclamation which promised "utter destruction" to the Japanese homeland if they did not surrender unconditionally. When the Japanese ignored the ultimatum, the use of the new bomb was inevitable.

At 8:15 on the morning of August 6, 1945, the first atomic bomb was dropped on the city of Hiroshima. In a matter of seconds, tens of thousands were killed and an entire city was obliterated. Three days later a second bomb was dropped in Nagasaki with similar results.

Finally, on April 14, 1945, Emperor Hirohito, in a recorded broadcast to his people, accepted the terms of the surrender. After six long years the most destructive war in history was over.

Photo courtesy of U.S. Navy

- LEWIS JACKSON -

Lewis Jackson graduated from Stamford High School in 1941 and worked for the First Stamford Bank and Trust Company. At the end of 1942, he enlisted in the Army Air Corps and was assigned to the 39th Bombardment Group of the 20th Air Force. In 1945, his B-29 flew 26 bombing missions over Japan.

I enlisted in December of 1942 and when I was sent to Fort Devins, it was the first time I was ever away from home. From there we were taken to Miami, Florida, where, strangely enough, we were put up in hotels. We stayed at the Blackstone Hotel, and I could remember that at the time they had rooms for $96 per night. We were there for three months, and then I travelled all over the country: California, Denver, Fort Meyers, Florida and Kansas. In Kansas, we were assigned to a permanent crew and I stayed with that crew until the end of the war. We were one of the few crews who flew every single mission together.

At that time, the B-29 was still being tested. It wasn't like the B-17 which was wide open. Our plane was pressurized so we didn't have to wear the big heavy suits to keep warm at the high altitudes. It was a new concept, a lot like the planes that fly today.

We had a crew of 11 just like the B-17. I was the CFC (Central Fire Control). I was located at the top of the plane, under a blister of glass. I controlled the top guns and the other guns. I could see 12:00 to 6:00 and that was my responsibility. The name of our plane was "One Weakness." It was taken from a character in "L'il Abner" called "One Weakness Jones."

In April of 1945, we flew from California to Hawaii and from there we were supposed to fly to Guam. But first we had to land on a small island, Kwajalein. Kwajalein had to be timed with the tides because we needed as much runway as possible, and at high tide we couldn't land. I don't think the island was 10 feet above sea level. We lost one of our crews on the way out there when they missed the runway and the entire crew was killed. From Kwajalein, we loaded up with weapons because on our way to Guam we'd be flying over Japanese territory. From this point until the end of the war, Guam was our home base.

The B-29 was designed for high altitude bombing from 20 - 30,000 feet. At that altitude, the fighters were less effective and the anti-aircraft had less of a chance of hitting us. The problem was, at that altitude the bombings were less accurate too, so when General LeMay took over, he decided that we should bomb from 7,000 feet. He personally led the first raid from that altitude and made sure everyone did it the right way. You see, some of the guys were practicing what we called "kick bombing." That means that rather than flying right over the target, some planes would make a sweep over and drop the bombs as they veered off. General LeMay made sure there was no more of that.

Every time we took off from Guam, we did so at one minute intervals. At the end of the runway, there was a 200 or 300 foot drop off a cliff, so halfway down the runway you always prayed that you had enough speed to take off. Sometimes you'd see a plane look like it dropped right off the cliff, and then a moment later it would pop right back up in the air once it was over the sea.

Almost all of our flights were 14-16 hours, depending on where in Japan we were going. All were bombing raids on the mainland, except that on most flights we were never over land for long. We were only over the target for a few minutes. The biggest danger for us was the anti-aircraft.

We flew both day and night missions. At night we'd take off around dusk. You never flew in formation at night because there was too much danger of collision. Everyone went up separately and you were assigned different altitudes. For example, if we went out in what was called an M.E. (Maximum Effort), the 39th Group would be assigned 7,000 feet. That meant that all 45 of our planes would be at that altitude. The danger was that if another squadron flew faster or slower than they were supposed to, there was always a danger that they would be underneath you when you dropped your bombs.

On the night runs, the Japanese would aim their searchlights up at the sky, and their fighters would simply ride the light beam up and try to hit us. We would have strips of tin foil, like Christmas wrapping, and dump it out of the plane. Once it got out of the plane, it would unfold and the search lights would pick that up instead.

Toward the end of the war, we began fire raids. We had big clusters of napalm that would bust open and drop fire all over the city. Since most of the structures in Japan were wooden, some of these fires were an unbelievable sight. Before we got over a city, our pathfinders would usually locate the target by dropping fire bombs over in an "X" pattern. By the time we got to the target, there would be a huge flaming "X", and you could see it for miles and miles. We bombed Tokyo this way 3 times, and after the third time it was totally destroyed.

One of the dangers of these fires below was getting sucked downward by a thermal updraft. On one of our Tokyo missions, we lost a crew that way. The fires down below could be so severe that they would create a vacuum, almost like a tornado, and it could just suck a plane right down. A few times we were bumped around by these firestorms.

We were hit a few times, but fortunately never seriously. When we were hit or low on fuel, we would have to land on Iwo Jima. We did this at least four or five times. On one mission, we had to stop there after dropping 500 lb. demolition bombs. Usually after you dropped your bombs, the radio operator would check the bomb bays and if they were empty, he'd say, "Bombs away". Well, once flying onto Iwo we had a very rough landing and the plane was shaking and vibrating. When we rolled to a stop at the end of the runway, everyone just disappeared. There was not a soul in sight. What happened was that one of our bombs had not dropped out and when we hit the runway, it dropped right down on the runway. They had to get a demolition crew out to disarm the bomb, and boy, did we get chewed out for that.

Once when we were at Iwo, a plane was coming in and it was badly damaged. I think that 5 guys on board were already dead, and the other 6 had to bail out. I remember the plane; it was called "Behren's Brood" and instead of going down, the plane stayed in the air and was flying around. Two Black Widows were finally sent up to shoot it out of the air. Everyone was just standing there watching this whole thing go on.

Our daylight missions were all "strategic raids." We flew in formation and were after a specific target. It was just like the movies. We'd go in for our briefing, and they'd show us the target and tell us the routes to take in and out. You were usually in danger for a few minutes before and after you hit the target. After that you were over water. If you went down over the water, submarines were usually located at 10 mile intervals and they would search for survivors. One of my best friends went down over the Pacific and was picked up by a sub.

Without a doubt, the most memorable and the most frightening thing I remember is when we bombed Osaka, a Japanese fighter was headed right for us. He wasn't even trying to fire at us, he was just going to ram us. I saw him coming in at 12:00 and shot him down. One image I'll never forget was the fighter plane miraculously peeling off and as the plane was rolling over, I could actually see the pilot.

One of the greatest pleasures I had was flying over the "Missouri" on September 2, 1945, as the Japanese were signing the surrender. We had a photographer assigned to the plane that day and he took a lot of pictures. Seeing all the planes in the air and the ships down below was the prettiest sight I ever saw.

You know, I think the war brought out the best in people. At Christmas time, when I was in California before I went overseas, a few buddies and I were walking around town. It was Christmas time and a man and his wife approached us and started talking to us. They told us that their boys were overseas and said, "How would you like to have Christmas dinner with us?" They said that they didn't think anyone should have Christmas dinner away from their families. We accepted immediately. On Christmas day, we had a wonderful dinner with this family and under each of our plates was a $20 bill. I just can't imagine that happening today.

Lewis Jackson returned to Stamford and married his high school sweetheart, Jane Buckley, who had served in the WAVES. He returned to work at First Stamford National Bank and remained there until his retirement in 1989. He received the Distinguished Flying Cross, the Air Medal with two Oak Leaf Clusters and a Distinguished Unit Citation.

Jackson (front row, 4th from left) and the crew of "One Weakness"

- DOUGLAS NORTHROP -

Probably no hometown boy epitomized the "All American Boy" more than Douglas Northrop. A handsome, popular student and an outstanding athlete, he went on to Yale where he became a track star and captained the 150 pound football team. When he joined the Army Air Corps in 1940, he rose quickly from Captain to Major to Lieuten-ant Colonel. When he was on leave he would often return to his neighborhood in Glenbrook and buy all the youngsters ice cream or thrill them with stories of flying. In the early years of the war, Northrop was commended several times for his hazard-ous work in the Atlantic on submarine patrol, and in 1943, he and his crew were credited with sinking an Axis submarine.

When the war in Europe was over, Northrop was sent to the Pacific. There, he participated in 20 bombing missions over Japanese cities and is believed to have been in the lead plane during the initial bombing of Tokyo. He was also credited with locating a group of American flyers downed in the Pacific, who were subse-quently saved.

On April 27, 1945, Northrop flew his last mission. At first it was believed that his plane went down in the Marianas, and that he had managed to stay alive. But by the end of the war, all hopes had dimmed and Northrop was officially declared dead.

Today, the Little League field in Northrop's old neighborhood in Glenbrook, is named in his honor.[1]

- JIMMY NESTOR -

Jimmy Nestor left high school during his junior year in 1944 to enlist in the U.S. Army. He was trained in underwater demolition in preparation for the assault on mainland Japan. However, when the war ended in August of 1945, he became a member of the occupational force. Assigned to the 24th Infantry 5th Ordinance Heavy Machinery Company, he observed, first hand, the damage done to Japan by American bombing.

We were supposed to be the backup force for the invasion of Japan. But when we were on Guam, they dropped the bomb, so by the time we reached the mainland, the war was over. I traveled all over Japan with the 5th Ordinance, and we had to inventory all of the equipment that came in and out. This equipment was going to be used to rebuild Japan.

A lot of the Japanese were impressed with our heavy equipment, and they would hang around and watch. Many of them were nice old men. Nobody would admit that they were in the military though. After a while we learned to figure out who the soldiers were by the clothes they wore. Times were tough and things were scarce, so if you saw someone wearing a nice pair of leather boots, you knew they had to be an officer or something.

The first place we went was Sasebo. It was messed up real bad. Then we went to Fukuoka. We were told not to trust the Japanese because they might still try to kill us. We were expecting problems, so we always had live ammunition. But there wasn't too much trouble.

We were ordered not to fraternize with them. We weren't even supposed to talk to them. A lot of the people were scarred and burned, and many of them didn't know what to expect of us. They thought we were going to kill them.

One time we saw a Japanese soldier wearing American gunner's wings with "Tex" on them. We had a guy in our outfit from Texas whose brother was killed in the war, and when he saw this, he went crazy. He went after the guy and tried to kill him. He was sent back to the states and discharged.

Overall though, we were kind to the Japanese, and as a matter of fact, the best P.R. for the U.S. were the young American soldiers themselves. We'd have chocolate bars and chicklets and give them out to the kids. One time we had a bunch of kids singing, "You are My Sunshine." Later, we took them to a USO show, and they sang it there.

Believe it or not, I think a lot of the people there were not in favor of the war. The people with small businesses, the jewelers and craftsmen, didn't want the war, just like a lot of Americans didn't want Vietnam. A lot of these people were our interpreters and they'd let us know who the imperial staff and officers were. I think they resented the military. Sometimes they would signal us by putting two or three fingers on their shoulders, to signify stripes. That told us somebody was an officer. One time we were driving a truck, and we had a bunch of laborers in the back. They saw a military truck coming and kept signaling us to run it off the

The American bombing damage at Yokohama

road. We honked the horn and squeezed the car so that it had to go off the road, and these guys let out a big cheer. They also loved it when we made the officers work along side the other people.

I spent a lot of time around Hiroshima and Nagasaki. We kept hearing about radiation, but what did we know about it? One of the guys said it must've had something to do with hot water like a radiator. And Fallout? One guy said that was the dust the bomb made when it hit. What did we know?

Hiroshima was just flattened. They wouldn't let us go into the core of the city because they were still doing tests. We were told to wash anything we used, but we had one guy who kept eating oranges. He never washed them. We were given big canvas "lister bags." You were supposed to add quinine and wait a few hours before you drank the water. We found no dead fish, like we were told. There were still plenty of animals, dogs, cats, and seagulls in the city. There was no big crater that everyone was talking about.

We always talk about the Atomic bombs but some of the other cities looked even worse. The B-29'a devastated those cities. Some of the places were still smoldering. Tokyo was leveled. It took me almost a day to cross town because of all the rubble. People were digging, looking for good bricks they could use to rebuild. A lot of the GI's would help with the big equipment or give them wood or gasoline.

Yokohama was just as bad. I still think that Yokohama and Tokyo were the worst. The thing you noticed was the smell from the bombs. It was still there, all over the cities, like the smell of fireworks. By the time we left though, things were starting to look pretty good.

I lay down on the couch some nights and think about some of the things that I saw. I actually saw Tojo during the war crime trials. We parked the jeep in Yokohama one day and there he was being marched into court.

We also saw Hirohito one time in Tokyo. Our interpreter told us that it was at a ceremony for firemen. At the time, we couldn't care less about the emperor. We were more impressed with the 1936 Ford fire truck that was there.

One time while I was in Kobe, a Japanese soldier came up to me, and in perfect English asked me where I was from. I told him I was from Stamford, Connecticut. He told me he was an engineering student at Yale, and he knew where Stamford was. I said, "Go ahead, tell me where it is." And he drew a little map on the ground and showed me New Haven and Stamford. He also told me that he often took the train to New York and visited Stamford sometimes on weekends. But before I left he said one thing I'll never forget. He said, "We're a humble people, but we will fight again."

Jimmy came back to Stamford in 1946 and later opened up his own auto body shop. He has worked as a claims adjuster for many years, but his passion has been the Springdale Fire Department where he has volunteered for over forty years and retired as Fire Chief. At present he is also the Commander of the Springdale VFW Post.

- TWO TRAGIC FATES -

Two Stamford men survived the war only to meet with tragic accidents after the war had ended. John Scalzi, a fine athlete, saw action in Africa and Italy with the U.S. Navy Armed Guard. He was transferred to the Pacific and an Amphibious Landing Ship where he travelled to Leyte, Pelileu, Okinawa, Tokyo, and Yokohama. On October 24, 1945, while en route home, Scalzi was knocked overboard and killed. He was only 20 years old at the time of his death.

Leonard Volpe left for Europe in 1943, three weeks before his son Leonard, Jr., was born. He saw action in France and Germany and at the end of the war he returned to Fort Devins, Massachusetts, where he was discharged. On December 27, 1945, Volpe and four friends took a cab to Boston, where he was then going to make the return trip home. Ironically, before the cab could make it to Boston, it was struck by an Army truck and Volpe was killed. He never had a chance to meet his 22 month old son.[2]

John Scalzi

Leonard Volpe

POSTSCRIPT

On May 27, 1994, over forty veterans of World War II attended a "Veterans' Symposium" at Darien High School. This event, held just before the Memorial Day weekend, had become an annual tradition in my history classes. In addition to its obvious important historical value, another aim of the program was to give the students a greater appreciation for the true meaning of Memorial Day.

One of the speakers that morning was Robert Patton, grandson of the great General George S. Patton, Jr., and author of a book on the General's life. As Patton looked at the young people in the audience, he recounted a story which had been passed down to him through two generations of this family. During World War I, his grandfather, anxious to see action in the war, voiced his fear that the conflict would be over before he had a chance to prove his courage. At that point, he was taken aside by British Field Marshal Edmund Allenby, who imparted a bit of wisdom to the 31 year old Colonel. He told young Patton that every generation produces more heroes than it requires, and while all of them were not always needed, they would be there, if called upon, to demonstrate the heroic qualities necessary to meet the challenge.

As I looked around the room that morning, I realized just how much Allenby's axiom applied to the World War II veterans. At a very young age, the same age, in fact, as the young students in the audience, their entire generation had already struggled through a terrible Depression and was now being called upon to fight in a great war. Their education took place, not in a high school classroom, but on the battlefields of Europe and Asia. In the prime of their youth they encountered hardship and tragedy that is incomprehensible to most of us today. In short, this generation was called upon to be heroic and, thankfully, they rose to meet the challenge.

Today, we have been given all of the advantages of a privileged society. We live in a free and democratic nation with boundless opportunity. We are more affluent, more educated, and fancy ourselves as more enlightened and sophisticated than our parents and grandparents. I am greatly humbled, however, each time I ponder a single question: If faced with the same challenges as our parents and grandparents, would our generation and those that follow it respond with equal courage? Will we produce the heroes that the times demand? Although I am comforted somewhat by Allenby's words, only the future holds the answer to these questions.

Fifty years after the conclusion of the Second World War, we need to be reminded that much of what we take for granted today and much of what we pass on to our children, is due to the heroic actions of a remarkable generation of men and women. It is important now and in the future, to remember their courage and aspire to equal it.

- A NEW HOME FOR THE UNITED NATIONS -

At the end of the war, as plans were being made to establish the United Nations, a permanent site for the new international organization was sought. In December of 1945, a U.N. Investigating Committee determined that the permanent headquarters would be located somewhere in the eastern part of the U.S. Almost immediately, Stamford's First Selectman George Barrett announced that he would make a "strenuous bid" for the town's selection and proclaimed the Mianus Gorge area as his choice for the site. His idea was soon endorsed by Congresswoman Claire Booth Luce, Senators Thomas Hart and Brian McMahon, and Governor Raymond E. Baldwin. All touted Stamford's proximity to New York and Boston, its natural beauty, and its accessibility by highway, rail, sea, and air.

In early 1946, a U.N. Site Committee was formed with representatives from China, Iraq, Uruguay, the UK, and France. It was chaired by Stoyan Gavrilovic of Yugoslavia. Over the next several weeks, as the committee visited many sites along the east coast, from Boston to New York, Stamford remained in contention and was visited three different times by the committee. Each time Stamford was given an extremely favorable review.

Finally , on February 1, 1946, the U.N. Site Committee announced that it was recommending the Stamford-Greenwich Mianus Gorge area as the permanent site of the U.N. Soon, however, opposition in both Stamford and Greenwich began to gain momentum and several local organizations went on record as opposing the selection.[3]

Ultimately, the opposition would prove costly as the U.N. General Assembly finally voted to locate in New York City. But while Stamford was not destined to host the United Nations, all of the factors which made it attractive to the Site Committee, namely its natural beauty, accessibility, and proximity to New York and Boston, would transform it into one of the nation's leading corporate headquarters in the second half of the twentieth century.

---

[1] "Superfort's Leader Downed in Attack on Japanese Mainland". Stamford Advocate, June 1, 1945.

[2] Stamford Advocate, August 20, 23, 1993, p.1.

*I*NDEX

Editor's Note: This index does not include the KIAs listed on page IV and V in the introduction since they are already in in alphabetical order.

A
Aiello, Joe 76
Albonizio, Dominick 142
Attanasio, Emilio 12
Austin, Laura 125

B
Baldwin, Raymond E. 237
Balog, John 28
Baran, Leo 111
Barrett, George 152, 237
Basilone, John 72
Battinelli, Carl 62, 87
Belasco, Gustave 38
Benevelli, Al 141
Bliss, Charlie 118
Blume, Karl 94
Bocuzzi, Mike 157
Boone, Carl R. 4
Brett, George 102
Burnes, Mabel 176
Buttery, Chet 58

C
Callahan, Daniel 38
Carella, Angelo 97
Conti, Arthur 202
Coppola, Ralph "Cappy" 30
Coughlin, Billy 61
Crane, James 102

D
D'Ademo, Joe 33
Debrisco, Lou 153
DiBlasio, Bill 158
DiPreta, Tony 80
Doman, Joan 52

Doyle, John B., Jr. 50
Dzilinski, Leon 133, 143

E
Ekstowicz, Nelly Kijek 125
Etzler, Ann 4

F
Farrell, Joseph 155
Feulner, John 35
Fielding, George, III 92
Fogio, Flavio 91
Foley, Richard 208
Fox, Myles 53

G
Genovese, Fred 210
Gillmore, Howard 45
Ginter, John Jay, Jr. 170
Giordano, Bruno 124
Godlin, Eugene 180
Golden, Jack 60
Good, Tony 61
Grabarz, Walter 14
Grabowski, Joe 126
Guinta, Charles 77

H
Hart, Eugene 108
Hart, Thomas 237
Hawkins, Bill 47
Horan, Audrey Vivian 17
Horan, Vincent 17
Hyland, Everett J. 3

I
Ichiba, Sam 137

J
Jackson, Jane Buckley 120
Jackson, Lewis 228
Jessup, Ralph 61
Johnson, Fred 84
Johnson, Howard 162

K
Kaslikowski, Stanley 132
Kijek, Anna 125

Kohn, Herb 113
Kovacs, Edward 191

L

Lacerenza, Peter 213
Lambo, Jerry 22
Laney, Frank 152
Lannie, Lucy 191
Lapinski, Benny 126
Lapinski, Frankie 126
Lapinski, John 126
Lichack, Elwood 8
Lodato, Phillip 204
Loveland, Frederick 125
Luce, Claire Booth 237

M

MacDonald, Robert 105
Manjuck, Edward 55
McKeithen, David 74
McMahon, Brian 237
Miller, Ruth Maurer 123
Mitscher, Mark 35
Moore, Charles E. 152
Mownn, John 92

N

Nestor, Jimmy 232
Northrop, Dougie 17
Northrop, Douglas 231

O

Obuchowski, John 4
Oefinger, Hawley 10
Ofiero, Gene 217
Ostaszewski, Helen 16

P

Page, Eddie 166
Pagliano, Lenny 200
Palmer, Jack 62
Patton, Robert 236
Pia, Tony 149
Poltrack, Edward 65
Preu, Roger 160

R

Raymond, James 41

Rewak, Ted 196
Rodansky, Harold Yale 52
Rosa, Danny 146
Roumeles, Sam 193
Russo, Sammy 24

S

Schade, Arnold F. 45
Shawinsky, Joe 69
Short, Walter 4
Smith, Henry 43
Stolfi, Jimmy 224
Sullivan Brothers 125

T

Tamburri, Dominick 147
Thomas, William O'Neill 3
Trower, Arthur "Jim" 72
Turpin, Clement 184

V

Vanech, Harry 177
Vitka, Stephen John 47
Vivian, Donald 20
VonEpp, Franz Ritter 195

W

Westcott, Walter 175
Westerberg, Alice 117
Wise, Madolyn Disesa 129

Z

Zurman, George 220

Printed in the USA
CPSIA information can be obtained
at www.ICGtesting.com
JSHW082159140824
68134JS00014B/317

9 781596 527775